D0176816

"Real women dealing with real issues—how refreshing! This book is for any woman who wants to get out from under her circumstances, walk *through* the valley, and up on to the mountain of hope, faith, and joy."

PAM FARREL
Author of best-selling *Men Are Like Waffles, Women Are Like Spaghetti; Woman of Influence;* and *10 Best Decisions a Woman Can Make*

"A wonderful collection of 'ah-ha!' moments . . . these moving, embarrassing, or humorous stories will enrich everyone who reads them. You'll know you aren't alone in your spiritual struggles."

GAYLE ROPER
Author of *Winter Winds; Autumn Dreams; Summer Shadows;* and *Spring Rain*

"Even if the writers were happy shallow, there is nothing shallow about this book. Every story captured my attention. . . . *But Lord, I Was Happy Shallow* is an easy read you are sure to enjoy."

Carole Lewis
National Director, First Place

"Each real-life story is an inspiring example of how God works all things together for good in the lives of those He has called out of the shallows and into the depths of Himself."

Karen O'Connor
Author of *Help, Lord, I'm Having a Senior Moment*

"Marita has done a great job of pulling together wonderful stories that will bless anyone and everyone. Give it as a gift; it will be appreciated!"

Kathy Collard Miller
Popular conference speaker
Author of *Princess to Princess*

"Dailiness often is the chisel that carves within us greater resiliency—so the next time you're frustrated with the cotton pickin' flow of your life, reach for *But Lord, I Was Happy Shallow*. You'll feel understood and encouraged."

Patsy Clairmont
Women of Faith speaker
Author of *I Grew Up Little . . . Finding Hope in a Big God*

"Standing still really means you're moving backward. And God intends for us to continually move forward—deepening our relationship with Him. This collection of 'lessons' may be just what you need to move forward into the deep!"

KENDRA SMILEY
Host of the syndicated program Live Life Intentionally
Author of *High Wire Mom* and *Aaron's Way: The Journey of a Strong-Willed Child*

"What a wonderful, heartfelt collection of God's continued love and constant care! You will be glad you read this book."

MAMIE MCCULLOUGH, PH.D.
Author of five books, including the life-changing *I Can. You Can, Too!*

"*But Lord, I Was Happy Shallow* is a wonderful collection of stories illustrating the many ways God transforms His children into the likeness of His Son, Jesus. Every stumbling block can become a stepping stone to a deeper walk with the Lord."

CANDY DAVISON
Women's Ministry Coordinator, Sandy Cove Ministries

"When struggling with life's unfairnesses, we need the encouragement you are offering."

LEE EZELL
Author of *Finding God When Life's Not Fair*

But
Lord, I Was
Happy
Shallow

Books by Marita Littauer

Come As You Are* (Bethany House, 1999)
Co-authored with Betty Southard

Getting Along With Almost Anybody (Revell, 1998)
Co-authored with Florence Littauer

Giving Back* (Here's Life, 1991)

HomeMade Memories* (Harvest House, 1991)

The Journey to Jesus (Hensley, 2004)
Co-authored with Florence Littauer

Love Extravagantly* (Bethany House, 2001)
Co-authored with Chuck Noon

Personality Puzzle (Revell, 1992)
Co-authored with Florence Littauer

Shades of Beauty* (Harvest House, 1982)
Co-authored with Florence Littauer

Talking So People Will Listen (Servant, 1998)
Co-authored with Florence Littauer

Too Much is Never Enough* (Pacific Press, 1992)
Co-authored with Gaylen Larson

Your Spiritual Personality (Jossey-Bass, 2004)

You've Got What It Takes* (Bethany House, 2000)

For more information on the ministry of Marita Littauer,
visit www.maritalittauer.com.

*Title out of print

Lessons Learned in
the Deep Places

But Lord, I Was Happy Shallow

Marita Littauer
general editor

Raelene Searle, project coordinator
Sherri Buerkle, style editor

Kregel
Publications

But Lord, I Was Happy Shallow: Lessons Learned in the Deep Places

Published by Kregel Publications, a division of Kregel, Inc., P.O. Box 2607, Grand Rapids, MI 49501.

Library of Congress Cataloging-in-Publication Data
Littauer, Marita.
    But Lord, I was happy shallow: lessons learned in the deep places / by Marita Littauer, editor.
        p. cm.
    1. Suffering—Religious aspects—Christianity.
2. Christian life. I. Littauer, Marita.
BV4909.B88   2004
242—dc22   2004009071

ISBN 0-8254-3160-3

Printed in the United States of America

1 2 3 4 5 / 08 07 06 05 04

Contents

Acknowledgments **15**

Introduction **17**

Part 1: Dailiness

A Bug Story | *Kim Garrison* **23**

Finding the Hand of God
 with My Feet | *Bonnie Compton Hanson* **26**

Born Again . . . Again | *Anne Worth* **30**

Bruised and Smoldering | *Gail Snow* **33**

Canceling the Pity Party | *Patricia Lorenz* **37**

Idle Words | *Kathryn Robbins* **40**

The Wrong Story | *Debbie Robbins* **44**

Pack Rat | *Brenda Hughes* **46**

Riding Betty Boop! | *Amanda Graybill* **49**

Roots | *Erin K. Kilby* **52**

That Was Just the Green One;
 the Gray One Is Coming | *Jan Bryan* **55**

Those People | *Renee Coates Scheidt* **58**

Five-Year-Old Me | *Marlene Bagnull* **62**

Earning My PMA Degree | *Patricia Lorenz* **64**

The Fruit Room | *Caryl Jones* **67**

Time Spilled Out | *Mary Lapé Nixon*   **70**

Mathephobia | *Jason S. Wrench*   **73**

Part 2: Education/Teachers

Chicken Pox Typing | *Jeanne Zornes*   **79**

Jesus, Jungle Gyms, and Me | *Dena J. Dyer*   **83**

Lessons for the Teacher | *Doris Schuchard*   **87**

My Gift from Miss Clara | *Lanita Bradley Boyd*   **90**

Part 3: Love/Marriage

A Frisky Frosty | *Anna Jones*   **95**

A Sporting Wife, Who Can Find? | *Jan Coleman*   **97**

Attitude Adjustment | *Marita Littauer*   **100**

Adventures in Camping | *Tonya Ruiz*   **103**

Love Extravagantly | *Marita Littauer*   **107**

Preaching Lessons | *Verna Davis*   **109**

Ironing Woes | *Bonnie Skinner*   **112**

Shaky Landings | *Ginger Plowman*   **115**

Socks in Bed | *Sherri Buerkle*   **118**

The Battle of the Sexes | *Tonya Ruiz*   **122**

The Parable of the Coffee Filter | *Nancy C. Anderson*   **125**

The Power of a Confession | *Kathy Collard Miller*   **128**

The Things We Do for Love | *Gena Maselli*   **130**

Part 4: Health

What a Celebration That Shall Be! | *Janet Lynn Mitchell*   **135**

Buckle Up for the Ride | *Deborah Fuller Thomas*   **138**

Divorce Is Not an Option, but Murder Is | *Amanda Rankin*   **141**

Grandma Wore High Tops | *Lisa Copen* **145**

Poor, Poor, Pitiful Me! | *Jeff Friend* **148**

Taking Up Space or Giving Grace | *Evelyn W. Davison* **151**

The Rubber Band Master | *Karen J. Olson* **154**

Wake Up, Sleeping Beauty! | *Cynthia Komlo* **158**

Part 5: Family/Parenting

Father Knows Best | *Linda LaMar Jewell* **165**

Fighting Fire with Water | *Patricia Lorenz* **169**

Important Things to Do | *Tonya Ruiz* **172**

Leading Our Children | *Tim Burns* **175**

Butterfly Summers: The Art of Letting Go | *Patricia Evans* **177**

Raisin' Great Kids | *Raelene Searle* **180**

Spoiled | *Lanita Bradley Boyd* **184**

When the Night Patrol Roamed | *Karen H. Whiting* **189**

Where's My Teeth? | *Patsy Dooley* **192**

Part 6: Prayer

Forbidden Fruit | *Lori Wildenberg* **197**

The Bicycle Prayer | *Jennifer Moore Cason* **200**

The Wrong Prayer | *Debi King* **203**

Part 7: Moving/Houses

Even Atlanta | *Deb Haggerty* **209**

Spinning Gold into Hay | *Donna Jones* **211**

High Heels or High Tops | *Daphne V. Smith* **214**

I Don't Want to Go! | *Betty Southard* **216**

His Name Shall Be Wonderful | *Kirk Hine* **219**

My So-Called Pseudo-Life | *Kim Johnson*   223

Mine or God's? | *Lynne Cooper Sitton*   226

Out of the Ditch and into His Will | *Neva Donald*   229

A Prayer Meeting for My House | *Judy Wallace*   233

The Dynamite List | *Mary Maynard*   236

Wasting Away and Knee-Deep in Sewage | *Martin Babb*   239

Yesterday, Today . . . and Tomorrow | *Peggy Levesque*   242

Part 8: Church Life

No Big Deal | *John Leatherman*   247

Pride Comes Before a Fall | *Sharen Watson*   250

Proof in the Pudding | *Lynette Sowell*   252

Special Rick | *Elaine Stone*   255

Strung Along at Center Stage | *Craig Sundheimer*   258

The Wrong Rub | *Barb Loftus Boswell*   262

What's *Your* Name? | *Elaine Stone*   264

Part 9: Garden/Outdoors

Fences | *Raelene Searle*   269

Flowers That Walked and Talked | *Bonnie Compton Hanson*   272

Why Bother? | *Georgia Shaffer*   276

Part 10: Holidays

A Lavender Thanksgiving | *Nanette Thorsen-Snipes*   281

A Treasure in the Trash | *Gayle Team-Smith*   284

Christmas Elf | *Gail Cawley Showalter*   287

Mother's Day—Not! | *Bonnie Compton Hanson*   291

The Year of the Toaster Oven | *Patricia Lorenz*   294

Three Red Dresses | *Golden Keyes Parsons* **298**

Valentines and Vacuums | *Patricia Evans* **302**

Part 11: Career/Employment

Knee-Deep, but Able | *Judy Dippel* **307**

A Clear Conscience | *Kitty Chappell* **311**

For the Sake of the Call | *Jennie Bishop* **315**

First Things First | *Chuck Noon* **318**

My Not-So-Perfect Plans | *Gaylynne Sword* **320**

Oxygen! | *Chris Karcher* **323**

The Rest of the Story | *Laurie Copeland* **326**

Unless the Lord Builds the House | *Paula Friedrichsen* **329**

Part 12: Friends

Dinner with Sinners | *Tonya Ruiz* **335**

Resentful or Rejoicing | *Gayle Roper* **337**

Sally Time | *Elaine Britt* **340**

You Can't Walk Through a Closed Door | *Daphne V. Smith* **343**

Part 13: Older but Wiser

A Field Day with My Face | *Lauren Littauer Briggs* **349**

A Really Bad Hair Day | *Verna Davis* **353**

Razing Eyebrows | *Marlene Barger* **356**

Part 14: Travel/Road Trips

Café Olé! | *Lilly Allison* **361**

My Noncrisis | *Carolyn Brooks* **364**

Freeway Frenzy | *Elaine Hardt* **366**

Directionally Challenged | *Laurie Copeland*   **369**

Oil Trouble | *Faye Landrum*   **372**

Rushin' Roulette | *Cindy L. Heflin*   **374**

Sitting at the Feet of Jesus | *Florence Littauer*   **378**

Part 15: Sports

In the Zone | *Trish Porter*   **383**

Learning to Receive | *Raelene Searle*   **386**

Manly Man | *Craig Sundheimer*   **389**

The Lady with the Hose | *Kathy Boyle*   **393**

Contributors   **397**

Permissions   **411**

Acknowledgments

Thank you to all the contributors who have helped me make my dream a reality. It has been my joy to see so many of you excited about your first published work. I have been honored to give your wings to your dreams. I hope that your stories published here are the first of many.

To those of you who are already multipublished and have books of your own, thank you for taking the time to contribute to *But Lord, I Was Happy Shallow*. Your presence has added depth and credibility.

Each member of my critique group has read numerous stories, offering their comments and improvements. They have also each contributed their own stories. Thank you all; your expertise has enhanced this project.

Two members of my critique group have been of special service: Raelene Searle and Sherri Buerkle. Raelene has been of great support to me as project coordinator. Once I had selected the stories and reworked them as needed, she handled all of the back and forth logistics between me and the writers—and me and the publisher. With the myriad of deadlines I have had upon me, I fear this book would have never happened without Raelene. Sherri is an aspiring novelist. In our critique group we always agree with Sherri's corrections to our work. With her novelist's "eye," her input always brightens up our nonfiction writing. As this project neared completion, I asked Sherri to review each story, perk it up with fiction techniques, and adjust the style to give each story a similar voice. If you enjoy reading this book, Sherri is greatly to be praised.

Introduction

One of my favorite memory verses from childhood is James 1:2–4 from The Living Bible, "Is your life full of difficulties and temptations? Then be happy, for when the way is rough, your patience has a chance to grow. So let it grow, and don't try to squirm out of your problems. For when your patience is finally in full bloom, then you will be ready for anything, strong in character, full and complete." Whenever my mother would moan or groan about some difficulty, my siblings or I would spout this verse at her, asking, "Is your life full of difficulties?" Our perky words were never met with a very positive response.

Somehow, when we are faced with life's daily problems, we don't want to be cheered up or challenged. What we want is someone who understands; someone who will cry with us. As the cliché reminds us, "misery loves company."

We all know that the lowest valleys of life are where our faith deepens. Yet knowing the end result doesn't make it any easier to be "happy," as James admonishes, when difficulties and temptations come. We continue to resist even the most daily of stresses.

I have had this book on my heart and mind for several years. Interestingly, it came to fruition during the hardest year of my life— one that was full of difficulties and temptations. During that time, I received cards, notes, and letters from well-meaning friends who gave me platitudes and cheer. I know their hearts were right, but none of their good intentions helped. Instead, they only increased my frustration. Those who helped me the most where the ones who put their arm around me—even if only figuratively—and felt my pain. As I have worked on this book, I have been reminded daily of its importance and place. While the good words people in my life offered often did little to lift my mood, the stories in this book did. Reading through the escapades of others was like having a good cry with a close friend. Each happy ending showed me God's hand in the midst of a rough time and left me with a smile. I was encouraged with the knowledge that "this, too, shall pass," leaving me stronger in character, full and complete.

The concept for this book was born when, after a particularly problematic phase of my life, I bumped into someone I had not seen in a few years. After chatting for a while he commented, "I don't know what has changed in you, but there seems to be a new depth." Knowing that this "new depth" was a result of my recent difficulties and temptations, I looked to the sky, raised my hand toward the heavens, and quipped, "But Lord, I was happy shallow." Since that time, I have often repeated that line as life's uninvited stresses have entered—or even overwhelmed—my life. Even though those trying times always result in growth, I can't help feeling that I was happy being shallow.

In the last few years, and especially this past year, each recitation of the line has sparked a kinship between me and those within earshot as their own life circumstances cause my comment to hit home. These are the people I have invited to share their stories; those who have—at least in essence—cried out, "But Lord, I was happy shallow." Here they let you in on the entertaining, real-life stories of difficulties they've faced and the deepening of their faith that resulted. In spite of all they've learned, they're still the first to admit that they were just fine before the "difficulties and temptations" came. True, their faith has grown deeper, but they were happy shallow.

In these pages, I have collected over one hundred stories of those who have grown "when the way is rough"—and lived to laugh about it. Rather than being a theological tome or a psychological treatise, *But Lord, I Was Happy Shallow* is a fun book that will lift you up when you are feeling down and remind you that through it all you will grow and will become "ready for anything, strong in character, full and complete."

This lighthearted collection features stories from noted authors, the CLASSeminar staff, CLASSeminar Graduates, and other writers. It can be read all in one sitting, such as during a long flight, or read a little at a time when you need encouragement. Each true-life story includes an important biblical truth that is exemplified by the story and the applicable Scripture.

If your life is full of difficulties and temptations, *But Lord, I Was Happy Shallow* will help you be happy—or at least bring a smile to your face. As you read each story, your faith will grow as you learn from the lessons others have been taught. Like them, you will grow to be "ready for anything, strong in character, full and complete." While you may have been happy shallow, wouldn't you be happier deep?

Like each of the stories included in *But Lord, I Was Happy Shallow*, I write this introduction with a happy ending. The difficulties and temptations of the last year have passed—leaving me stronger in character, full and complete. I know that there will be other times when the way is rough and my patience has a chance to grow. But I pray that by remembering the experiences shared in *But Lord, I Was Happy Shallow*, I will stop trying to squirm out of my problems and will embrace James's admonition to be happy.

There is a poster on the wall near my desk that I have kept with me for years and years, and through many a move. It says, "I have been rich and poor. Rich is better." After reading these stories, I can truly say, "I have been happy shallow and I have been happy deep. Deep is better." I hope that in the end, you can say the same.

Part 1

Dailiness

A Bug Story

Kim Garrison

But store up for yourselves treasures in heaven, where moth and rust do not destroy, and where thieves do not break in and steal. For where your treasure is, there your heart will be also.

—Matthew 6:20–21 NIV

Ugh. A worm! I did a double take when I noticed it crawling up the pantry door. I grabbed a tissue, smooshed the intruder, and deposited its remains in the trash. I gave the incident no further thought—until a couple of days later when I saw two more of the same type of worm, one on the inside of the pantry door and the other on the floor. "Ewwww! More bugs!"

This was not a good sign. I had a flashback to a previous episode when ants invaded my pantry, but this invasion would be even worse if creepy crawly worms were involved. I was in a rush, though, and didn't have time to do more than grab a tissue, squish the two worms, and throw them away. In the back of my mind, I made a mental note: *After Christmas, clean out the pantry!*

A few more days flew by, and holiday preparations and shopping and cleaning and gift wrapping consumed my time. I hadn't been paying much attention to my pantry because I was buying more fast food than usual. But once I opened the pantry door, I was startled by a moth that was perched on the wall above some boxes! "Yuck, what are you doing in here?" I said, and went for a tissue.

I had a bad feeling that there might be a connection between the creepy worms and the moth . . . but I still didn't want to deal with the implications of that thought. I closed the pantry door and assured myself, "*Soon*" *I'll examine my pantry more carefully and clear out any* "*problem.*"

That evening, my sixteen-year-old daughter went to look for a snack. "Mom!" she shrieked when she spied a worm crawling on a bag of chips! Her alarm shook the whole house. "There's a larva of some sort in the pantry!"

My teenage daughter had identified what I'd failed to confront—the worms I'd been avoiding were moth larvae! Now I had no choice but to inspect the cabinet thoroughly and deal with whatever I found. Did I mention it was 10:15 at night?

The next two hours were disgusting! I pulled on some plastic gloves and emptied the shelves in the pantry. A raging infestation of moth larvae wriggled on three of the five shelves. Grabbing a large garbage bag I filled it with ruined boxes of cereal, baking mixes, flour, sugar, and more. Some of my staples were stored in airtight plastic containers, but larva had crawled into the crevices of the lids and made cocoons! Others had attached to the outsides of boxes and bags. The two moths we'd seen were evidently the first to hatch, and there would've been hundreds over the next week or so.

Two hours and four garbage bags later, my pantry was empty and the shelves wiped clean with ammonia. The task would've taken much longer, but my fourteen-year-old son volunteered to help out. He actually had fun talking to the worms—just before spraying and killing them!

I piled the few unharmed items—canned goods and a few unopened airtight products—on my kitchen island, planning to leave the pantry bare for several days to make sure no more larvae were hiding out. Then I'd lay down fresh shelving paper before restocking. I was glad this all happened about a week before Christmas, instead of on Christmas Eve when I had to entertain family.

At 1:00 A.M., I hopped into the shower to wash off the smell of ammonia—and any stray larvae. Exhausted, I prayed, "God, why did this have to happen? What could you possibly teach me from this?" Immediately I felt God reply, "I'm glad you asked!"

I then saw an analogy.

The larvae could be compared to bad habits—let's say, becoming lazy with my regular quiet time. Like one little larva in the pantry, skipping one day of quiet time didn't seem to be any big deal. "Lord, You know how busy I've been! Just this one day . . . I'll make up the time tomorrow."

Two little larvae in the pantry, two more days of neglecting God's Word were a more significant warning. "Lord, I miss our time together, but after the holidays, I promise, I'll get back on track." Left to its own end, though, laziness can become a whole pantry full of grief! By neglecting time with God, my life could become infested with little worms of negativism, self-centeredness, impatience, and irritability. That's where I was headed if I didn't do something about my increasing bad habit of laziness.

But it wasn't just a bad habit. Like I avoided admitting that the worms in the pantry could be larvae, I avoided naming my laziness as sin.

Right there in the shower, I prayed. "God, forgive me. I've been sinning in my lax attitude about our quiet time together. I'm sorry, and I pray that You'll help me to do better, starting today."

With that, I felt renewed. I spent the rest of the Christmas season with a fresh spiritual commitment—and a fresh clean pantry, too.

Finding the Hand of God with My Feet

Bonnie Compton Hanson

God has blessed you forever.

—Psalm 45:2 NIV

"Your reservation is under 'Don,'" the restaurant hostess announced with a bright smile. "We should have a table for you in about ten minutes."

I sure hoped so. We eat at fine restaurants only on very special occasions, and today was one of them. It was lunchtime the day after Valentine's Day, and we were celebrating our anniversary.

But only half of my mind was celebrating; the other half was taken up with problems. Bathroom problems. Bad ones. Don had worked on our guest bathroom that morning, using plunger, drain cleaner, and all the rest without success. We needed a plumber. That meant megabucks. Sigh.

After about twenty minutes, the hostess called, "Don, table for two." We jumped up—just in time to see another couple hurry off with our waiter.

Puzzled and a bit put out, I asked the hostess, "Excuse me, but did you have two *Dons* on the waiting list?"

She glanced at her list. "Oh, dear. That call was for you. *John* must have thought it was for him. Don't worry; we'll get you a table."

Which they did—another twenty minutes later. And after a few bites of steaming chicken pot pie, I quit being so bent out of shape.

After lunch, we headed to a shopping mall to look for my anniversary present—a pair of shoes. That might not sound particularly romantic, but I have horrible bunions—calloused and misshapen—from too many years of too-tight high heels. The bunions are so awful that my grandson Daniel asked, "Grandma, are your feet growing thumbs on the side?"

So my one request for an anniversary present was to shop for shoes. And as much as Don hates shopping, he agreed to come along.

The first mall we went to was closed due to construction. The second one was packed, forcing us to park in practically the next county. By the time we reached the mall my feet hurt, and I needed to use the ladies' room. So, it seemed, did dozens of other shoppers, most with little children. The line to the bathroom stretched down a hallway.

Finally, it was my turn. As I left the stall, I held open the door and looked around, "Anyone need this?"

Just then a mother rushed in with a little boy. She flashed me a smile. "Thanks!"

"Hey!" another woman shouted and flew across the room. Her arms were full of shopping bags. "I was here first! Get out!" She raised her bundles as if she were about to whop the child on the head. "It's mine! Now get out!"

I'd never heard such screaming and cursing. Finally, she flounced into another stall and slammed the door shut.

I rushed out of there, completely disgusted by the whole affair. "Honestly, God. This is supposed to be my anniversary. Why are You putting me through all this? All I want is a happy, uneventful day."

When I arrived at the shoe department, I wandered from table to table and shelf to shelf. I didn't expect much, knowing that my bunions would make a good fit nearly impossible. Yet, while Don sat waiting patiently, I got excited as I cruised the shelves. Soon my arms were full, and I sat down by Don.

I could hardly believe it. Out of the pile I'd collected, I found six pairs that fit. Six pairs! I'd never had that many pairs of new shoes in my entire life! "Look, Don!" I cried happily. "They're all on sale. I'm going to take them all!" Then I took back the other ones I'd tried on and rejected.

When I returned, an attractive young blond sat by my husband, chatting away. Her eyes sparkled and her smile lit up the whole area. For just a moment I was jealous—until I realized she wasn't in a chair, but in a wheelchair. It turns out, she had multiple sclerosis, and her doctor had told her that she could never walk again. But her disease hadn't kept her from being enthusiastic about her work, her family, and life itself.

Leaving her and Don in deep conversation, I gathered up the shoes I wanted and headed for the counter. But when my clerk went to check on a price, another clerk grabbed the cash register and entered someone else's purchases on my bill. What a mess! And on top of that, a third salesperson had taken my shoes and put them back on the shelves. By the time I got everything straightened out, I was burning. I stomped away with my bags to find Don and get out of there.

He was still talking to the young lady. Turning to me, she said, "I understand you've both had serious health problems. But look at you . . . here on your anniversary, enjoying life and each other. Isn't God wonderful?"

Still grumpy, I retorted, "Wonderful? I've just spent thirty minutes straightening out a mess, and all because of my stupid bunions."

At that, she grinned and kicked off her shoes. "I know just what you mean," she said.

I gasped. Young as she was, her bunions were far worse than mine.

"Be thankful for your blessings," she said.

Boy, did God ever convict me just then. I'd let my feelings of frustration overwhelm me. Never once did I think of all the blessings that God has shown me—having Don at my side ten years after his major heart attack, His healing me of cancer, giving us forty-five years of togetherness and love. Instead, I'd concentrated on the ugliness of life. I needed a heart change—a blessing awareness change.

Next time I start moaning about my lot in life, I'll remember I have bunions, but I can walk. I may feel ill, but my cancer is cured. I may feel unappreciated at times, but I've been married to a wonderful man for forty-five years.

In order to appreciate my blessings, I must have a heart willing to recognize them. A soft and willing heart pleases God, because He wants nothing more than to bless us forever.

Born Again . . . Again

Anne Worth

*Therefore, if anyone is in Christ, he is a new creation; the
old has gone, the new has come!*
—2 Corinthians 5:17 NIV

I prided myself on being a self-sufficient woman. Through counseling and recovery groups, I overcame an abusive childhood, alcoholism, and several divorces. I was finally doing great—I had a successful career, a beautiful home, and a sleek new car—and I thought I'd done it all on my own. *"I can do anything I put my mind to,"* I thought. But when I became ill with lupus, I met my match. The doctor's prognosis sent shivers down my spine: incurable, debilitating, possibly fatal!

The illness made it difficult for me to stay out of bed for more than a few hours at a time. In despair and fear, I thought of killing myself, but as difficult as living was, I had a greater fear of dying. Lurking in the shadows of my childhood was the thought that I'd surely go to hell.

In my early teens, I became convinced I'd never be good enough to go to heaven, so I ran as far as I could from the church. After I'd set out to convince myself that Satan and hell were ridiculous concepts, lots of people were more than happy to help me believe it.

But faced with impending death, I was terrified that the few Christians I'd known might have been right. But I couldn't just snap my fingers and overcome my anger toward Christianity. What could I do to reconcile my feelings and fears? I had no idea, but God had a plan.

Through a series of strange "coincidences"—events where God remains anonymous—I ended up walking into a hotel to spend *eight* days with a church group. Nobody but God could have orchestrated that. I felt more than a little scared . . . like a lion being thrown to the Christians!

During the days that followed, I was surprised to be validated by the group's leaders. They were upset at the judgmental, perfectionist, legalistic, kind of Christians who'd sent me fleeing as a teenager. I heard the Good News for the first time without feeling condemned. I heard that God wanted me to be saved, that He loved me beyond my comprehension, which at that time was pretty small. I still had no idea how God could help me.

At one session, I heard a song about how God had created me before the beginning of time, knitting me in my mother's womb, inspiring my first breath, being there when I first smiled and took my first step. You'd think that hearing how special, how wonderfully I was made, would make me happy.

It didn't. My rage erupted like a volcano. If God had been there all along, why hadn't He done something to help me? I threw a plain old fit. The feelings of being betrayed by God spewed out in tears and frustration, then hardened into a barrier that kept His words from getting into my heart.

Even though the group leaders were a bit shocked at the intensity of my outburst, they helped ease the anger and pain out of my heart. They talked quietly with me, saying, "Trust us; if you'll let Jesus come into your life, it will never be the same." Their words began to give me hope and soften my heart. They told me again how Jesus had suffered and died so that I could be forgiven—and that I really needed that forgiveness.

As the group leaders talked with me, I held my face in my hands, weeping and feeling exhausted, but still resistant. Suddenly, in my imagination, I saw Jesus standing in front of me. I almost stopped breathing. He was a gentle but powerful presence, His warmth spreading into my heart and around my body. He stood patiently waiting for me to decide what I'd do.

Slowly, He extended His hand toward me. In the blink of an eye, I was whimpering against His chest and the pain of the past was flooding away. In place of fear and anger, I began to feel sweet, quiet, contented joy. I received the gift of believing. He was *real*.

Instantly, in the depth of my being, I knew that I'd never be alone again. I knew beyond a shadow of a doubt that He would be faithful, and my life would never be the same. I didn't have to figure everything out on my own—I could lean on Him, and He would give me new understanding, new hope, and a new future. Yes, a future. I knew healing waited for me in my future.

He healed my feelings—of anger, resentment, abandonment—feelings that ran as deeply as my body was broken. But He also healed my body enough so that I'm at work serving Him as a biblical counselor. I never thought that God would use *me*. But He knew that when others heard my story, their hearts would shelter hope for their own healing.

I, even I, am an instrument of God. I am made whole, and I am a new creation for His pleasure and His purpose.

Bruised and Smoldering

Gail Snow

*A bruised reed he will not break, and a smoldering wick he
will not snuff out.*

—Matthew 12:20 NIV

In May of 1997 I ran away—for the second time. The first time I ran away from home, I was seventeen and, now, as an adult, I found myself reacting the same way to unexpected hardships. At seventeen, I didn't want to live the life God was asking me to live. And at forty-four, I was once again refusing to accept what God had brought into my life. I decided I'd leave that life and start over again.

I'd been dealing with depression and anxiety for almost a year, and nothing in my life seemed to be getting better. In fact, trouble had snowballed. I tried putting my trust in the Lord, but just when I felt I could trust again, something else would happen: a daughter's unexpected pregnancy and marriage during her senior year, an unborn grandchild lost, a criminal charge brought against one of my children, my husband undergoing five-way heart bypass, the estrangement of one of my daughters . . . the list seemed never ending. It was more than I could handle.

I charged a one-way ticket to a credit card, took my brokenness, and left without saying a word to anyone—not even my husband. I convinced myself that everyone would be better off without me. They were having a hard time dealing with my depression anyway, so they'd probably welcome my being gone.

I really didn't have a plan—other than getting away from my problems. I rented a motel room the night before my plane was to leave. As I lay there, feeling sorry for myself, the thought of suicide went through my mind. Since I'd left with only the clothes on my back and my purse, I was a little confused about how I'd end my life. I had no pills, no sharp objects, not even a belt! I looked at the window: *Let's see,* I thought. *I could stand on a chair, wrap the drapery cord around my neck and jump.* I pictured it in my mind, but I saw the drapes—rod and all—yank from the wall and tumble with me to the floor. Then I imagined the large bill from the motel for damages. I decided instead to stick with my plan of getting on a plane.

As the plane took off, I thought of my husband and kids, and I wondered if they'd even noticed that I was gone. When we'd been in the air for about twenty minutes, I noticed a little girl in the next row, staring at me. She smiled when she saw that I'd noticed her, and I gave her a weak, but friendly smile. She continued to stare.

I glanced out the window and thought how perfect everything looked from up here. Neighborhoods formed perfect square blocks, the way the farmers' crops were laid out actually made sense, and mountains looked different when I gazed down at them instead of up. I said sarcastically to the Lord, "This is the problem God. From Your viewpoint, everything looks perfect, everything makes sense. You should try living down there in the chaos for awhile, then You'd see."

I'd barely finished my remark when I was reminded that He *had* lived down there and, better than anyone, He *knew* the chaos that existed on planet earth. A tiny bit of shame passed through my soul.

The little girl was still smiling at me, and I smiled in return. This time, though, the smile was humble.

We'd been in the air for about thirty minutes when the thunder and lightening began. The lightening flashed all around us, and I was frightened. But the little girl wasn't. She just continued to smile.

As the thunder rumbled, the story of Jonah suddenly flashed through my mind. I looked at the innocent little girl in front of me, and then I glanced at the others sitting next to me and across the row. Tears filled my eyes, and I started to pray. I asked God to keep all the people around me safe, to not punish them because I was running away. I told Him how sorry I was that I was once again running from my problems and not facing them with faith and trust in Him, like I should.

I worried about the people on the plane, especially the little girl with the big smile. I was just about to jump up and yell, "If you throw me off the plane this storm will end!" Then I heard the pilot say, "It seems we're flying into a storm, so we're going to change course and fly around it. We shouldn't lose more than ten minutes." Saved from a death plunge! Thank You, Jesus.

When I got off the plane and entered the airport, I noticed a large sign: "Someone misses you, call them, 1-800 Call ATT." I started sobbing. I called my sister-in-law, too ashamed to talk to my husband. I'd been gone for nearly eighteen hours, and I was sure he'd be very angry with me for making him worry. I knew what I had to do. I made plans with my sister-in-law, asking her to come get me and escort me home.

When I arrived home to a worried husband and children, a change had taken place in my heart. Although I was returning to the same problems I'd ran away from, I felt that, with the Lord, I'd be able to go on. I could see how God had been at work the whole time I was away, right down to the AT&T sign. I knew He must really love me to guide me all the way back home, but I wasn't sure I could put my whole trust in His plan for my life.

A small pile of mail had arrived while I was gone, including the recent Crossing's Book Club selection of the month. I opened Max Lucado's book, *He Still Moves Stones*. As I flipped through it, I found a chapter titled "Bruised Reeds and Smoldering Wicks." The chapter started with a verse from Matthew 12: "A bruised reed he will not break, and a smoldering wick he will not snuff out" (v. 20).

As I read that chapter, I saw myself battered and bruised by life's circumstances. Once a woman-on-fire-for-the-Lord, I was now timid and lacked faith, reduced to a smoldering wick. At the end of the chapter, Max wrote, "Let's ponder the moments when Christ met people at their point of pain. We'll see the prophecy proved true. We'll see bruised reeds straightened and smoldering wicks ignited."[1]

At that moment, I knew I'd be made whole again. God had met me in my pain, and I would return to Him, trusting with all my heart, mind, and soul His plan for me.

---

1. Max Lucado, *He Still Moves Stones* (Nashville, Tenn.: Word Publishing, 1999) 7.

Canceling the Pity Party

Patricia Lorenz

Yes, happy are those whose God is Jehovah.
—Psalm 144:15 TLB

I wasn't looking forward to my fifty-seventh birthday. The angst I felt at the milestones of thirty, forty, and fifty was nothing compared to my dread of the fifty-seventh.

My mother died at age fifty-seven of Lou Gehrig's disease, ALS; and my hitting the age that she died crashed into my psyche with the force of a locomotive. I could hardly believe mother was so young when she died. *How many more years do I have?* I wondered.

I spent the first half of my birthday with my daughter Julia and her three youngsters—which normally would have redeemed the day. But Julia was in the middle of an exhausting divorce, and seemed to have been in a bad mood for nearly ten months. By the time they left for their two-hour drive back home, I, too, was exhausted from the stress and tension that seemed to surround them.

After I waved them down the driveway, I walked into my house alone and promptly began a grand pity party. Did I do anything at all to pull myself out of the doldrums? Of course not. The pity party rules demand that you make yourself as miserable as possible.

No presents, no cake, and the cards from my relatives and friends had all come in the mail two and three days earlier. My oldest daughter in California hadn't even called that day. As usual, she thought my birthday was the fourteenth instead of the twelfth.

My pity party continued, complete with tears, a bit of anger, and then wishing the remaining hours of the day would end quickly. I even talked aloud to God: "Okay, God. I'm a nice, happy, fun, pleasant person. I have lots of friends, great kids, wonderful relatives. Some of them must remember that it's my birthday. So why am I alone tonight? I do stuff for other people on their birthdays. Is there something You want me to learn from this dismal experience?"

In a last-ditch effort to do something productive that evening, I gathered the trash and took it out to the garage. On my way back into the house, I spotted my old bicycle in the corner. An old boyfriend had given it to me for Christmas ten years earlier. I never did like that bike. It didn't fit me right, and lately the gears were slipping in spite of a tune-up a few months earlier. Now, I kicked the back tire and said, "You're about as worthless as I feel. I wish I had a new bike."

That's it! I'm going to buy myself a birthday present. A new bicycle! I'd wanted one for three years, but for sixteen years in a row I'd had kids in college, and I couldn't think of extravagant purchases for me. But my black mood pushed me over the edge. I was going to indulge myself!

A new bicycle! Yes! I'll go shopping for it Monday morning. Since it's the fall season, they'll probably be on sale. I practically skipped into the house, feeling thirty years younger and filled with anticipation for a brand-new bike. I was a kid again, dreaming of a sleek new, lightweight bike with shock absorbers and a comfortable seat.

That night, before bedtime, I paged through the book of Psalms, trying to find a good definition of happiness. I found it in Psalm 144:12–15 (TLB): "Sons vigorous and tall as growing plants. Daughters of graceful beauty like the pillars of a palace wall. Barns full to the brim with crops of every kind. Sheep by the thousands out in our fields. Oxen loaded down with produce. No enemy attacking the walls, but peace everywhere. No crime in our streets. Yes, happy are those whose God is Jehovah."

The verse perfectly described my sons and my daughters. I thought,

I'm healthy, have plenty to eat, no enemies attacking my walls, no crime in my streets, and I have a wonderful friend in the Lord. This birthday is just another day and, most definitely, all is right in our world.

Monday morning dawned, and my excitement over a new bicycle hadn't waned. I drove to the bike shop and found a beauty—sleek silver and white, lightweight aluminum frame. Riding it around the store I felt as excited as when I got my *first* bike, at age seven. The bike of my dreams was even on sale, so I pulled out my checkbook and paid in full.

Since then, whenever I feel a pity party coming on, and if the temperature outside is at least forty-five degrees, I hop on my twenty-one-speed beauty—with the shock absorbers and a spring-loaded seat for extra comfort—and head for the bike trail that starts just a block from my house. An hour later, with another ten miles under my belt, my sunny disposition has returned.

Every time I hop on that bike, I'm reminded of the joy, well-being, and health that God and that bicycle have brought into my life.

Who needs a big birthday celebration? Next year, I'll skip the pity party and invite all my friends to a birthday celebration. Even better, maybe I'll call my friends up tomorrow and we'll take off on a twenty-mile bike jaunt. When you're a child of God, every day can be a celebration.

Idle Words

Kathryn Robbins

*I pray that out of his glorious riches he may strengthen
you with power through his Spirit in your inner being.*
—Ephesians 3:16 NIV

I sensed a victory at hand. My best friend and I were bundling up our
children to play outside in a Minnesota winter. We moms hoped
that we could enjoy a cup of coffee—without "help." Between the two
of us, we had eight kids under the age of eleven, so finding dry mittens
for every hand called for a *hurrah!*

I'd been struggling with depression since the birth of my fourth
son three years earlier, and I'd learned even the smallest of victories
needed to be celebrated. So enjoying a cup of coffee was definitely in
order—even if it was only five minutes before the first child came in
to go "potty."

As we enjoyed our coffee, my girlfriend and I picked up the threads
of an earlier conversation. "If I ever find myself pregnant again," I
said, "I know I'll handle it much better than I did the last time. Because of Steve's vasectomy, I'll know without a shadow of a doubt that
a baby would be God's will instead of our mistake."

Five years passed after I'd uttered those words in ignorance and
bliss. My youngest son was turning eight and in school full time, so I
thought I was free to plan my life. I told the Lord, "I'm bored and I

need an adventure." Presto! Bingo! My husband's company transferred him. We were moving to Orlando, Florida—lock, stock, and barrel. This wasn't the kind of adventure I'd had in mind. I was thinking of something more like a short-term mission trip to an exotic location of *my* choice. But here we were—leaving the frozen tundra to thaw out in the tropics.

Moving away from the snowbelt, though, was emotional for me. I was leaving my family, my closest friends, and my cultural roots. I felt like throwing up, and my head hurt, but I was too busy to think about it. One day, while packing, I told my mom, "If I didn't know better, I'd swear I was pregnant."

"Oh," she said, "that can't be. It's just stress."

Stress was good—I could deal with stress. But a month later, as I lay in my sunny Florida bedroom, my stomach turned cartwheels and my head pounded like an African drum. I realized this was not stress. I was either dying of a deadly disease or I was pregnant.

Scripture says that every idle word uttered from our mouths will be recorded in our book. I'm sure my book will be of epic proportions! My "I'll handle it so much better because I'll know it's God's will" must have been recorded in bold print. So it shouldn't have come as a big surprise that my own words brought me to my knees.

I can envision a scene in heaven like something out of the book of Job. Satan stands before the throne of God, listening to God's plans for me. "You can't be serious," snorts Satan. "You think You can use *her* to accomplish Your will? Look what a mess she was when You asked her to birth a few brats. I'll bet she'll curse You and want to die if You ask her to birth another!"

But God knows the end from the beginning, and He says, "She is Mine and I am hers. Love binds us to one another no matter what I ask of her. My will is being done. Watch and see."

My husband and I were stunned. Actually, *stunned* was an understatement! We stared at the two pink lines on the test strip, willing at least one of them to vanish. We walked around in a fog for weeks . . . no, months. My idle proclamation of eight years ago was just a whiff of hot air. I didn't deal with this pregnancy any better than the last one, even though I knew *without a shadow of a doubt this was God's will.* Because it sure wasn't mine!

I comforted myself with the hope that this would be the little girl I'd always longed for. But at twenty weeks the ultrasound tech proclaimed, "Oh, how exciting! Now you'll have five boys!" How could God do this to me? If this was my reward for serving God all my life, then I quit! I felt like my prison sentence had been extended another twenty years with no hope of parole. For the first time in my walk with the Lord I was having a Jonah moment. "You want me to do *what?*" This must be a bad joke! Our move to Florida had stripped me of everything—family, friends, home—and now my freedom.

I imagined Satan, wild-eyed with victory, racing into the presence of God to throw my failure in His face. "See! She's failed You! She's worthless, just as I—"

But in mid accusation, Satan runs smack into Jesus. "Silence! Satan, you're nothing but a lair. She has not failed. She has only had the wind knocked out of her." Turning toward His father, Jesus asks, "Father, would You send her the help and support she needs to carry this heavy task?"

God smiles, "Gladly." At His spoken word, ministering angels were immediately dispatched.

In the meantime, I spent hours lying in bed wrapped in self-pity, staring at the bare walls of our rented house. Funny, the only decoration that got hung up on any wall was a small wooden plaque that my cousin had painted for me: "In Thee Will I Put My Trust." Could I do that? Could I put my trust in the knowledge that God loves me and has my best interest in mind? I wasn't sure anymore.

But the still small voice of the Lord whispered, "I know this feels bad, but trust Me."

Trust. I'd seen that word a lot lately. The theme at our church that year was "trust"; every devotional I picked up admonished "trust." Okay, I knew the best thing was to trust the Lord, but I was going to close my eyes during the scary parts.

And that's where the ministering angels came in. God provided the best prenatal care with wonderful midwives who loved me no matter my mood, a house with a swimming pool that our four older sons enjoyed, a church that cared and prayed for us, and good friends that we love to this day. And to offset the postpartum depression that comes after birthing, He placed me where I could get natural therapy—sunshine. Not only were my needs met, but God also provided an ultrasound technician as an angel of excitement, who typed on our son's first picture, *BABY BOY NO. 5!!!* You'd think that he was part of *our* plan all along.

I learned that God is gracious, compassionate, slow to anger, and abounding in love. He provided everything I needed without any harsh words of reprimand for my self-pity. He simply loved me.

Eight years ago, my words were spoken in a state of ignorance, yet they became words of faith. They were translated into a firsthand experience of God's love and compassion as I struggled to honor Him.

I might not understand everything God has planned, but when I look into the face of this darling "Little General," I know without a shadow of a doubt—Satan better batten down the hatches, because this little one is up to the challenge of rattling the gates of hell.

The Wrong Story

Debbie Robbins

Do not consider his appearance or his height, for I have rejected him. The Lord does not look at the things man looks at. Man looks at the outward appearance, but the Lord looks at the heart.

—1 Samuel 16:7 NIV

My sister and I play this little game. We pretend that everyone we see is a character in a play. If you pass us at the mall, or take a seat near us in a coffee shop, your life may be rewritten. The plots we give our characters are always fabulous with spectacular endings.

Our imaginations really work overtime when we're traveling by airplane. We have a ball meshing together the stories of various travelers. Prime targets are those who wear outrageous clothes at 6:00 A.M., travel in what looks like their pajamas, or look too Wall Street or Rodeo Drive. By the time we're finished, the story could end up on the first page of the *National Enquirer*—next to the exclusive about the four-headed cow from Wisconsin.

My sister and I were on our way from Louisville, Kentucky, to Kansas City, Missouri, playing our "people watching" game. We chose a target just screaming for us to make up a wild story. A woman in her midthirties approached the gate waiting area, picked up her pass, and sat down. She was alone, but the ring on her finger said she was married. The look on her face showed she was tired and unhappy. But her demeanor wasn't what drew our attention—it was how she was dressed. She wasn't in pajamas, nor was she well put together. She wore short-shorts, high platform shoes, teenage accessories, and a tight T-shirt. Suddenly our "people watching" turned into gossip.

"The way she's dressed," I murmured, "she's perfect fodder for the Jerry Springer Show—*Thirty-somethings who dress like teenagers.*"

"Not quite," my sister replied. "No bare belly button."

When we boarded the airplane, we joked that we'd rather barricade ourselves next to the bathrooms than sit near *her*. But God, in His wisdom, had a different plan. The flight was sold out and, because Starr and I were near the end of the boarding line, the only seats available were the two rows that faced each other: three seats facing forward and three seats facing the back. By the time our thirty-year-old teenager boarded, the only seat available was right across from us! My sister and I exchanged a look of horror.

Attempting to disguise our discomfort, I pasted on a huge smile and rattled off the first thing that came to mind. "So . . . where are you from?"

She was from Louisville, and she'd returned home to attend a funeral—her baby sister's funeral. She'd just buried a beautiful nineteen-year old girl, who had lost a two-year battle with leukemia. Remembering our malice and gossip, my little sister and I couldn't have felt more embarrassed . . . or so we thought.

The thirty-something woman, married and a mother of two, told us, "I usually don't dress like this. Today I wanted to wear my baby sister's clothing. I just needed to feel close to her."

Humbled and ashamed, my sister and I never again played our "people watching" game.

I'm thankful that, when I come before God, He doesn't look at what I'm wearing or at any of my physical characteristics. He isn't swayed by man's opinion, and He doesn't gossip with His angels about the poor choices I've made. I'm deeply grateful that, instead, He looks at my heart. And I'm even more grateful that He forgives without condemning.

Pack Rat

Brenda Hughes

For where your treasure is, there your heart will be also.
—Matthew 6:21 NIV

Have you ever heard the old proverb, "Use it up, wear it out, make it do, or do without"? It was my grandmother's favorite. My earliest memories are filled with the chorus of, "Don't throw that away; you'll never know when we might need it," and the ever popular "Don't throw that away, it might be worth money some day." We saved everything!

Such frugality is admirable. At least, that's what I thought. So I became the ultimate collector. I saved it, stacked it, and stored it. As time passed, it became more of a challenge to take care of my growing piles of valuables. By the time my second son was born, it took me hours upon hours to clean my house, and for the life of me I didn't know why. I knew I was organized, so I must be missing that one elusive tip that would make my life a cinch. Or could it be some deep-rooted psychological malady that was sabotaging my efforts? So began the collection of the self-help wing of the library.

I was given a new revelation. As a working mother of two young children, I just needed to work harder at pampering myself. In my dictionary, pampering equals chocolate and wicked desserts. How else is a young mother to keep up her energy? And so the "diet without exercise or deprivation" collection was born.

During this amassing of gadgets, inner wisdom, and the perfect diet, I also became a Christian. Old habits are hard to break, and once again I was off collecting all things Christian—books, music, and knick-knacks. How on earth would I get this Christianity thing right if I wasn't well equipped and accessorized?

Don't think, though, that I only collected. I actually read and applied the wisdom found in my collection of books and magazines. In one of my diet books, the author posed a unique question; she asked if the reader had a tendency to hoard food.

Hoard food? Hoard—that's a coarse, barbaric, unladylike word. Webster says, "it's a hidden supply or fund stored up." Now that doesn't sound so bad—actually it sounded like a good thing. Something stored up, yet it didn't sit well with me. What was it about this word?

I remembered a parable in Luke chapter 12 about the rich fool. He thought that by building bigger storehouses he'd be able to, "take life easy; eat, drink and be merry." But that very night, his life was going to be asked of him. The parable teaches, "This is how it will be with anyone who stores up things for himself but is not rich toward God."

Ouch. I already knew I hoarded food, and I wondered if I was guilty of doing the same thing in other areas of my life. So I asked, "Lord open my eyes to the things I hoard, help me to see these things as You see them."

Remember the old cliché? "Be careful what you ask for because you just might get it." God did just that. All of a sudden, the wonderful collections of items I'd amassed over the years revealed their true nature—dusty piles of junk I'd hung around my neck like millstones.

The Lord nudged me in the most gentle way. *Daughter, do you really need all of these books and magazines? Does not My word say that I freely give wisdom to those who ask? Do you trust Me to provide wisdom when you need it?*

How do you argue with that? The stuff definitely had to go. But what if I need to know fifty new ways to redecorate my bathroom? What if I need to reread that old college textbook? But I loved appearing so well read. Nope . . . they had to go.

Each week, God revealed the storehouses I'd built for myself. You may have them too—the "skinny wardrobe" you just know you'll get back into, piles of knick-knacks, unused kitchen gadgets, the list goes on and on. As the clutter left the house, lo and behold, my home became easier to care for. Housework that had taken all weekend, now took a couple of hours. God removed the millstones and set me free.

You may think I now live in a vacant house with no amenities, but I didn't have to go that far. God just wanted to teach me to hold loosely to the things of this world, and that obedience brought freedom. He is *Jehovah Jirah,* my provider, the giver of every good and perfect gift. I know now that my treasure is in Him.

Riding Betty Boop!

Amanda Graybill

The LORD himself goes before you and will be with you; he will never leave you nor forsake you. Do not be afraid; do not be discouraged.

—Deuteronomy 31:8 NIV

I love hopping on a motorcycle and feeling the ocean breeze hit my face. I began riding a year ago and never dreamed how learning to ride would parallel the rest of my life. One day, I rode Betty Boop—that's what I call my red '95 Yamaha Virago—to the gas station to fill her tank, and I forgot to put the kickstand down. As soon as I let go of the handle bars, she clattered to the cement. Looking around to see if anyone saw what happened, I lifted her from the ground.

Another day, I decided to ride to work. I took the back way along the beach just to feel the sea mist on my face. When I turned into the office driveway, I hit some gravel and forgot to apply both front and back brakes at the same time. Down I went—hard! I broke my right pinky—which would heal—but didn't put a scratch on Betty Boop. Embarrassed, I began to wonder if I needed training wheels.

With each accident, I was tempted to give up. But, as any bronc rider will tell you, you have to get back on. Sometimes when life's struggles hit, it feels like taking a hard fall. But Betty Boop taught me to get back on and ride!

My life was cruising along just great on January 1, 2003. Both my sons were home together for the first time in a few years, one on leave from the U.S. Marine Corps and the other home from college.

The joy ride ended, though, with one phone call. I knew it when I picked up the receiver and the first sergeant asked for my eldest son. As I handed the phone to him, my heart ached because of what the phone call meant. We'd hoped and prayed it wouldn't happen, and had been trying hard to capture our special moments together. But his tour of duty for the war front was imminent, and our New Year's celebration hit the skids.

The next crash resulted from a call from a local reporter. He asked his question and my heart stopped beating. "How do you feel about your son going to war?" I wanted to scream into the receiver, "How do you think I feel?" But instead, I simply said, "I'm proud that my son will be fighting for our freedom." Hanging up the phone, tears streamed down my face and I lifted up a prayer: "Lord, I feel so empty right now. Please fill me with Your presence."

As I prayed, I thought of all the times I complained about having to fill up the tank on my motorcycle, and about how quickly it ran dry. At that moment I felt that my spirit, too, was running on empty. For weeks I didn't know where my son was. Watching the news became almost an obsession as I searched for any evidence of him. Yet God continued to fill up my spiritual tank, saying to my heart, "Trust Me, there's not a place your son can be that I am not with him." I clung to that promise, and soon received a ten-minute morale call from my Marine. Even on the other side of the world, in a war torn city, God was holding our son in His loving hands.

During the next four months, I faced the loss of my best friend and the loss of my father, but God stayed faithful. He filled my tank each day with His loving-kindness, other people's encouraging notes and phone calls, and a peace in the midst of the storm. He returned my son with only a few scratches—which would heal—and a lot of close calls.

Now, whenever Betty Boop needs refueling, the Lord also reminds me how often I need Him. When I forget to put the kickstand down in life, He's there to uphold me, and even though I may fall, God picks me up. I still ride Betty Boop into the sunset, but now my eyes are focused on the Son! Hop on His Harley and you'll never have to worry about riding alone. He's always there in front of you, steering you through the rough patches of the road.

Roots

Erin K. Kilby

Then you will know the truth, and the truth will set you free.
—John 8:32 NIV

"We finally got it finished, and just in time for your visit!" My mother proudly displayed room after room of shiny hardwood floors, softly papered walls, and an elegantly tiled foyer. Her taste was exquisite.

"It's fabulous, Mom," I replied, and I meant it. But secretly, I felt a pang for the house I grew up in.

Upstairs later, I unpacked my suitcases in my old room, now decked out with a vanity, coordinated daybed, and a tasteful area rug to warm the hardwood floors. I reminisced about the décor from my youth— threadbare-green carpet, worn couches with missing buttons, peeling gold fleur-de-lis wallpaper in the bathroom. My mother, though, must have longed to make these changes.

"Remember this?" My sister-in-law Julie appeared behind me and giggled as she handed me a photograph. "When your mom had the bathroom torn up, we found it on the sheet rock behind the medicine cabinet."

The photograph showed childish bubble letters scrawled on the wall: "Erin loves Rob," and next to that I'd written in a show of rebellion, "I couldn't resist, Mom." I was thirteen at the time.

I grinned halfheartedly. Poor Mom. She and I had always gone head-to-head on everything. I challenged her constantly. How many sleepless nights had she spent worrying about my next escapade? I was always in trouble, always breaking rules, and never listening to her. She and my father were faithful in taking us to church, and had even managed to involve me in the youth group. Yet nothing would stem my wildness. I seemed hopeless.

As an adult, past visits to my childhood home had brought back to me all my foolish choices and the lessons I'd learned. Every doorknob, crayon mark, and rip in the carpet was significant. They were stories of me, of my life, my growth as a person. Now, with all the fresh clean surfaces, I felt like my foundation was all gone.

"Mom's starting dinner." My brother Andy came and whisked Julie away.

I sighed and pulled up the blinds. Outside the window stood a huge leafless maple tree. The winter had stripped it bare, but it was still lovely. The branches reached up past my window and toward the sun. It stood taller than the house now, and I smiled as memories of this tree came flooding back.

I was ten years old, running out into the autumn chill. My mother was calling, "You stay out of that garage, Erin! Your dad doesn't want you messing with his tools. Besides, it's dangerous in there!"

A neighbor's maple tree was shedding its seed pods, and I was fascinated. Hundreds of the pods were spinning through the air like whirlybirds. I had an overwhelming urge to collect every one of them. But I needed a bucket from the garage, and a shovel too, so I could gather them. I didn't blink before doing exactly what I was told not to—poking around the garage and my father's tools to find a bucket and shovel.

A few hours later, I'd filled the bucket several times and torn every seed out of its whirly bird pod. My mother came outside, looking for me and calling. "Erin, it's time for dinner!"

I panicked. The bucket and shovel from the garage would give away my disobedience. I needed a place to hide them—fast! I tossed the bucket, shovel, and whirlybird seeds in a nearby flowerbed behind some bushes. And then forgot about them . . . until spring.

My mother was planting flowers late in spring when she discovered the rusted remains of a bucket and shovel. She also found several maple saplings. The clues led her to the obvious conclusion, and she summoned me to explain the evidence.

I did what any self-respecting ten-year-old would do. I lied. "I don't know who did that. Maybe it was daddy. They're his bucket and shovel."

My mom knew me too well. She didn't buy my story. "Erin, you're being dishonest. Do you know how I can tell?" She pointed out the telltale saplings. Instead of the punishment I so richly deserved for lying, she asked me to plant the sapling in the yard . . . just outside of my window.

"A lie can be hidden only for a time," she explained. "But, as the seasons change, the lie will grow . . . just like the sapling. In time, it will become so large, that everyone will notice it. It's better to plant the truth. When it grows, you can be proud when everyone notices it."

For many years, the lesson was lost on me. And as the writing on the bathroom wall testified, I still broke rules, lied, and rebelled.

Now, looking at the tree outside my childhood window, a revelation washed over me, and my despair over the "old" house left me. I'd thought that the lessons I'd learned in my childhood were tied somehow to the house. But, like this maple tree had done in the soil of the backyard, the truths Mom and Dad taught me had taken root in my soul. And with every passing season, those truths grow stronger as I stretch upward toward the sky.

That Was Just the Green One; the Gray One Is Coming

Jan Bryan

With God's power working in us, God can do much, much more than anything we can ask or imagine.

—Ephesians 3:20 NCV

We were elated! My husband and I wanted to have a large family, and I'd found out that I was pregnant with my fourth child. I was even more excited because after three boys, we had a girl! It was so much fun. Instead of blue accessories, we had pink—and dresses and curls and ribbons and socks with lace.

With the addition of our little one, though, we discovered new dimensions. We were now a family of six, and we no longer fit anywhere! We didn't fit in restaurant booths. We didn't fit in people's homes (so we were never invited as a whole family). And worse, we didn't fit into the family car.

Our car was designed to fit four adults comfortably. The three boys sat in the back seat, and since we had bucket seats, my husband and I sat in the front. My daughter sat on my lap—those were the days before car seats and seat belts. My daughter's sitting on my lap was fine when she was an infant—very convenient, in fact; I could breast-feed her at any time.

As she grew older, though, she grew bigger and heavier. Until eventually she and I would arrive at our destination looking wrinkled and disheveled. We were a happy bunch, but we were definitely crowded in that little car.

One day while jammed in the car, we noticed a big car for sale. It was beautiful. It was green. It was a station wagon. My husband and I exchanged glances, and we knew—we had to have a closer look at that car.

We piled out of our rolling sardine can, and in minutes we were plunked into the biggest car I'd ever been in. It had seats galore, with a few to spare! In fact, it was a nine-passenger car. Even though it was used, the seats weren't ripped, and the carpeting was like new. I was beside myself with joy when my husband told me this palace on wheels was in our price range, and if we traded our car in, we could buy it. I knew it was a gift from the Lord. I'd always trusted that He would supply all my needs, and sure enough it was happening again.

We immediately jumped back into our little car and drove home. My husband felt we should present our car in the best condition possible, so our mission was to wash it inside and out. We all were assigned a portion of the project, and we worked hard. Finally, cleaned and buffed, our old shone like new. It was time to go back to the car lot and offer our trade-in on the green station wagon. The excitement had mounted while we cleaned the car, and now we were all giddy with the vision of us driving away from the lot in that beautiful green machine.

When we got to the dealership, my husband, in his great wisdom, told us to stay in the car. After all, we might not all fit in the salesman's office. He went in and we could see him through the glass talking to the salesman. When he came out, he had a somber look on his face. He sunk behind the wheel and told us. "The car is being sold to that man standing inside."

We missed the car by five minutes. "Oh, why did we go home?" I lamented.

I can hardly describe the disappointment that shrouded our happiness. We were stunned. We'd been so sure that the Lord was providing that beautiful green car for us. We'd already been praising Him and planning our victory party. How could this be? The Lord certainly wouldn't dangle a carrot in front of our starving faces and not let us eat!

I hate to admit that at thirty-nine years of age, I broke into tears. I cried all the way home. Over the next few days, I had lots of tearful talks with the Lord. But the disappointment shadowed me and wouldn't leave. I didn't understand. Where was the Lord, and what was He doing?

About a week later, my husband called. He'd tracked down a dealership that carried the same make as the green car. He wanted me to go to price that particular model and let him know the cost of a *new* car.

The following week, we picked out a brand-new car. It was gray with blue interior—my favorite color. It was a nine-passenger like the older green model, but the new model had a better design for the rear seat passengers. It was fancy and luxurious, and even had electric windows! The dealership worked the finances with my husband and made it affordable.

As we drove home in our new vehicle, the light began to dawn. The Lord had shown me the green model, in order to raise my awareness and expectation. Without seeing the green car, we would've never thought of making the change. I didn't even know that type of car existed! Then, He gave me the best.

Since that day, God at times seems to open a door, but if it shuts, I know it's because He has something better waiting behind another door. I no longer burst into tears of disappointment when a door closes for me or for a friend. I just smile and say, "Oh . . . oh that. That was just the green one. The gray one is coming!"

Those People

Renee Coates Scheidt

God resists the proud, but gives grace to the humble.
—James 4:6 NKJV

There is none righteous, no, not one.
—Romans 3:10 NKJV

It sneaks into our hearts before we realize it. That's how deceitful pride is. We even find ourselves proud that we've not been proud! If we don't stay alert to pride's devilish ways, we'll fall into its clutches. How easy it is to tell ourselves, "I may not be perfect, but at least I'm not nearly as bad as 'those people.'"

"Those people"? Exactly who are "those people"? We all know the kind. They're the ones locked up behind the prison doors, the ones condemned by society.

These were the thoughts that echoed through my mind the day I approached the tall chain-link fence with rolling barbed wire along the top. *What am I going to say to these prisoners? This is definitely way out of my comfort zone. Besides, with this cold, my voice is nearly gone.* Sounded like a good excuse to me to run for the hills. But for some reason, I didn't leave.

Suppressing a shudder, I pressed the button to enter the maximum-security correctional institute. With reluctance, I entered through the heavy double doors and, the tone of my voice reflecting my discomfort, I announced, "I'm here for the crusade."

"Just have a seat, and I'll page the chaplain," the clerk replied, and motioned me to a seat. The chair was as cold as the atmosphere. In just a few minutes, the chaplain appeared. "Thanks for coming to help," he said.

"Thank you for the invitation," I responded. I felt duty bound to be at least polite, but I still struggled with thoughts of, *What am I doing here?* Trying to hide my discomfort, I quickly continued, "This is my first time to be inside a prison. I'm not sure what to expect."

Without hesitancy, the chaplain said, "Just tell them about the Lord, like you would anyone else. They're no different from the man on the street."

I smiled, again to be polite, but I bit my lip to keep from saying what I really wanted to say: "I don't think so! The people I know and associate with aren't so bad that they're locked up! How can you put us in the same category with them?"

We soon arrived at the prison gym, and a sea of men dressed in orange coveralls sat before me. The gospel band cranked up with strains of, "I saw the light, I saw the light, no more darkness, no more in night. . . ." As I slipped onto the second bleacher, I heard behind me a beautiful voice that stood out from all the others. I turned to see a young African-American male, totally absorbed in the worship. His voice rivalled any professional singer. Questions raced through my mind, but fear kept me from asking what I so wanted to know. Things like, *Why are you here? What caused you to do something so bad that you were willing to risk prison if you were caught? Was it worth it?*

Finally, I summoned up my courage and spoke, "You have such a beautiful voice. Do you mind if I ask you some questions?"

"Not at all," he answered, and he held out his hand to shake mine. "My name is Ben."

"What brought you here, Ben?"

He ran his hand across his throat. "I cut a man for tricking me on a drug deal. If someone hadn't come along when they did, he'd be dead. I'm in here for three years for doing that."

"How do you feel about what you did now?"

"Oh, I regret it alright. I was wrong. My dad is a preacher, and I was raised in a good Christian home. But when you're strung out on drugs, you forget all that. You do what you have to do to get what you need at that moment. I'm clean now though, and I plan to stay that way."

By now I was more relaxed and decided to press on. "Have you thought about what you want to do when you get out?"

"Exactly what *they're* doing right now," he answered, pointing to the praise band. "I want to let others know about Jesus, and that His way is the only way to really live."

By then the chaplain was preparing to introduce me and our time was gone. "Thanks for sharing with me. I really appreciate your honesty and openness."

I hurried toward the platform. No longer did I wonder what to say. The music began and I started to sing, "What can wash away my sin? Nothing but the blood of Jesus."[1] A confidence and energy beyond my own seemed to carry me through the next fifteen minutes as I shared the message of God's grace and mercy. When I finished, I knew God had spoken—even through a hesitant, skeptical, proud, cracked vessel like me.

When the program was completed, and the customary thank you's and good-bye's said, I was escorted to the thick doors that opened to the outside world. By this time, I could no longer contain the thoughts flooding my mind, and I kept up a one-sided conversation with the guard. "You know, I was so scared about coming here today. I thought these men would look different—like the outcasts of society. Yet they looked so normal! I struggled with, what does a person like me, who tries to obey the law, have to say to those who've broken it? But now I see the truth—they're just like me! There but for the grace of God, go I. My sin might not have put me behind these walls, but I'm just like them—just another sinner in need of the saving grace of the Lord."

The officer nodded in agreement as he watched me step outside to a free world. Light rain pattered on my face, but it didn't quench the

---

1. Robert Lowery, 1876, public domain.

warmth flowing from my heart. The person who walked out of that prison was different than the one who'd entered just hours before. Where pride walked in, humility now exited. From the depths of my soul, I hummed a church song that I had learned in my childhood. "Sing it o'er and o'er again. Christ receiveth sinful men. Make the message clear and plain. Christ receiveth sinful men."[2]

Even Ben.

Even a prideful soul like me.

2. Erdmann Neumiester, 1718, public domain.

Five-Year-Old Me

Marlene Bagnull

I keep working toward that day when I will finally be all that Christ Jesus saved me for and wants me to be.
—Philippians 3:12 NLT

W*hy did you do such a dumb thing?"* I scolded my twelve-year-old. Debbie shrugged her shoulders. "I didn't mean to."

I sighed. "I just don't understand you. Sometimes you act so grown up, yet at other times you act like you're five years old."

Later that day, I was forced to admit that there's also a five-year-old in me.

I'd fought a mob of people in the grocery store, waited for an eternity in the slowest checkout line, then I threw my bags of groceries into the car and slammed the door. After giving the empty cart a shove, I had to chase after it to keep it from banging into someone else's car. I had an adult temper tantrum!

At home, as I rushed to put away the groceries (including several broken eggs) and get dinner started, the phone rang. I hate sales calls, but I couldn't even talk back to this one. It was a recorded message! I slammed down the receiver.

That evening I ranted and raved, trying to balance the checkbook. "This new statement is impossible! Why don't they give me something I can understand?" I sounded like my eight-year-old when he's struggling with homework.

I didn't feel very good about myself when I finally crawled into bed. I'd accused my twelve-year-old of acting like a five-year-old when I was just as guilty! And that day hadn't been an exception. More often than I care to admit, I respond to situations in an immature way and end up taking out my frustration on my loved ones. I say things I wish I could take back. I yell and scream instead of dealing with situations quietly and rationally.

"Lord, forgive me," I prayed. "Help me to grow up—to set a good example for my children."

I still haven't outgrown all my childish behavior. Like the apostle Paul, I don't always understand why I do what I don't want to do, or why I avoid doing what I earnestly want to do. But I'm learning to apologize to my children when I fall short, and to be more patient with their "five-year-old behavior."

The pressures of life have a way of bringing out the five-year-old in all of us. There'll be days when we fail miserably—when our behavior causes us to feel embarrassed and disappointed in ourselves. But I praise God for the gift of His forgiveness and for the strength He gives me to try again. And I'm getting fewer skinned knees as I'm starting to put childhood behind me.

Oh dear. I wonder how I'm going to cope with adolescence?

Earning My PMA Degree

Patricia Lorenz

For them all sorrow and all sighing will be gone forever;
only joy and gladness will be there.

—Isaiah 35:10 TLB

I believe in the "save now, buy later" philosophy. I was raised by parents who could stretch a dollar twice around the block, plus I was given the daunting task as a single parent to get four kids raised and through college. That's probably why I'm a frugal, money-saving soul who's never paid interest on a credit card in her life.

In 1987, I paid cash for the only new car I've ever purchased, and I'm still driving that little red wagon. Granted, at well over 185,000 miles, the ol' "bucket of bolts"—as my Dad refers to it—suffers a number of shortcomings. The air-conditioning system went kaput in 1996. The tape player bit the dust two years before that. The rear speakers put out more static than music. The gas gauge hasn't worked since 1989.

For the past two years, to adjust the heat inside the car I had to pull off to the side of the road, raise the hood, and adjust a little lever up near the windshield. This past winter, my brother, Joe, came up with something ingenious. He put a lawn mower cable inside the car on the floor near the gearshift. Now "fast" means "hot" and "slow" means "cold," but at least I don't have to jump out of my car to adjust the heat every time I get a hot flash.

"'Lil Red," as I like to call her, is still sound mechanically, and she doesn't have much rust, even after seventeen years on Wisconsin's salty streets. But I knew it was time to start saving for my next car. Then I received a check for $5000 from a publisher for the reprint rights to two stories I'd written. An unexpected windfall, to be sure. *Whoa!* I thought. *This is going right into the bank for a new, "used" car fund.*

I started dreaming of cars. I imagined one with a CD player instead of a broken tape player. I mused about the comfort of driving with air-conditioning during the summer instead of having all four windows rolled down. How wonderful to arrive with my hairdo in tact instead of looking like I'd been in a desert storm. I even drove past a few car dealerships that day and gazed lovingly at some shiny late-model used cars.

The day after the check arrived and my new car fund began, I picked up my tax returns. After writing a check for $210 to the tax preparer's office, I walked as fast as I could to my car. Safely inside, I let the tears well up and stream down my face. I was in shock. I owed the federal government $3,367; I owed the state $128. And instead of my having to pay $150 for my quarterly estimated taxes, the tax man said I had to pay $1000 to the federal government and $40 to the state. "Both of those checks are due this April fifteenth," the tax man reminded me.

When I got home, I'd just written out the four checks to the federal and state revenue departments when the phone rang. "Hi, Mom, it's Andrew," said my youngest. "I desperately need a loan of two-hundred dollars to pay my utilities and part of my rent. My paycheck is late." Andrew was also a freelancer of sorts, doing camera and grunt work for ESPN's major league baseball coverage. As a beginner on the crew, he even had to pay his own airfare to the cities where the games were held, so borrowing money from Mom had become a frequent activity for Andrew.

When I'd finished writing the checks that day—$210, $3,367, $128, $1000, $40, and $200 for Andrew—I had exactly $55 left from my $5000 new, used car fund. With $55 I couldn't even buy a motorized kiddy car.

I stared at the wall in front of me and nearly started crying again. But then I remembered something I'd been sharing with friends, family, and strangers for years: "You have to earn that PMA degree! It'll change your life" (PMA = Positive Mental Attitude).

"Okay, Patricia," I said to myself. "It's time to stop blubbering and start practicing what you preach. It's time to turn this wailing around one-hundred-eighty degrees. It's time to understand that God has blessed you beyond measure. Four thousand forty-five dollars worth of unexpected bills came to you, and God blessed you with a check for five-thousand dollars to take care of it! It's time to really, truly believe that you're the only one responsible for your happiness and your attitude. You can choose to whine, complain, and feel sorry for yourself, or you can choose to be happy, knowing that God will always take care of you."

I'm proud to say that I have earned my PMA degree. I'm also happy to report that 'Lil Red is behaving beautifully without a whine or a whimper. I think we both have a lot more miles left in us. After all, I need to enhance my PMA degree. Five or so more years with 'Lil Red ought to do it, don't you think?

The Fruit Room

Caryl Jones

In God I trust without a fear. What can man do to me?
—Psalm 56:11 RSV

I started to feel uneasy. I was about twelve years old, and my sisters and I were finishing dinner. Mom had said, "Let's have canned peaches for dessert. I don't have any up here. Caryl," I held my breath as she turned to me, "would you go down to the fruit room and get a jar?"

It was the very thing I feared most. Inside I screamed, *The FRUIT ROOM! Anything but the fruit room! Why do I have to go?* Outwardly I muttered, "Sure," and left the table.

The only thing worse than facing the fruit room alone at night would be having anyone know how afraid I was.

We lived in the country, and every summer we canned so much fruit and jam there wasn't space for them in the house. Instead, we put them in a cool room in the basement of the garage. It was only a short walk from the house—outside to the garage, then down one flight of stairs.

It should've been a cake walk—um—fruit walk, but I'd let my imagination scare me until that short trip was filled with terrors. As soon as I stepped out on the porch and closed the house door, two things always startled me. Number one, the darkness. The porch light helped a little, but it was still so dark that nothing looked familiar. Even the big old trees had turned into spindly, spooky creatures. Number two, the dogs. We had three, but they could bark like a hundred. They probably would've stopped when they realized it was me, but by then the other dogs up the road would start howling, and ours would answer back.

I'd walk as quickly as I could to the garage, dodging treacherous tree limbs and wild dogs. Sometimes I took a flashlight with me, but batteries always seemed to be something Mom "forgot to buy."

The garage itself was an eerie place—more like an old barn, unfinished and used mostly for storage. I was sure half the bugs and spiders of the world lived there. There were birds too. During the day they looked like swallows, but at night . . . well, isn't that when vampires came out? I'd open the garage door and duck, just in case they were waiting to swoop on me. Then I'd start down the stairs. They were the kind with open backs, and the space underneath the stairs was big enough to hold one medium sized monster, three escaped prisoners, or a pack of man-eating wild animals.

The fruit room was right at the bottom of the stairs. After pushing the door open, I'd paw through cobwebs trying to find the light string, listening to strange rustling noises from the shelves. Snakes and mice wouldn't be nearly so bad to live with if they'd just stop popping up suddenly—always trying to make a person scream.

Our well was in one end of the fruit room. When the door was open, that corner was completely hidden. I watched John Wayne movies, and I knew that wild Indians liked to live near water and food; it seemed like a perfect hideout.

As soon as I was in the fruit room, I'd grab any jar and jump back out before the door could swing shut behind me. But I still had to face the worst part of all. Going back up the stairs. Anyone or anything that I'd stirred up on my way down would be waiting. I could almost feel icy fingers reaching through the steps, grabbing my ankles.

After racing up the stairs, I'd dash toward the house, bound onto the porch, and leap into the house. Then I'd try to calm down before handing the fruit to Mom.

"Oh, you got cherries instead."

I knew my fear was getting out of hand. I'd even considered refusing to go. But if my sisters ever figured out why, I'd never hear the end of it. Then one night, I discovered a Bible verse that turned out to be a life saver. Psalm 56:11: "In God I trust without a fear. What can man do to me?" I understood that God would take care of me. Sure I trusted Him—but without a fear? My imagination told me what a man or monster could do to me.

But God's Word was stronger than my imagination. I decided I didn't want to be afraid anymore. I sat in my bedroom, with every light on, and relived my journey step by scary step. Safe in my room, I knew it was silly to believe in monsters. I knew the bugs and snakes we had weren't poisonous. Our noisy dogs wouldn't allow any wild animal—let alone a convict—near the place. No person alive, no matter how brave, could endure living in that damp, dark room.

I started to feel calmer, and I didn't have to wait long for the real test. "Caryl," my mom said the next evening, "would you run down and get some strawberry jam for supper?" The familiar panic started to rise, until I remembered my verse.

In God—I stepped into the dark, forcing myself to walk slowly while the dogs howled around me;

I trust—shaking the flashlight as its beam faded;

without a fear—into the garage, down the dreaded stairway;

what can—standing inside the infested room, carefully choosing a jar of strawberry jam;

man do—taking a deep breath, then walking at a moderate pace up the open stairs;

to me?—bounding onto the porch, this time in triumph.

I felt like a hero! I'd battled and won. I don't remember ever volunteering to go to the fruit room, but the fear no longer controlled me.

And the bonus? I got exactly what I was sent for—every time!

Time Spilled Out

Mary Lapé Nixon

Therefore, I urge you, brothers, in view of God's mercy, to offer your bodies as living sacrifices, holy and pleasing to God—this is your spiritual act of worship.

—Romans 12:1 NIV

I love perfume, but not just because it smells so nice. I can trace the seasons and milestones of my life through fragrance—a random whiff in a mall or elevator conjures memories and emotions of the past. In the scent of Lauren, I can experience my carefree college days; in Fendi, the early stages of my career, in Red, the courtship of my husband. During the first years of our marriage we savored Dolce and Gabbana, which remains a favorite today. This special luxury is always a welcome gift, and the pure "parfum" is the culmination of science and art in liquid form.

So the gift I received from my husband several years ago was, indeed, special. The velveteen red box opened like an oyster bearing a precious pearl. Nestled in a bed of red satin laid the treasure—a small square flask. Its glass middle was shaped like a woman's figure whose womb bore the fruit of liquid gold.

Although it was too fine for everyday use, I wore it to work anyway. Its extravagant fragrance transcended the mundane details of life. One morning I was running late, and while throwing on my clothes, I knocked over the open bottle. Stunned, I watched the perfume drip to the floor and saturate a newspaper.

I couldn't discard the paper, so I kept it as a room deodorizer. Every day I'd smell the sweet perfume on the floor and be reminded of my blunder. I saved the precious bit left in the bottle for special occasions; no longer could I slosh it on every day.

But I wondered, why was I careful now when I had been so careless before? The depleted bottle now reminded me that time and the phases of life are much like expensive perfume. As I'd squandered the precious scent, so had I in my youth carelessly squandered time, which I'd perceived as limitless. As long as plenty of perfume remained in the bottle, as long as I had health and vigor, I took time for granted.

Slowly, the level of perfume decreased; life's flame flickers. I tire easily and remember with difficulty. So much has now been spilled; how can I redeem time in these days, when so many details cry out— a dusty house, grocery shopping, tending the yard? Because I can't do everything, frustration hounds me.

There yet remains in the spilled bottle, though, enough to savor; it cries out to me, "Don't lose hope. There's still some left." As long as I wake up each day there's a chance to begin life afresh. Although I was angry and frustrated yesterday, I need not be today. Although the past *can't* be changed, my attitude *can*.

And just as the spilled fragrance greets me anew each morning, so does each day. Still, the fragrance of spilled perfume will one day evaporate, but the sweetness of God's forgiveness and hope remains forever.

The remaining perfume is a warning, too, against opportunities lost—from fear, laziness, or just inertia. If I hide away what remains of the precious fragrance, I'll never enjoy it. If I fail to take risks, I'll never enjoy life. Does the fear of catching a cold stop me from hugging and kissing someone? Do I fail to attend Bible class because I'm fearful— or just reluctant—to go alone? In caution, do I take the greatest risk of all—not risking anything?

The perfume in the bottle, the perfume that's been spilled, reflects how God might perceive the days of my life. They will either be a sweet bouquet to Him or else a foul odor. In squandering time, I spill the bottle that holds the days He has allotted to me. So I must savor each day, one precious day at a time, just as I savor, drop by precious drop, my perfume.

Jesus—the Author and Finisher of our faith—lived thirty years as a sweet savor to the Father. Likewise, each life—whether long or short—should strive to emanate that fragrance, ascending heavenward, a reflection of His unfading, incorruptible, and unspeakable glory.

Mathephobia

Jason S. Wrench

There is no fear in love; instead, perfect love drives out fear, because fear involves punishment. So the one who fears has not reached perfection in love.

—1 John 4:18 HCSB

I was having problems. It was my junior year in high school, and I couldn't sleep. I was gaining weight, my grades were slipping, I felt I was slowly going insane. I thought there might be something seriously wrong with me, so my father took me to his physician. After getting a complete physical and donating most of my blood for lab tests, the evidence was conclusive—there was nothing wrong with me.

It wasn't a physical problem, we decided, it must be a psychological problem. I saw a Christian counselor, and he had me fill out psychological evaluations. They indicated that I should be a bus driver or a minister—interesting choices.

The counselor and I talked a lot, but mostly we talked about my dread of math. I hated math. I loathed math. I wished math would disappear from the face of the earth. I just knew that Algebra II, the class I was taking that year, was going to be the end of my life. I was, in fact, so frustrated with math, my anxiety had manifested itself in physical ways. That's why I couldn't sleep and was depressed, which caused me to eat more. Grades in my other classes were slipping because I spent most of the day either dreading or recovering from math.

We looked at how I'd responded to math for my entire life. Two years before, I'd actually had a nervous breakdown in my geometry class. The teacher had given a test on the very first day of class, and I didn't know anything about geometry. I freaked out.

Yes, math literally made me sick. The psychologist ultimately determined that I had—and I kid you not—mathephobia, or the fear of math.

I ended up failing math that year—the only class I've ever failed. I felt so defeated, like such a loser. The next year I had to retake Algebra II but with a different teacher. I was surprised, though, that I did better the second time around. Not only better, but a lot better. I ended up with an "A" average.

Why the big change? In retrospect, it's easy to see what changed. I no longer had the fear of failing—I'd already done it. For so long, though, I'd striven to be perfect. I had this warped perception that if I were perfect, people would like me more, my family would love me more, and maybe—just maybe—God would love me more. So when I faced something that I wasn't perfect at, I physically and mentally shut down. But when I failed, I somehow learned that I would never be perfect, that I don't have to be perfect at something from the minute I start studying it. Instead, I became open to learning and growing.

I did get better at math as time went on, and I allowed myself to grow no matter how slow the process. I also learned that God loves me, no matter how imperfect I am. Now, I no longer fear math, or fear that I'll never be the Christian I want to be. I realize now, that's a slow process too. I still get frustrated, over both math and my Christian walk, but tackling either no longer makes me anxious. In my college statistics classes I, in fact, made A's. I've gone on to become a social scientist working in the areas of communibiology and behavioral genetics, both of which rely heavily on the ability to use statistics. I've actually taught biostatistics to medical students and residents and statistical research methods to undergraduates. I'm even in the process of writing a statistics research methods book.

Who would have thought that could happen?

Apparently, only God.

Part 2

Education/
Teachers

Chicken Pox Typing

Jeanne Zornes

*An anxious heart weighs a man down, but a kind word
cheers him up.*

—Proverbs 12:25 NIV

It happened when I was fifteen—that time of life when the size of your self-esteem is inversely proportional to the number of zits on your face. So far, I'd survived adolescence without buying a crate of acne medicine, so my self-esteem was holding its own. Plus, I had one other thing in my favor; I belonged to the "Scholar Clique." My friends and I didn't flaunt letterman jackets or get asked to the junior prom, but when report cards came, we dominated the top of the honor list.

I realized, though, that my "seek-and-ye-shall-find" method of typing wouldn't take me far in life, so I enrolled in typing class. This was back in the days of old-fashioned manual typewriters; the keys were stiff and they constantly jammed. I assumed that typing class would get me an easy "A," that I'd race through it as easily as the quick brown fox jumped over the lazy dog, and that my scholastic standing would be secure.

I didn't anticipate, though, struggling to memorize a keyboard that wasn't arranged in alphabetical order, with A to Z lined up left to right. Worse, I landed a taskmaster for a teacher. Old and bent, Miss Jones had thin white hair, and she wore thick, outdated glasses that made her eyes look twice their size. At the sound of the bell, she shut the classroom door and, in her sensible shoes, clomped to the front of the class.

Within a few weeks, she took us from picking out easy words like *hit* and *owe* to doozies that made us look for *q* and *x*. Soon, we were performing timed typing tests to measure speed and accuracy. I felt as clumsy and nervous as a mile runner on crutches.

"Now students, it's time for the timed test," she'd announce in her scratchy voice.

Rat-ta-tat-tat-tat-tat—some of us waited, but almost everybody started in ahead of the timer.

"Do not start until I say go," Miss Jones said above the clatter of pounding keys.

Regardless of when we started, five minutes later, we all felt like our fingers had been doing push-ups for an hour.

Ding! Time's up.

"Now students, please quit typing." A few always got in some extra words. Poor Miss Jones was doing her best, but she couldn't control the cheaters.

Just as I was actually pushing twenty-five-words-a-minute, I woke up sick one morning with suspicious spots on my abdomen, neck, and face. Funny, they didn't look like zits. My fever was high, and as my mother quarantined me to my room, I remembered—I'd helped in the church nursery a couple weeks earlier. Chicken pox was going around.

At the grand old age of fifteen, my time for chicken pox had come. The doctor suggested I might get it "harder" than the little rug rats who'd exposed me. That was an understatement. In a few days, I was a raging, itching mess. I had pox in unmentionable places. Some on my face became infected and broke, leaving deep, oozing pits that were worse than any acne scar.

After two miserable weeks and still splotched with calamine lotion, I went back to school. But all I wanted to do was pull up a stone and participate in Job's Old Testament pity party.

I'd kept up with most of my class assignments that were sent home.

But there was no way to make up two weeks of typing. My friends had long ago left *quick brown fox* and were typing as fast as a fox being chased by hounds. My stellar GPA was plunging like a meteor. I had to do something—fast! I approached Miss Jones with a form permitting me to drop out of typing and go to study hall.

"That's really a shame," she said, looking at me with her bigger-than-life eyes. She never flinched at my splotchy face, and there was real kindness in her voice. I was surprised to see someone real and caring. She continued, "I know you can improve on your own. You were one of my best students."

I couldn't believe it. Had she really noticed me? Had she noticed when the others cheated? Had she understood why my typing speed wasn't at the top of the class?

Whatever her reason, I knew she believed in my ability to overcome, and I wanted to prove her right. I asked God, "Please help me learn on my own what I couldn't learn at school." At home I practiced typing, pushing myself to get faster and better. Eventually my pretzel fingers began picking out the keys naturally and rhythmically.

Nearly forty years later, I'm still typing, but I rejoice that computers have replaced old manual typewriters, making composing so much easier. I smile when I think of my adolescent trauma with chicken pox and the resulting scars. My happiness then depended upon grades and a clear complexion. I've added more scars—physical and emotional—through life's inevitable trials: joblessness, both parents dying when I was thirty and still single, waiting until thirty-four for marriage, tight finances, cancer scares, getting hit by a drunk driver, a father-in-law's ten-year struggle with Parkinson's Disease, major business disappointments.

I could've dropped out of life at any of those times, but I chose to push through—with God's help. I return to the lesson from my typing-class days and remember how my teacher looked beyond those horrible pox scars. She wasn't young and chic, but she turned out to be an unlikely messenger of encouragement. She helped me turn a negative into a positive and find deeper happiness in my circumstances.

I can do the same and use kind words when I'm around people

who are discouraged by setbacks. God can use even little words of encouragement, like, "I really appreciate how you did that," "You're getting better all the time," "I'm impressed by your progress," and "I know you can do it."

I've discovered an even better sentence to practice when typing: "I can do everything through him who gives me strength" (Phil. 4:13 NIV).

Jesus, Jungle Gyms, and Me

Dena J. Dyer

Permit the children to come to Me; do not hinder them;
for the kingdom of God belongs to such as these.

—Mark 10:14 NASB

What a guy! Jesus calls His followers "little children," and the Gospels show Him as a man who loves kids and loves to teach. Imagine that—He even loves to *teach* kids. When I instruct children, my back tightens, my eyes narrow, and my head starts to spin. It's like Mr. Rogers meets the Exorcist. Not a pretty sight.

The funny thing is, I enjoy teaching adults and teenagers. They're clean, quiet, and interested in the lesson. Especially when I bring donuts.

Still, God has used my experiences with kids to make me aware of—and somewhat at peace with—my less-attractive qualities. I try to relax when I help at my son's school or go to a birthday party. I hug the kids, ask them questions, and listen to them. And I have a notebook handy for all the funny and amazing things they say.

Once, while leading children's theater classes, I had in the group a six-year-old cutie with blond curls, sparkly blue eyes, and a mischievous grin. I never knew if she would spout something totally ridiculous or incredibly wise.

During an audition for our year-end production, I noticed her pounding her head with her notebook.

"Ann!" I exclaimed. "What in the world are you doing?"

"Hitting myself on the head," she said.

"I can see that, but why?" I asked.

"My finger hurts, and this makes me forget about it."

Another golden moment came when the church nursery was overrun with kids, and the workers desperately needed help. Too many adults apparently think that teaching children's Sunday school is like being sent to Alcatraz—once you go in, you never come out. As a minister's wife, I thought I would set a good example for the other adults and help with the prekindergarten class for a while.

Some of the kids were eligible for "Oldest-Child-Still-in-Diapers" in the *Guinness Book of World Records*. When one of them asked me for help in the bathroom, I turned in my resignation.

One Sunday, a little girl named Katie interrupted the Bible story with something "very important" she needed to tell the class. I let her speak, thinking she'd been overcome by a mature spiritual revelation—brought on, of course, by my excellent teaching.

"What is it, sweetheart?" I asked.

"Happy Birthday, Elvis!" she yelled.

I think that was my last Sunday in the elementary age class.

Children can be difficult at times. And so can teachers—like my third grade teacher, "Mrs. Morose."

As a child, I was known as teacher's pet because I got straight A's, turned everything in on time, and strived to obey. In other words, I tried to be perfect. Yet, my most vivid memory involves Mrs. Morose and a playground "curly" slide.

To understand the importance of a curly slide—the kind that starts way up high and twists and turns like a roller coaster—you have to realize that I grew up in Dumas, Texas. There, the most exciting event all year was when the Lions Club members rolled up the local beauty queen in meat packing paper (seriously!) the night before the annual barbecue.

Anyhow, after a day spent inside studying—or, rather, listening to the construction crew work on our new playground—I was selected by Mrs. Morose, along with several other kids, to go outside and check out the jungle gym in progress. We were instructed to glance at the playground, come back in "without saying a word," then calmly report to the class what the crew was doing.

But when we saw the slide, which looked like a giant multicolored curly fry, we couldn't contain our joy. Along with the other students with me, I jumped up and down, clapped my hands and shouted, "A curly slide! A curly slide!"

Mrs. Morose was instantly at my side with ruler in hand. She grabbed my elbow and steered me toward the door, hissing, "I told you to look quietly at the playground! You'll be punished for this!"

And we were. We had to stay after school, writing on the blackboard one hundred times something like, "I will obey my teacher and not get excited over things kids naturally get excited about."

I'm not bitter, though. Really, I'm not.

Through my experiences with kids and teachers, God began to show me my perfectionist tendencies and unrealistic expectations about myself and others. When I had my own child, those expectations got thrown out with the baby's daily bath water!

Gradually, through journaling, counseling, and lots of chocolate therapy, I made peace with myself as a person. I learned that as hard as I try to be perfect, I'll never get there. I'm not a perfect mom or wife, teacher or student, and (shocker!) there are no perfect teachers or students.

Well, I take that back. There is *one* perfect teacher: Jesus.

A lot of people picture Jesus as being like Mrs. Morose—a stern instructor who hates merriment, who carries around a sharp instrument, and is ready to whap you if you get out of line. In all honesty, I used to think of Him that way myself.

But the more time I spend with Him, the more I believe that Jesus resembles bubbly Ann rather than Mrs. Morose. I imagine Him having sparkling eyes, a mischievous grin, and a great sense of humor. His disciples, in fact, never knew whether He was going to say something incredibly wise or, in their opinion, totally ridiculous.

I also think He's a little like Katie, not that He necessarily celebrates Elvis's birthday, but because He loves a celebration. His first miracle was performed at a wedding!

I know that Jesus is a lot of fun. The Gospels often show Him inviting the children to come near. Can't you see Him—like some magnetic jungle gym—laughing as the moppets climb up, around, and behind Him?

I'm thankful that God has worked on me when it comes to kids. I'm feeling so peaceful, in fact, that I'm actually volunteering as a "helper" for Vacation Bible School this year. No teaching involved, just assisting. After all, it's only . . . five days!

Oh, dear, what have I done?

Lessons for the Teacher

Doris Schuchard

Do not fear; you are of more value . . .
—Matthew 10:31 NASB

I'd always dreamed of following in my parents' footsteps. They both were teachers, and I played "school" with my younger sisters, took along educational games when I baby-sat, and taught children at summer camp. So I was excited when I graduated from the same college as my parents and began my teaching career.

Four years later, I was ready to quit. "I don't know if I can do this much longer," I sighed one morning at school.

Kelly, my student teacher, looked up from the juice cups she was filling. "But you're so good with the children! I can't wait to be a teacher."

"The kids are great, the parents supportive, and I don't know what I'd do without you," I smiled. "But still . . ."

I thought back to that first year of teaching when it all started. "Let's draw a picture of the trees we saw on our Autumn walk," I suggested to my students. I rolled out the mural paper on the floor, but when I tried to get down and join my kindergartners, both knees throbbed and refused to bend. Even twelve aspirin a day and rest didn't help. Over the next few months, my other joints became stiff, sore, and inflamed. My handwriting looked like scribbling. It hurt even to turn my head to look out the car's rear window. Dusting a low shelf became impossible.

The day I didn't have the strength to get out of bed finally drove me to a doctor. "You have a classic case of rheumatoid arthritis," the orthopedic surgeon concluded.

"Arthritis? I'm only twenty-three!" Yet somehow I would adjust, determined not to let it interfere with my teaching. At school I sat on a child-sized chair instead of the floor; I asked fellow teachers for help with heavy lifting in the classroom.

Still, I wondered if I was doing the right thing. "These kids deserve a healthy teacher—I'm afraid I'm just not good enough."

Our conversation was interrupted as twenty, three- and four-year-olds crowded around me, all talking at once.

"Hi, Miss Doris, what are we going to do today?" asked Stephanie as she bounced up and down.

"Yeah, are we going to use finger paints?" asked Trevor.

Kelly set the juice tray down and clapped her hands. "Let's line up for music time."

Soon the children were marching behind this Pied Piper, laughing and singing, "If you're happy and you know it, then your face will surely show it. If you're happy and you know it, clap your hands!" A few laps around the classroom and they all tumbled around Kelly on the rug, ready for story time.

"People have many feelings. Sometimes we're happy, sometimes we're sad, and sometimes we're afraid," explained Kelly. She opened a book to read about a little boy who was fearful of the monsters in his closet.

"One time I was scared a monster was under my bed," volunteered Amy. "But Mom squirted it with 'monster spray' to make it go away."

"Did you know that even grown-ups can be scared?" replied Kelly. "I just found out I have a sickness called lupus. When my legs hurt, I use crutches. And when my hurt makes me afraid, do you know what I do?" she smiled. Twenty enthusiastic voices sang, "If you're scared and you know it, then your face will surely show it. If you're scared and you know it, pray to God!"

Who was the teacher and who was the assistant that day? Kelly's simple faith spoke to my own heart. If this young woman could trust God with her future, who was I to limit His working in my life?

What should I plan for my children tomorrow? Finger paint, build a fort, write a class story? There were so many possibilities, but suddenly I knew. There would be time for all that and so much more—I was their teacher, after all!

My Gift from Miss Clara

Lanita Bradley Boyd

"For I know the plans I have for you," declares the Lord, "plans to prosper you and not to harm you, plans to give you hope and a future."

—Jeremiah 29:11 NIV

The small group took their places at the front of the room, but my thoughts were elsewhere. Tall imposing Miss Clara, her gray hair tightly pulled back into a bun, settled herself and gave the group her full attention. I slipped out of my seat, pulled the shoebox from under my desk, and crept to the back of the room. Crunched on the floor behind a bookshelf that formed a work area, I carefully took out my paper dolls and spread them on the floor.

These were not ordinary paper dolls, but ones I'd made myself. My Aunt Mae would give me the page of Betsy McCall paper dolls from her *McCall's* magazine, and I'd cut them out to play with them. I'd even create my own dresses for Betsy. I took them to school and played with them when I was finished with my seatwork, which was always well ahead of the other students.

My "works of art" fascinated the other third-grade girls, and the spirit of free enterprise possessed me. I began selling my handmade dolls and dresses. For the enormous sum of two pennies, Velma Wright could have her own Betsy McCall paper doll and outfit. Judy Wiseman would give me special orders for outfits to match her own. For the price of her lunch cupcake, Betty Austin could have a doll and four outfits. I had a booming business, and each night I worked on new clothes and dolls—and deposited my newfound wealth into my piggy bank.

But the inevitable moment finally arrived. I looked up from the floor where I was selling my wares to see Miss Clara towering above me. Never had she seemed so tall or forbidding. But she doled out no chastisement, verbal or otherwise. She only regarded me with a long piercing, thoughtful look as she collected my box of paper dolls and pennies.

I never knew how my parents found out. I was given no note to take home; we had no telephone in those days. But they knew. I could tell by the long meditative looks that they gave me. So when would the explosion come? When would I be punished? I prayed to God to get it over with, but He seemed preoccupied elsewhere.

A few weeks later, Daddy said he and Mother needed to talk to me about school. My stomach catapulted.

"Miss Clara has talked to us. She's very concerned that you're not being challenged to meet your potential. We've all discussed this and decided that when you return to school next week, you'll go to Miss Sue's fourth grade class. What do you think?"

What did I think? I hated the idea! I was hysterical. I refused to go. But my parents had prayed over this and the decision had been made. I changed grades and thus friends and experiences. I was mad at God and Miss Clara and my parents for ruining my life. I actually had to work and earn my grades! No longer could I float through classes, feeling condescending toward those who had to work so hard.

I still don't know if the decision was right from an educational or parenting point of view, but I now appreciate the strength of character that the decision forced upon me—and the experiences that came from it. Had I entered college a year later, I wouldn't have sat by my future husband at daily chapel and in two classes. He would've been a year ahead of me and we might never have met—and how totally different my life might have been. No other life could have been as good as the life I have.

I now thank God that my path was altered so completely when I was in third grade. God had abundantly responded—in His own unique way and time—to my prayers, my parents' prayers, and Miss Clara's quandary.

What I saw as punishment at the time, became a special gift—a gift from God, through Miss Clara.

Part 3

Love/Marriage

A Frisky Frosty

Anna Jones

I belong to my lover, and his desire is for me.
—Song of Songs 7:10 NIV

An illustrated book on sex caught my attention. I'd been meandering through the children's section in our local Barnes and Noble, and had chosen *Frosty the Snowman* for my kindergartner's Christmas book exchange. Not far away, I'd spotted this very adult material in the self-help section. Surprised at how prominently it was displayed, I found myself flipping through the pages.

The bookstore was crowded and I was embarrassed to be seen reading something so salacious. I placed my newfound item underneath *Frosty the Snowman* and headed to the Christian section, where I could "safely" view my book. I found it difficult, though, to manage my wallet, *Frosty,* and my new book in a way that I could discreetly view the pages. So I placed my wallet on the shelf.

A young lady began searching the shelves around me. Could she see what I was reading? More engaged in the book than I'd like to admit, I tucked it within the pages of *Frosty* and looked for a private spot to read. I found a nice little chair wedged in the corner of the store where I could finish perusing the book to my satisfaction.

It was an eye-opening read, one I admit I found interesting. Yet I wasn't eager for the entire bookstore to know my business. So I carefully planned my route to reshelf the book; hidden under *Frosty* it would be easy to replace without attracting anyone's attention. I deposited the book and headed to the checkout. Reaching the line, I suddenly realized I didn't have my wallet. I knew right where I'd left it. Not yet in a panic, but a little concerned, I briskly walked to the aisle. "Oh no!" I checked each shelf. "It can't be. It's gone!" Had my sin found me out? Surely my credit cards and $250 of Christmas cash had been stripped from me. With my heart racing and my legs trembling, I rushed to the checkout and stopped before a bearded, longhaired gentleman. "Did anyone turn in a brown wallet?"

In the gentlest manner, he handed the wallet to me, saying, "I found it in the Christian Section."

I drove home, pondering the experience. Had it been wrong for me to look at the book? If not, why did I feel the need to hide it behind *Frosty?* If I hadn't done anything wrong, why was I so embarrassed? My mixed reaction to the book certainly chilled my thoughts, but I couldn't help but smile at the humor in the situation.

I went home to my husband and relayed the details of my experience. To my surprise, he was totally unconcerned about my wallet, but he teased, "Did you learn anything?" My husband obviously prefers me frisky rather than frosty.

Well, I thought, *what did I learn?*

In my next quiet time, I prayed and spent time in the Song of Solomon, contemplating my mixed emotions. That's when God turned up the heat, and the frost began to melt. I learned that God meant for married sex to be pleasurable—but the world has corrupted it. God compares an earthly marriage to His relationship with the church. He wants us to desire Him with the same degree of intensity that we would desire a lover. Our relationship with Him is intimate and exciting, and in the same way that our marriages need nurturing, our relationship with God requires time and effort to nurture it.

I rejoice in my nine years of marriage (which is pretty good these days). And I rejoice, too, in the message that God has given to me: *I belong to my lover, and His desire is for me.*

A Sporting Wife, Who Can Find?

Jan Coleman

Be agreeable, be sympathetic, be loving, be compassionate, be humble.

—1 Peter 3:8 THE MESSAGE

Carl waited until after the wedding to inform me of his fervor for fishing.

"That's great, dear," I replied. "Every man needs a passion."

"I hoped you'd take up the sport and go with me."

I cringed as an old memory bubbled to the surface. It was a family outing in Yosemite, and my cousin's first catch of the day was my neck. I was ten years old, and a crowd of adults tried to extract the barb while I screamed and flinched. Then we made a trip to the hospital through winding mountain roads, where I lost my lunch.

"No, thanks," I smiled. "I'm not into fishing."

The gleam of hope faded from his eyes.

Carl had been single for many years and thought he'd finally found in me a midlife soul mate, a woman who loved to banter over politics and travel back roads on mountain bikes—a woman willing to brave adventure and try new things.

Or so I'd claimed before the wedding.

We'd both been down the road of rejection, and God had given us a second chance. In my first marriage, I molded myself to my spouse's expectations, trying to keep up with his demands for perfection. Maybe then he'd stop stepping out on me. He left me anyway, and I'd lost my true self. After twelve years on my own, and with God's help, I'd found "me" again. The idea of learning to fish to make a man happy caused me some jaw clenching.

But for Christmas I got a collapsible rod and waist pack with various pockets for all the tackle. "Just in case." Then one day, I came home from the post office to find Carl practicing his cast. "It's all in the wrist," he coaxed. "Here, you try it. There's nothing like the thrill of fishing."

The following spring, he invited me to spend the day fishing with him. "Okay," I said. "I'll try it, but I'll bring a book in case I get bored." Fat chance. Carl kept saying, "We've got to keep moving. They aren't biting in this spot." After trekking a mile upstream, I resorted to my best whine, but it didn't seem to faze him.

In early summer, Carl came home with a friend's borrowed boat in tow—twelve feet of dents with a grease-caked motor most likely manufactured when Kennedy was in the White House.

"These old things were built to last." He gave it a friendly bang. "I've rented a mountain cabin for the weekend. I know that hiking along a stream through the wilderness isn't your idea of fun, so I thought we'd try some lake fishing."

Three days later, I found myself floating on a gorgeous canyon lake. The place was deserted except for a graceful bald eagle perched atop a pine tree. I marveled at the scenery while Carl primed the pump and yanked on the frayed cord to start the engine.

"Not sure what's wrong," he said, taking apart the cover to investigate. "We've got plenty of gas."

Choke. Spit. Sputter. The motor refused to cooperate. Had God heard my prayers?

I contained my growing glee. "That's too bad, honey." A good book on a sunny deck was my idea of the perfect getaway weekend, and it looked like a strong possibility. Maybe Carl would give up and be content with a subscription to *Field and Stream*.

Just as we were rowing the crippled boat to shore, a Department of Fish and Game truck backed down the boat launch, and a man in uniform hopped out. "Hey, don't leave yet!" He shouted. "I'm about to dump four thousand fish in this lake."

Suddenly, my heart gave a stir. All those fish coming straight toward me? I grabbed my rod and some bait.

"Hold it, Jan," Carl said in all seriousness. "This isn't sporting."

"Huh? What do you mean?"

"These are fresh out of the hatchery. They haven't had a chance to survive in raw nature."

"I thought you brought me out here so I could feel the thrill of a bite on my line?"

I had him there. He smiled and shrugged, then placed the oars back in their slots. I sat waiting, watching the dark swell of trout circling our boat in the shallow water, cautiously making their way to the deep. My pulse throbbed as the perfect cast landed in their midst and my first prey was lured to the orange, glittering bait.

And then it happened—one took the bait. I jerked to set the line as Carl had taught me, and it began—the battle of wills between me and my catch. I followed Carl's coaching; let the fish tire out, keeping my line taut so I could net him. Over the next few minutes I caught four more.

Then something sparked in me—a thrill I'd never known. And I've not been the same since.

To Carl's surprise, I'm now a convert to this water-tug-of-war. And we bought that old boat from our friend—Carl was right, lake fishing is tailor-made for me.

God changed my heart that day on the lake, but the message was not, "Submit to thy husband's outdoor yens." Rather it was, "Respond in love."

I experienced the kind of love that makes a marriage great; one that doesn't insist on its own way, one that considers what's right for the other and makes adjustments. A love with no conditions attached. Carl would love me whether I fished or not. But, lovingly, compassionately, he gently persisted in finding a way for me to share in his passion, and it paid off.

For both of us.

Attitude Adjustment

Marita Littauer

If possible, so far as it depends on you, be at peace with all men.

—Romans 12:18 NASB

My husband doesn't like it when I travel. Traveling has been a part of my life, though, for all my adult years. When I met Chuck, I was teaching seminars all over the country and still am. You'd think he'd be used to it after twenty years of marriage. Instead, he likes it less and less.

While on the plane ride home from seminars, I often enjoy escaping into a romance novel. As I read, I picture Chuck meeting me at the airport terminal with roses in his hand, or at least dropping what he's doing when I walk in the door at home. Then he hugs me and kisses me and confirms how much he's missed me. Not.

In reality, the plane lands. I deplane and walk alone through the terminal, get my baggage and go to my car. I wait in line to pay for my parking and drive home. Because I like to get home from a trip as soon as possible, I frequently arrive late at night rather than the next day. So Chuck is often asleep. I tiptoe in, drop my bags, and undress in the dark. I crawl into bed beside him and he wiggles his foot against my leg to welcome me home. Hardly the romance-novel scene I'd painted in my mind.

One year, my trip had me scheduled to arrive home on the day of our anniversary. It was our sixteenth, and I really wanted that romance-novel scene I'd so often dreamed about.

I'd arranged to have flowers sent to his office with a card that said "Happy Anniversary! Hurry home after work!" (The flowers would be delivered in the morning in case he forgot what day it was, and they'd remind him to do whatever he needed to do.) I'd also planned to arrive home before he got off work, so I'd have time to shop for the ingredients to make a lovely dinner.

When I got home, I headed straight for the kitchen, did the dinner prep work and put it all aside. When I went into the bedroom, I found something small and black hanging on our four-poster bed with an anniversary card. (He hadn't forgotten after all.) After relaxing in a bubble bath, I put on my present and lit some candles in the bedroom. Next, I put something bubbly in a silver bucket, and placed it, along with two crystal flutes, next to the bed. When it was nearly time for him to come home, I crawled up on the bed and read my romance novel—and waited. The dogs barked and I heard his car door. I tucked the romance novel away and arranged myself artfully across the bed.

From the results of my efforts, I could now write a romance novel of my own! He was excited to see me, glad I'd come home. While the night left me breathless, I thought it through in the morning. That was the reaction I'd like every time I get home!

Romans 12:18 tells me that it's my job to do the changing, not to change him. What could I change that would bring about the desired effect? First, I could change my schedule so I came home before he did, instead of after he was asleep. I could fix a special dinner and bring on the bubbly. I could put on one of the many "little some-things" he's given me over the years that I know he likes, and I can place myself across the bed as if in a lingerie catalog. Yes, I could do that.

And my next trip, I did just that. It worked again—even without the special day and without the flowers. My next trip, I tried it again, and it worked again. I'd created an attitude adjustment.

While Chuck is still not crazy about my traveling, he sure loves my coming home! But without travel, would I be putting forth the home-coming effort? Perhaps not. Perhaps being apart makes being together that much more exciting. Perhaps travel isn't so bad after all.

Adventures in Camping

Tonya Ruiz

Love suffers long and is kind; love does not envy; love does not parade itself, is not puffed up; does not behave rudely, does not seek its own, is not provoked, thinks no evil; does not rejoice in iniquity, but rejoices in the truth; bears all things, believes all things, hopes all things, endures all things. Love never fails.

—1 Corinthians 13:4–8 NKJV

Laughter is the shortest distance between two people.[1]

—Victor Borge

"Pumpkin, I've got good news," said my husband of only three months. "We're going camping!" I could tell by his voice that he was really excited.

But dread quickly overwhelmed me. "Ron," I told him, "I've never camped before."

"Don't worry, sugar," he said in a soothing voice. "I'll take care of everything."

"Look," I sweetly said, "in my family roughing it meant sleeping with a window open at the Hilton." We both laughed. I was dead serious.

---

1. QuoteWorld.org, http://www.quoteworld.org/author.php?thetext=Victor%20Borge (accessed 17 March 2004).

For weeks he shopped and packed. I'd never seen him so enthusiastic about anything. On the appointed departure date, we drove off with our camping gear tied atop our white Ford Escort. He was smiling; I was in charge of reading the map. Only three hours into our journey, we were lost.

"Okay," I said, "don't get frustrated. I'm doing the best I can. Which way is East again?"

"Sugar pie," he patiently explained, pointing with one hand and driving with the other, "North, South, East, and West. Didn't you take geography in school?"

"Sure," I said, "and I got an A."

He rolled his eyes, pulled the car over to the side of the road, and took the map away from me. Instantly, he solved the problem. "It would have been easier to follow," he scolded, "if you hadn't had the map upside down."

Already tired and weary, we reached our planned camping site. "When you get away from the city lights, it sure is dark," I told Ron as we looked up at the stars. "I keep hearing noises and they make me nervous."

"Don't be silly, muffin, we're in the middle of nowhere. Do you think a chain saw murderer would come all the way out here?"

"Of course not," I lied.

At sunrise, he walked to the lake to do some fishing and I headed to the showers. Upon returning to our campsite he found me in the tent crying. "Why aren't you cleaned up, yet, honey bun?" he inquired.

"There are bats hanging from the ceiling in the shower," I sobbed.

"They won't bother you, muffin."

The second night it rained and our air mattress turned into a life raft. We decided to move to a new location.

Ron chose a scenic spot by a stream. It was warm in the sun, and I decided a dip in the water would refresh me. Slowly, I waded into the stream. Snakes, snakes, and more snakes, gathered around me, their beady eyes watching my every move. I walked on water. Once on the bank, I yelled for Ron. Inspecting the menacing serpents, he assured me, "Nothing to worry about, cookie, those are just little water snakes."

Again, we moved to a new location. We stopped the car and pulled over, looking for a place to pitch our tent. Ron liked it. "Look, honey, we can camp here on the hill, and in the morning I can catch you breakfast from that stream."

Either I was dizzy or the ground was moving. After my eyes adjusted, I realized the ground was blanketed with amphibians.

"Don't worry, cupcake, those newts are just migrating," he said.

I ran for the car and Ron followed. "I will not sleep with those things crawling all over me. Get me a hotel room, or take me home!"

After finding the only lodging within a hundred miles, Ron rented a little cabin for us. *It may look slightly rustic,* I consoled myself, *but at least I won't be sleeping with the newts.* Ron went out to collect kindling for the fireplace, the shack's only redeeming feature. I decided to crawl into bed to get warm, only to find it was already occupied—by dozens of tiny arachnids! I used the pillow to brush them away, and then crawled in. The bear's visit to our porch didn't scare me too much. He made a lot of noise, but I knew he wanted the outdoor trash can and not me. At least the cabin had a lock on the door.

Around two in the morning, I heard scratching sounds. Tiptoeing over to the light, I switched it on. Mice scurried in every direction. I ran screaming and jumped onto the bed.

Ron awoke with a start and reached for his hunting rifle. "What in the world is wrong?"

"Mice," I whimpered as I sat in the middle of the bed, my head covered with the blanket.

"Don't worry, cream puff," he said. "They won't get on the bed," and resumed his snoring.

I shook him awake. "I thought you were Prince Charming, but I was wrong. You're Grizzly Adams."

He pulled me under the covers and nuzzled me with his beard.

"I just don't get it, dumpling," he said over breakfast. "What more could you want. Fresh air, peace and quiet, and mountain streams full of trout?" He was invigorated by this adventure and I was deflated.

"We should have discussed this in premarital counseling," I said. "I love you, but a lifetime is going to be a long time if camping is involved. And please, stop calling me foods!"

Grizzly said, "Okay, kitten, I have a solution."

The next day, we found a small town with a decent hotel. Ron bought me a lawn chair that he dubbed, "the queen chair," and he found a perfect spot for it—right next to a lake. He put my chair in the sun and his manly camping chair next to it.

"I am not putting that worm on the hook," I complained as he taught me how to fish. At dusk we headed back to town. "I won't tell anyone my trout were bigger than yours," I promised. After a lovely dinner at a restaurant and hot showers at our hotel, I asked Ron, "If you still want to rough it, I could open a window." We both laughed.

Our twenty-year marriage has been like that first camping trip. Learning to give and take, and working together to find solutions to our problems. There have been good years and bad years, and we've learned to compromise. The next year we found a beautiful cabin near a lake and across the street from a day spa.

Other than the moth invasion and the mouse incident, it was an almost perfect vacation.

Love Extravagantly

Marita Littauer

Observe how Christ loved us. His love was not cautious but extravagant. He didn't love in order to get something from us but to give everything of himself to us. Love like that.

—Ephesians 5:2 THE MESSAGE

I'll never be able to entertain again," I wailed. The huge, Red Baron type biplane was covered in dry cleaning bags and hung above my desk. How could I write with dry cleaning bags, emblazoned with bright yellow and black advertising, hovering over my work area? The airplane had hung there for years without incident. But this was different.

The Folker D7 had been a part of Chuck's life for over twenty years. He'd built it and had too much of himself invested in it to risk flying it. With a five-foot wing span, it can't be tucked just any place. So it hung near the peak of the cathedral ceiling in the family room, above my desk.

I like my home to look like a showplace, and big red airplanes are not a part of my decorating scheme! As you can imagine, even having the airplane there was an act of compromise and love. Since it was important to Chuck, I accepted it as a conversation piece—and you can be sure it generated quite a bit of conversation!

On this day, Chuck had taken the airplane down to take it to a model airplane show. He'd spent hours cleaning off the dust that had settled onto every surface. The plane had been very popular at the show, and he'd discovered just how valuable it really was. Before he put it back on its hook, he wanted to protect it, so he covered the body and wings with plastic dry cleaning bags, advertising and all. He felt it was a good solution. I disagreed.

Just days prior to my outburst, during my personal Bible study time, God had told me to take on Ephesians 5:1–2 as my personal mission statement. He said my mission was to love my husband with extravagance, not to get, but to give everything of myself. As I cook breakfast or dinner, as I do the dishes, as I do the laundry—all of these things are something of myself I can give, not expecting to get in return. God reminded me that Chuck has had a rough time. He was not in a place to be able to give much. But I was. I wrote the verse out and taped it to the mirror in my bathroom to remind me that, although it was my mission, it was contrary to my human nature.

I knew my outburst to seeing the red airplane was an overreaction. So I went outside to cool down. There, I trimmed my roses, and as I took a deep breath, *love extravagantly* came to mind. Does it really matter if the airplane has a bag over it? What's more important—that my husband be happy or that I have a lovely home? Hmmm . . . that was a tough one.

Love extravagantly, I told myself. I came back in and apologized— ready to accept the dry cleaning bags. Chuck pointed up.

Chuck had decided that I was right, that the bags really were ugly. He'd taken the plane down, removed the dry cleaning bags, and replaced them with clear plastic wrap, which clung tightly to every curve and didn't even show!

Ah, *extravagant love*—certainly contrary to human nature. But, oh, what power as a personal mission statement!

Preaching Lessons

Verna Davis

Submit to one another out of reverence for Christ.
—Ephesians 5:21 NIV

I'm married to a minister. His presence in the pulpit is awesome, and his preaching is filled with humor, insight, and great spiritual truths. As a public speaker, I often find myself jealous of his ability to capture his audience with his eloquence.

Over the years, I've learned quite a bit from Doug's preaching. I constantly take notes not only on what he says, but how he says it, what examples he uses, how he delivers his point. As a result, my speaking career has benefited from what I've learned from Doug's preaching techniques.

I've also learned how *not* to preach. One day, Doug and I were engaged in our version of verbal domestic warfare. In short, we were fighting. Loudly. I hope it doesn't shock you to find out a preacher and his wife argue, but perhaps that's why it's best to call the parsonage before you drop in for a visit!

We were in the midst of our marital dispute when Doug spotted his Bible on the dining room table. It was lying open at the fifth chapter of Ephesians. With a look of immense satisfaction, he picked up God's Word and started to quote. I guess that would've been all right if he hadn't also started to pound the pages with his finger to emphasize his point. And even that would've been all right if he hadn't used his best preacher voice in the process. Call me sensitive, but it hurt my feelings.

"Wives, submit to your husbands as to the Lord," he said smugly. "For the husband is the head of the *wife* as Christ is the head of the church, his body, of which he is the Savior. Now as the church submits to *Christ,* so also *wives* should *submit* to their husbands in *everything.*" (Emphasis is Doug's alone, trust me!)

That was the wrong Scripture at the wrong time. Or maybe I'd received one too many personal sermons delivered to me by my minister. Or maybe I just wanted Mr. Smug Doug to have a taste of his own medicine.

I snatched his Bible from his hands. "Very good, *honey,* but you only read three verses to me; Ephesians 5:22–24." I admitted they were good instructions for a wife on her relationship with her husband. "*But,*" I pointed out, "the rest of the fifth chapter of Ephesians involves the husband's relationship with his wife. Pretty good instructions— all *eight* verses worth!"

I delivered my ace-in-the-hole, my *coup de grace* with a sweet smile, at least as sweetly as I could with anger dripping from my lips. I said, "Look at this verse, honey." I had my own finger ready to pound. "*Husbands,* love your wives, just as Christ loved the church, *and gave himself up for her.*" After reading this to him, I placed the Bible on the table between us and waited for the next blow from Doug. I thought he might eventually win the battle, but this round belonged to me!

To my surprise, Doug leveled his finger at my face and said, "Verna, thou shalt *not* preach to the preacher!"

I couldn't help it and neither could Doug. We both burst out laughing. We laughed so hard we had to hold each other for support. Then we just started holding each other. To this day, neither one of us can remember what we were arguing about.

Through our laughter that day, we promised each other we'd never again use God's Word as a tool to hurt the other. Scripture is foremost a gift from the breath of God, and we are to use it for all kinds of training so that we may be equipped for good works. Although God's

Word is as sharp as a sword, that sword should never be used to pierce another child of God.

Doug and I have devised a way to discipline each other if we're ever tempted to do so again. The offender is to stand twenty paces away from the offended. The offended will load a self-righteous Scripture-shooter with Holy Word pellets and shoot the offender in the middle of his/her cold, cruel heart.

And during this procedure, the offended is to shout—what else?— "Fix these words of mine in your hearts!"

Ironing Woes

Bonnie Skinner

But strive first for the kingdom of God, and his righteousness, and all these things will be given to you.

—Matthew 6:33 NRSV

I'd lived an exciting life. I worked my way through college, enjoyed many extracurricular activities, including being the homecoming queen during my sophomore year. Immediately following graduation, my parents drove me to Washington, DC, where I worked as a secretary to a United States senator from our state. Within a few weeks, I was taking dictation in our nation's Capitol! Back in the early 1950s, this was a major feat for a twenty-year-old girl from Sand Mountain, Alabama.

I immediately joined a church in DC and became active in the single's department. Once each month, I worked in the church kitchen, helping serve free meals to military men stationed in the area. Since this was during the Korean Conflict, those dinners were well attended. On my first Saturday night at work, I served a plate of spaghetti to a handsome young man who was attending Officer's Candidate School in nearby Fort Belvoir, Virginia.

We became friends and later enjoyed sightseeing every Sunday after church. As time passed, we became engaged. Jack received his shiny Second Lieutenant's bars four months later. Shortly thereafter, we were married and left Washington, DC, for Jack's first military assignment as an officer at Fort Leonard Wood, Missouri.

Several weeks later, I laundered Jack's military uniforms. This was before spray starch and Martha Stewart were household terms. I remembered watching my mother make starch from scratch on our Alabama farm. I poured boiling water into a large pan as mother did and added what I thought was enough flour to make starch for Jack's khaki uniforms. I remembered the importance of removing the sticky film covering the cooled starch in the pan; I did not, however, remember that mother added more water to dilute this concoction.

I dipped each pair of pants and each long-sleeved shirt into the starch mixture, wringing out the excess liquid and hanging them on an outside line to dry. (This was also before clothes dryers became a household appliance.) I then sprinkled water on each dried garment, rolling it up tightly to maintain the dampness for easy ironing, after which I tucked all the uniforms into a pillow case in preparation for next day's ironing.

The following day, I ironed one leg of the first pair of pants. I was impressed how these pants would certainly have *body*. But by the time I finished ironing that one leg was so stiff it stuck up in the air. As I struggled to iron the other leg, tears formed in my eyes, and I sat down and cried. I knew Jack needed a new uniform for the next day, so I attempted to iron the shirt with the same results. The stiff arms were flailed like a harpooned octopus as I tackled one of the front panels.

That was in the summer of 1952, and there was no air conditioning in our apartment in hot, humid Missouri. As I stood at that ironing board with perspiration trailing down my face and legs, I regretted that I'd ever married. This was not at all what I'd anticipated as the life of a newlywed! I'd gone from being a secretary in Washington, DC, to being a laundress for one of America's soldiers. *This*, I reflected bitterly, *is not the life for me!*

As a final insult, a brisk wind suddenly swept through the open door, blowing up the skirt of my nylon dress (another fifties thing), and the nylon stuck on the flat surface of the hot iron! I turned off the iron, looked down at my dress, and saw a gaping hole in the skirt.

Scraping the partially melted pieces of nylon off the iron's surface, I knew the dress was ruined. I'd simply have to toss it into the trash. This dress had been one of six that I'd purchased for my trousseau and had paid out on layaway. So much for my attempt to be a Betty Crocker bride.

As I continued to iron, I needed a distraction, so I turned on the radio (no TV in those days), only to hear that Adlai Stevenson had selected my former boss, Senator John Sparkman from Alabama, to be his running mate for the upcoming Democratic presidential race. When I heard that, tears spilled down my face. If I'd remained in Washington, DC, I might have ended up in the White House. Oh, woe is me!

Where was God in all this?

Jack arrived home full of enthusiasm, looking forward to seeing his new bride. To his amazement he found the Homecoming Queen standing in the center of the room, wearing a dress with a big hole in the skirt, and holding a shirt so stiff that one arm actually saluted! When Jack realized my dilemma, he plucked up his uniforms and said in a calm voice, "Don't worry, honey, I'll take them to the base laundry from now on. I'll wear this uniform again tomorrow."

I felt an immediate rush of love for Jack because of his attitude— and I began to understand unconditional love. The loss of my trousseau dress took a little longer to get over, but I remembered, "Lay up not your treasures on earth, Bonnie. Remember to always seek your solace in our heavenly Father."

Many times I've remembered that day and how I wanted to be a perfect bride and make sure Jack was impressed with my wifely capabilities. That day taught me that what really mattered was how eager Jack was to get home to me. He could have cared less about having four sets of uniforms neatly hanging, appropriately starched and ironed.

Through our almost fifty-two years of marriage, I've learned that the most important thing I can do is take care of myself in all possible ways—mind, body, and soul—so I may be a good partner for Jack. A wonderful marriage was given to me. Occasionally I'll fail my husband, but I know God will never fail either of us. All we need to do is keep Him first in our lives, and He takes care of the rest.

Shaky Landings

Ginger Plowman

"For I know the plans I have for you," declares the LORD, *"plans to prosper you and not to harm you, plans to give you hope and a future."*

—Jeremiah 29:11 NIV

It's funny how the personality traits that first attracted us to our husbands later drive us crazy. Take my husband, Jim, for instance. He's always approached adventure with reckless abandon. He enjoyed rappelling down steep mountains Australian style (upside down) and making 230-foot bungee jumps. His daring sent shivers of excitement and intrigue through my entire body—making him the most irresistible man I'd ever met. So I married him.

Thirteen years and two kids later, that adventurous attitude no longer holds the same appeal. One day I was frying pork chops, for instance, when Jim waltzed into the kitchen with that mischievous boy-have-I-got-an-idea-now look on his face. The zeal in his eyes told me I needed to brace myself.

"I want to fly airplanes," he grinned.

I wanted to cover my ears and chant, "I'm not going to listen to you. I'm not going to listen to you." But instead, I chose the mature approach. "Have you lost your mind? Do you think I'm going to offer my blessing? Do you think I want to seal my fate as a widow at the age of thirty-four? If you do this, I'm never speaking to you again!" (Stomp, stomp, stomp, slam.)

Two mornings and many prayers later, still in my pajamas, I planted one hand on my hip and waved my toothbrush with the other. "Okay," I proclaimed, "if you want to do this, it's fine with me. But let's get one thing clear, buddy. Neither I nor your offspring will ever get into that airplane with you!"

Three months later, I was climbing into the back of the airplane. Jim kissed my cheek and promised, "You're gonna love it." My excessive fear of heights, however, was screaming otherwise. To make matters worse, Jim's flight instructor announced, "Jim, today we're going to work on your shaky landings."

I leaned forward and tapped the instructor's shoulder. "Excuse me . . . but for a second there I thought you said we were going to work on Jim's shaky landings."

The instructor chuckled at my anxiety as Jim spoke some sort of numeric jargon into the microphone. "Auburn traffic Skyhawk eight-niner-eight-four-seven departing runway three-six." But all I heard was, "Mayday! Mayday! Mayday! We're all going to die!"

Trying to keep a calm demeanor, I squeezed my eyes shut while sweat poured down my face. The seat belt seemed flimsy and totally inadequate, so I assumed crash position. I braced myself, shoving my feet against the back of the front seats and pressing my palms on the ceiling—for when we rolled, of course. Confessing all of my sins, I begged for God's mercy. Then I felt the plane lift off the runway. Nothing happened. Ten minutes later, I peeked through one eye to see if I'd arrived at the pearly gates. Nope, it wasn't the pearly gates, but it was something that took my breath away: a thrilling and fantastic view of God's creation.

An overwhelming sense of peace washed over me as I basked in the beauty of it all. I began to see what attracted Jim to flying. The freedom of sailing with the clouds over the earth was like a glorious tour of God's handiwork—and my husband was my tour guide. Pride fluttered in my heart as I glanced at his handsome face etched with excitement. I was glad to share in his adventure that day, and landed safe and sound, in spite of his shaky landings.

I'd protested going flying with Jim, and in much the same way I often protest going somewhere that God wants me to go. When God first called me to speak and write on a national level, I wanted to cover my ears and chant, "I'm not going to listen to You. I'm not going to listen to You." I questioned, "Do You think I want to make a fool out of myself, speaking in front of large groups all over the country?"

Two years later, I was speaking at Saddleback Church in California, one of the largest churches in the country, and being interviewed on national television and radio. Was it against my will? At first, you bet it was. The fear and anxiety that plagued my heart every time I took the microphone threatened to overwhelm my obedience. Then one day, I opened one eye and looked around. I saw what God saw: the beauty of His handiwork through an obedient life.

Do I ever experience shaky landings? Yep. Once I was in the middle of speaking and an eighty-year-old man in the audience suddenly stood up. He yelled, "Hey, what's going on here? I thought this was where the prostate cancer support group was meeting!" Then he walked down the aisle, in front of the stage, and out the door. He mumbled something, like Tim Conway from the Carol Burnett Show, about "women having no business in a prostate cancer support-group meeting."

Then there was the time I swallowed a bug midsentence and nearly passed out from choking. Even in disastrous situations, though, God still fulfills His purpose when I surrender to His will.

We mustn't assume a crash position, fearful and anxious over what might happen if we move out of our comfort zones. We must obey God's calling on our lives, step out in faith, and allow Him to transform us. He has a perfect plan for our lives that can only be fulfilled if we're willing to fly with Him.

And in spite of a few shaky landings, the view is worth the ride.

Socks in Bed

Sherri Buerkle

It is better to live in a corner of a roof, than in a house shared with a contentious woman.

—Proverbs 21:9 NASB

My husband has never understood women. He never will. I've tried to teach him how our minds work, but he forgets, the way he forgets his pile of dirty work clothes that I stumble over in our bathroom. He insists he doesn't need to understand the female psyche. That's what I'm around for—to interpret.

But who is there to explain *me* to *him?*

Every year, when the cold wind blows and the sun hangs low in the sky, I can't get warm. I tote my hot cocoa from room to room, all the while complaining how chilly the house feels.

"It's an oven," my husband says as he flips from one football game to another.

"I'm cold," I'll whine. "Can we cuddle?"

He looks disgruntled and then a grudging acceptance crosses his face. "Ten minutes. That's all."

I take what I'm given, but it hasn't always been that way.

Growing up in North Dakota, you'd think I'd be immune to low temperatures, but living through a yearly ice age only seemed to make me hyper aware of it. Knowing my predisposition to shivering, I married a man whom I thought was a cuddler.

It seems the only reason my husband tolerated our cuddling when we were dating was because he had some hormonal imbalance that insisted he get close to me. After we'd been married for a few months, I seemed to have cured him of this malady, and his secret aversion to cuddling came to the surface.

At first when we cuddled, he'd say he was "a tad warm." As the weeks rolled by his language became stronger. "Sweetheart. I love you, but I'm getting . . . overly warm."

Immediately, I'd disengage, thinking it was just the summer heat that was bothering him. I mean, I'm not totally insensitive to his feelings. I could do the walk-by cuddle and hug. But I couldn't wait for winter. That's when the real toe-warming cuddles started.

Winter came, and to my surprise, my husband's mild objections didn't change. They became even stronger. Now he was "sweaty and uncomfortable" and that climbed to, "Honey, I'm blazing hot!"

My feelings were hurt. My husband didn't understand my need for the exchange of heat. I didn't just *want* to be cuddled, I *needed* to be cuddled. It's what makes me feel loved.

I wish I could say I was mature about it all. I wasn't. Instead of talking out the issue, a seed of mischief was planted in my brain. That night, when we crawled into bed, I put my bare, icy feet on his legs. You've never seen a man jump out of bed so fast.

"You're feet are freezing!" he yelped.

"They are?" I asked with false innocence. "But you're so warm and you like it cold, remember?"

"Cool. I like it *cool,*" he emphasized as he climbed back into bed. "Put some socks on."

I sighed. "I'm too tired." Again, I wiggled my feet under his thigh even as I heard him hiss in a breath of night air. I smiled perversely. "Besides, you're warm. As the man, you're supposed to take care of me."

I know. I was evil. I played on his manly duties to get him to subject himself to my torture. All through that winter, every night, I climbed into bed and slapped my frozen toes onto his warm skin. And like a trooper, he'd suck it up and bear this new burden.

It's fortunate for him that we all mature. He did so a bit quicker than I. Change started out subtly. First he bought me the most adorable slippers and placed them at the foot of our bed. I'd wear them, just until a half hour before bed. That's when I'd kick them off and make for the linoleum. Self-inflicted torture isn't to my liking, but revenge will make a person temporarily insane. I'd shuffle about, out of his sight, waiting for my feet to ice over. When my toenails turned blue, that's when I'd turn in.

Next, he left socks on my pillow. The old Dr. Seuss story came to mind, "Fox in Socks," and just like the sly fox, I was determined not to give in to Mr. Knox's suggestions to leave him alone. I'd fumble around and knock the socks behind my pillow. When he asked if I'd seen those blasted socks he'd left out for me, I'd shrug and snuggle further under the covers.

Not a dimwit by any stretch of the imagination, my husband scoured the Bible for answers to our dilemma. One night, while my toes were warming on his calves, he turned to me. "Why don't you wear socks to bed?"

"They feel icky." Which wasn't a lie. I disliked wearing socks to bed.

"I don't mean to complain, but I really hate it when you put your cold feet on me."

By nature I'm not a spiteful person, and because of my immature behavior, contrition had crept up on me. I had to come clean. "I know."

He blinked back his surprise. "And you do it anyway?"

"I guess it all started when you stopped cuddling me."

"I didn't stop cuddling you."

"Not entirely," I admitted, but his quickie cuddling was no cuddling at all to my mind. "You said cuddling made you too hot."

"It does."

"But I need to cuddle—a lot."

He pulled me close and began to chuckle.

I was not in a laughing mood. "What's so funny?"

"I was just wondering how Solomon did it. Thankfully, I only have one wife to contend with."

My heart sank. It's common knowledge Solomon had woman

troubles. His wives had not been a blessing, and neither had I. I'd been weakening my marriage by trying to manipulate my husband. "That's not funny."

My husband kissed the top of my head. "Tell you what. I promise to cuddle you if you stop warming your feet on my legs."

I couldn't believe it. Instead of getting angry, my husband gave me exactly what I wanted. Did I mention my husband was more mature than I?

I thought for a minute. "I can live with that."

"But there's got to be a time limit."

Restrictions and rules—it's such a guy thing. But I played along. "Ten minutes?" Less than that and I would feel cheated.

"That's doable."

We both fell asleep, more content than we'd been all winter.

My husband and I have been married over twenty years. I frustrate, confuse, and generally irritate him on a daily basis, as he does me. But that's okay. To this day, my husband uses the Bible to interpret my actions. God has shown him (and me) that when two completely opposite individuals want to love each other, they must sometimes meet on middle ground.

Dr. Seuss knew that. Just read "Green Eggs and Ham." In addition to the Bible, it's a fine book on marriage.

The Battle of the Sexes

Tonya Ruiz

*Again, if two lie down together, they will keep warm; but
how can one be warm alone?*

—Ecclesiastes 4:11 NKJV

*Nobody will ever win the battle of the sexes. There's too
much fraternizing with the enemy.*[1]

—Henry Kissinger

I think we're polar opposites," I said to my husband one chilly morning. As I turned the thermostat up past freezing, my husband turned it back down and told me, "You won't die of hypothermia, put on a sweater."

"Yes, sir!" I snapped, standing at attention (with my fingers crossed behind my back). This was a full-scale battle over the thermostat, and all is fair in love and war.

"I don't like being cold," I told him as I jumped into my clothes and shrugged into a hooded sweatshirt. When I pulled the drawstring tight around my face, I looked like the unabomber. I could see my breath as I said, "I suspect your grandfather was one-fourth Polar Bear." I was so cold, my nose was red enough to guide Santa's sleigh.

---

1. QuoteWorld.org, http://www.quoteworld.org/author.php?thetext=
Henry%20Alfred%20Kissinger (accessed 17 March 2004).

Ron, dressed in shorts and a T-shirt, and pounded his chest Tim Allen style. He was invigorated by the cold air.

He's not invigorated, though, by stimulating conversation. Over breakfast, I chatted about a story in the newspaper. My husband listened and responded with "Ah-huh" about every ten seconds. He got up and started walking away. "Wait," I told him, desperate for conversation, "I've only used three hundred words. I've got two thousand left."

Later that afternoon, after I returned from a luncheon, he asked, "Did you have a good time?"

I dove into a long narrative, but I could tell by his contorted face that he'd hoped for a "Yes" or "No" answer. I might as well have married Joe Just-the-facts-ma'am Friday from Dragnet. I phoned my girlfriend and spent the next twenty minutes reliving everything down to the color of the toothpicks in the hors d'oeuvres.

If his face registered dismay after my luncheon, it was twisted in agony later that evening. I'd announced, "Honey, I stopped by the video store and brought home a couple of movies."

He examined the cases and exclaimed, "They're both chic flicks! This could be the worst movie night of my life."

He slept through both love stories, and when I woke him I said, "I guess it's your testosterone. It won't let you watch a movie unless it is full of machine guns, sharks, or aliens."

"Honey," he said, "the only way we'll ever agree on a movie is if they come out with *My Big Fat Greek Gladiator*."

My voice dripping with sarcasm, I replied, "Maybe, we could hope for a *Sleepless in the Matrix*."

I headed for the bathtub and filled it to the brim with steaming water. Twenty minutes later, I climbed out lobster-red. Slipping into my warmest pajamas, I realized I was wearing more flannel than a lumberjack. But a girl's gotta do what a girl's gotta do.

After Ron's lukewarm shower, he flung his bathrobe off James-Bond style and climbed into bed. It was obvious he hoped for intimacy.

As he nibbled my ear, I asked, "Did you lock the front door?"

He grabbed his robe and grumbled his way down the hall.

"You're a veteran," I hollered after him. "It's your job to check the perimeter." I made a mental note to buy him camouflage pajamas. When he got back into bed, I planted my cold feet to his warm back. "Yiiiikkkeeesss!" he hollered.

"I'm confused." I told him, "Since it's so stinking cold in this house, how do you expect me to have warm feet?"

"By wearing more socks," he suggested.

"Hey, I've got an idea," I said seductively. "How about if I crank up the furnace and take off my Paul Bunyan pajamas. Then I'll slip into the nightie I bought for our anniversary." As I went into the hallway to change the thermostat, I said Arnold-Schwarzenegger style, "I'll be back."

We've declared a truce. Except for his ample supply of male hormones, we're not so different after all. We've been bunkmates for some time now, sharing our warmth, our laughter, and tears. Alone, I would have suffered, but sharing my days—and nights—with someone I love has enriched my life.

As I get older and my estrogen levels plummet, maybe I'll be warmer, talk less, and love *Dirty Harry* movies. Then Ron and I will almost be twins.

Of course, it'll be *ages* before I'm *that* old. Um . . . excuse me, while I go turn down the thermostat. It seems to be getting warm in here.

The Parable of the Coffee Filter

Nancy C. Anderson

A soft answer turns away wrath, but a harsh word stirs up anger.

—Proverbs 15:1 NKJV

I'm going home!" my brother Dan said. "Your bickering is making me crazy. You two fight constantly—and it wears me out."

I defended our behavior. "Hey, it's not like we disagree about *everything*. Ron and I agree on all the major issues. We hardly ever fight about big stuff like where to go to church, how to raise Nick, or who's a better driver (me). We just disagree about the little stuff."

Dan sighed and said, "Well, I'm sick of hearing you go to war over where to put the towel rack, which TV shows to watch, or who did—or didn't—use a coaster. It's all dumb stuff. None of it will matter a year from now."

"You're exaggerating," I said. "Besides, no one is mad."

"Oh yeah? I can tell Ron is, by the way he *stomped* up the stairs. Why did you have to criticize the way he mowed the lawn. I know it wasn't perfect, but couldn't you just let it go?"

"No," I replied. "We're having company tomorrow and I want the yard to be perfect. So I told him to fix it. Big deal. Anyway, I won. He removed it."

Dan shook his head. "If you keep this up, you may win the arguments, but you'll lose your husband."

I slugged his arm. "Stop being so melodramatic."

The next evening, Ron and I went out to dinner with some friends we hadn't seen in several years. We remembered Carl as being funny and outgoing, but he seemed rather quiet and looked exhausted. His wife, Beth, did most of the talking. She told us about her fabulous accomplishments and then, endlessly bragged about her brilliant, Mensa-bound children. She only mentioned Carl to criticize him.

After we ordered our dinner, she said, "Carl, I saw you flirting with that waitress!" (He wasn't.) "Caarrrrlll," she whined, "can't you do anything right? You're holding your fork like a little kid!" (He was.)

When he mispronounced an item on the dessert menu, she said, "No wonder you flunked out of college. You can't read!" She laughed so hard she snorted. But she was the only one laughing.

Carl didn't even respond. He just looked at us with empty eyes and a blank stare. The rest of the evening was oppressive as she continued to harangue and harass him about almost everything he said or did.

We said good-bye to Beth and Carl and left the restaurant in silence. As we walked to the car, my brother's comments echoed through my mind. When we got into the car, I spoke first, "Do I sound like her?"

"You're not *that* bad."

"How bad am I?"

"Pretty bad," he half whispered.

The next morning, as I poured water into the coffee pot, I looked over at my "Devotions for Wives" calendar.

"The wise woman builds her house, but the foolish tears it down with her own hands" (Prov. 14:1b NASB). *Or with her own mouth,* I thought.

"A nagging wife annoys like a constant dripping" (Prov. 19:13 NLT). *I was a nagging, annoying wife. How could I stop this horrible pattern?*

"Set a guard over my mouth, O Lord; keep watch over the door of my lips" (Ps. 141:1 NASB). *Oh Lord, show me how!*

I carefully spooned the vanilla-nut coffee into the pot, but I forgot the filter. The coffee was undrinkable, of course, bitter and full of grounds. I had to throw it away.

It struck me then. Coffee without filtering is like my coarse and bitter speech. I prayed, "Oh, please Lord, install a filter between my brain and my mouth. Help me to choose my words carefully and speak with smooth and mellow tones. Thank You for teaching me the 'Parable of the Coffee Filter.' I won't forget it."

An hour later, Ron timidly asked, "What do you think about moving the couch over by the window? We'll be able to see the TV better."

My first thought was to tell him why that was a dumb idea. *The couch will fade if you put it in the sunlight, and besides, you already watch too much TV.* But, instead of my usual hasty reply, I let the coarse thoughts drip through my newly installed filter. "That might be a good idea," I said calmly. "Let's try it for a few days and see if we like it. I'll help you move it."

He lifted his end of the sofa in stunned silence. Once we had it in place, he asked with concern, "Are you okay? Do you have a headache?"

I chuckled. "I'm great, honey. Never better. Can I get you a cup of coffee?"

Ron and I recently celebrated our twenty-fifth wedding anniversary and I'm happy to report my "filter" is still in place—although it occasionally springs a leak. I've also expanded the filter principle beyond my marriage. I've found it to be especially useful when speaking to telemarketers, traffic cops, and teenagers.

The Power of a Confession

Kathy Collard Miller

Therefore, confess your sins to one another, and pray for one another so that you may be healed. The effective prayer of a righteous man can accomplish much.

—James 5:16 NASB

W ell, honey," I said to my husband, Larry, "I'd really like our side yard to be all concrete. Then we can put the trash cans there."

Larry stared at me as if I were from outer space. "Why would you think that? I'm not even going to put the trash cans there."

My spirit deflated like a punctured balloon. His voice sounded so gruff. Did he really think my opinion wasn't worth anything? I shrank back and muttered, "Seems everything I say is worthless. I guess I just won't say anything."

The tension between us had grown since he'd retired and we'd moved to a newly-built home. He'd been around 24/7, we'd moved quite a distance from family and friends, and it seemed like thousands of decisions had to be made about the new place. We often commented, "We sure are under a lot of stress." Stress? Hoo-boy! But after almost thirty-two years of marriage, we somehow thought it couldn't affect us.

But it did—and I wasn't happy. Larry and I rarely initially agreed on anything for the house. And to make matters worse, my hormones were raging. Oh, menopause, here I come! I knew I was feeling super-sensitive to Larry's comments, and even when I expressed my wounded feelings and he said he hadn't meant to hurt me, I couldn't accept it. I viewed everything he did through a negative eye, perceiving him as my foe rather than my ally. I knew I was wrong, but I couldn't seem to stop entertaining thoughts about his faults and meanness.

Recently, I called Larry from one of my speaking engagements in a distant city. He asked how the program had gone, then he paused. "Kathy," he said, "the Lord has convicted me about something and . . . I want to ask your forgiveness. I've been thinking that your supersensitivity was your problem and you needed to deal with it. But I haven't been your spiritual leader by helping you. I'm so sorry. Will you forgive me?"

I couldn't believe my ears and couldn't respond.

"I want us to work on this together," he continued. "We'll do anything we need to do to help us overcome this challenge."

I felt like a burden fell off my shoulders. He really cared! He really was sensitive to the Lord. I was so pleased and expressed my appreciation.

But I didn't realize the difference it would make in my perceptions. When I returned home, I felt completely different toward Larry. My negative eye was gone, and I felt free to recognize his many positive qualities. I was freed, too, from the negative thoughts about him that had plagued me.

I fell back in love with this wonderful guy, and when I expressed my surprise at what had happened, Larry replied, "I'm not surprised at all. I knew my confession would break the bondage holding you. I hadn't been the spiritual leader in caring for you, and the Lord assured me that taking that leadership would give you the freedom you needed." He smiled, a bit smugly perhaps, but I couldn't have been more thrilled.

The power of a confession. Asking for forgiveness is a powerful healer and it breaks the bonds that hold us and cause destruction. James 5:16 says, "Therefore, confess your sins to one another, and pray for one another so that you may be healed."

I'm grateful that God gave me a spiritual leader, who obeyed the Lord and set me free.

The Things We Do for Love

Gena Maselli

*Be devoted to one another in brotherly love. Honor one
another above yourselves.*

—Romans 12:10 NIV

Standing among a few thousand starstruck preteen girls, I knew I'd
arrived. If I never did another self-sacrificing act in my marriage,
I was convinced I could still nab the Wife of the Year award. I'd fulfilled my promise to love, honor, and cherish through good times and
bad by becoming a pop princess wanna-be.

My husband is unlike most thirty-something men. Although we
don't have children, he's the author of charming children's books. While
some wives complain of competing with Sunday afternoon football
or being dragged to antique car shows, I don't. My husband isn't a
sports junky or a car buff, but he is a big kid at heart. His Lego collection is one of his most valued possessions, and an evening of munching on McDonald's while watching the Muppets would win out over
dinner at a five-star restaurant any night of the week. In addition to
all this, he's a teeny-bopper music junkie. To him, it's cheerful, clean
music that makes you want to dance.

So when my husband's thirty-first birthday came around, I asked
him what he wanted for a gift. He thought about it for a few days, and
then he heard the news. Disney Radio's Pop Till You Drop concert was

coming to town, and his favorite teeny-bopper band was the main show. That's what he wanted—tickets! I agreed, but wondered if I'd feel a little out of place. Maybe we could borrow a few children for the night as a plausible cover.

On the night of the concert, there we were, just the two of us—on the fourth row, dead center. The only other adults I saw had small children with them. It's fair to say we were in the D.I.N.K. (double income no kids) minority. Our only allies were three older, teenage boys who sat in front of us. One sheepishly looked our way before taking a seat and said, "Gee, I hope our little sisters show up before the concert starts." We laughed, knowing their virtual sisters were probably out and about with our virtual children. We were all on our own.

As the first band took the stage, four pretty, young girls—the oldest maybe thirteen years old—sang and danced their hearts out. I stared, questions flooding my mind. Was I ever that young? Are they really releasing their third album and still wearing braces? And more importantly, was my stomach ever that flat? I was in awe. To be that talented and that young; it was amazing.

"Please stand up and clap with me," my husband urged as I slouched in my chair trying to blend in. "I need you to be my recreational companion right now."

Ugh! This was not the time for a *His Needs, Her Needs* reminder, but I grudgingly stood and halfheartedly clapped my way through the first two bands.

During intermission, while parents stood in lines with their children to buy T-shirts or get autographs, my husband pushed us to the front of the lines to get our own keepsakes. He even developed a tag team plan for efficiency: "You stand in that line for that band's autographs, while I stand in this line for this one."

"Maybe no one will notice that we don't have children with us," I muttered.

"Don't worry," my husband reassured me. "People are gonna think our kids are somewhere in the arena and that we're standing in line for them."

It must have worked because a few minutes later a mother asked,

"All I want is a free book cover for my daughter. While I'm up there, do you want me to get your daughter one?"

"No, that's okay," I said with a weak smile.

As the evening wore on, I loosened up. Maybe it was singing "Who Let the Dogs Out" at the top of my lungs, or seeing my husband blissfully jamming to the beat. Whatever the reason, I got into the groove and had a blast. By the end of the night, my ears rang, my feet hurt, and my throat ached from screaming with the crowd.

During the ride home, my husband proclaimed it was the most fun he'd had in a long time. I had to agree. It was fun. Even more, I'd learned a lesson that night. I'd spent the weeks leading up to the concert, and even half the concert itself, worrying what other people would think. But then a big, neon news flash hit my mind: This was not about me. This was about someone I loved, about giving him a great birthday present and making a special memory. This was ultimately about serving another, about putting him first, even if it was a little uncomfortable for me.

Isn't that the kind of love God wants us to walk in every day? Doesn't He constantly remind us in His Word to love one another, encourage one another, and think of others first? Some may think going to a teeny-bopper concert falls outside the realm of God's love, but I disagree. The important issues are rarely the most obvious. Sometimes the question on the surface is, "Will you go to this concert with me?" when the issue underneath is, "Am I worth your time?" or "Is my opinion more important than the opinion of strangers?"

I can't count the times when my own self-centeredness has kept me from serving others, even the ones I love most. Learning to do so is a process, a process of daily dying to my own selfishness and putting my eyes upon God and the people who are the most important to Him.

Take it from me—a thirty-something, screaming, pop princess wanna-be. It's not the easiest road, but learning to see the way God sees is worth the ride.

Part 4

Health

What a Celebration That Shall Be!

Janet Lynn Mitchell

*Let the sea and everything in it shout his praise! Let the
fields and their crops burst forth with joy!*
—1 Chronicles 16:32 NLT

I felt numb as I left the hospital. Eight-week-old Joel and six-year-old Jenna had been admitted, and my husband, Marty, stayed behind to be with them. I headed for a grocery store, and since it was 11:00 P.M., only one place was open twenty-four hours a day. Turning the engine off, I rested my head against the seat.

What a day, I thought. With two of my young children in the hospital, and a third waiting at Grandma's, I was truly spread thin. Today I'd passed the infant CPR exam required before I could take little Joel home from the hospital. *Would I remember how to perform CPR in a moment of crisis?* A cold chill ran down my spine as I debated my answer.

In addition to the CPR exam, I'd spent the day learning the facts about Jenna's juvenile diabetes. Exhausted, I reached for my grocery list. It more resembled a scientific equation than food for the week. I'd been trying to accept Jenna's diagnosis, and I now knew how to test Jenna's blood and give her insulin shots. But I was terrified. There was so much to remember when it came to food choices; food needed to balance the insulin that would sustain Jenna's life.

"Let's go, Janet," I mumbled to myself while sliding out of the car. "Tomorrow is the big day! Both kids will come home from the hospital." My mumbling turned into a prayer.

"God, I'm scared. *What if* I make a mistake and give Jenna too much insulin, or *what if* I measure her food wrong, or *what if* she does the unmentionable—and sneaks a treat? And God, what about Joel's apnea monitor? *What if* it goes off? *What if* he turns blue and I panic? *What if* I can't handle this?"

My thoughts startled me and made me shudder. I redirected my mind away from the *what ifs* and gave myself an emergency pep talk, reciting what I knew to be true, "I can do all things through Christ who strengthens me. I can do all things . . ."

I grabbed my purse, locked the car, and entered the store. The layout of the store was different than the one I was used to. Uncertain where to find what I needed, I walked up and down each aisle.

Soon I was holding a box of cereal, reading the label, trying to figure out the carbohydrate count and sugar content. "Would three-fourths a cup of cereal fill Jenna up?" Not finding any sugar-free cereal, I grabbed a box of Corn Flakes and continued shopping. Pausing, I turned back. *Do I still buy Fruit Loops for Jason?* I hadn't even thought how Jenna's diagnosis might affect Jason, my typical four-year-old. *Is it okay if he has a box of Fruit Loops while Jenna eats Corn Flakes?*

I turned down the canned fruit and juice aisle. *Yes, I need apple juice, but how much? Just how often will Jenna's sugar "go low" so she'll need this lifesaving can of juice? Will a six-year-old actually know when her blood sugar is dropping?* The *what ifs* were again starting to take over.

I held the can of apple juice and read the label. *Jenna will need fifteen grams of carbohydrates when her sugar drops. But this can has thirty-two.*

My hand trembled, and I tried to steady the can when the tears slid down my face. Not knowing what to do, I grabbed a couple six-packs of apple juice and dropped them in my cart. Frustrated by feelings of total inadequacy, I crumpled up my grocery list, covered my face with my hands and cried.

"Honey, are you all right?" I heard a gentle voice. I dropped my hands from my face. I'd been so engrossed in my own thoughts I hadn't even noticed the woman shopping alongside me. She put her hand on my shoulder. "Are you all right, honey? Are you a little short of cash? Why don't you just let me—"

"Oh, no . . . thank you, ma'am." I looked into the eyes of the silvery-haired woman who waited for my answer. Wiping my tears, I tried to gather my composure. "I have enough money."

"Well, what is it, then?" she persisted.

"It's just that I'm kind of overwhelmed. I'm here shopping for groceries so that I can bring my children home from the hospital tomorrow."

"Home from the hospital! What a celebration that shall be. Why, you should have a party!"

Within minutes this stranger had befriended me. She took my crumpled grocery list, smoothed it out, and became my personal shopper. She stayed by my side until each item on my list was checked off, and she even walked me to my car, helping me as I placed the groceries in my trunk. Then with a hug and a smile, she sent me on my way.

Shortly after midnight, while lugging the groceries into my house, I at last felt the impact of what this woman had taught me.

"My kids are coming home from the hospital," I said with wonder and giggled with joy. "Joel is off life support," I shouted to my empty house, "and he's functioning on a monitor! Jenna and I can learn how to manage her diabetes and give her shots properly."

And just as God met my needs in a grocery store, He will meet each and every need we have. Now that was a reason to celebrate.

And what a party there will be![1]

---

1. From *A Special Kind of Love*. Copyright © 2004 Broadman and Holman Publishers. All rights reserved. Used by permission.

Buckle Up for the Ride

Deborah Fuller Thomas

*My flesh and my heart may fail, but God is the strength of
my heart . . .*

—Psalm 73:26 NASB

You've probably seen one—a snapshot of a family at the end of a
ride in an amusement park. They're in the throes of exquisite
terror after a free fall. My family's photo shows us careening to the
bottom of Disneyland's Splash Mountain. Our eyes are squeezed shut,
our mouths frozen in screams as we plunge into foam and mist. What
a wild ride!

Our photo was taken the summer of 1998. I know by the way my
left hand clutches my wig as we plummet. I feared it would be whipped
from my bald scalp to float like a drowned rat in Brer Rabbit's lagoon.

Six months before, I'd embarked on a wild ride of a different sort—
one over which I had no control. It promised a maximum fear factor,
and propelled nausea to an art form. I'd just been diagnosed with breast
cancer and was facing surgery, chemotherapy, and radiation.

Coming home from a doctor's visit, I was armed with brochures
and pamphlets describing all the possible scenarios connected with
my treatment. Sitting shoulder-to-shoulder with my husband, I read
one grim possibility after another. In my stunned and hopeless frame
of mind, I fixated on one thought: If all those side effects happened to
one person, wouldn't it be better just to die?

At that moment, the phone rang. My sister-in-law in Indiana had just heard about my diagnosis. Without realizing it, she gave me a completely new perspective—God's perspective. She simply said, "Don't take everyone's chemo stories as your own." She explained that her husband found his own chemo experience to be quite different from the horror stories friends had shared with him. Mine could be different too, and attitude, as you buckle up for the ride, can make all the difference in the world.

After the initial impact of my first chemo treatment, I learned to plan ahead to manage my nausea, keeping Jell-O and bland foods in the fridge, loading up on water beforehand to keep hydrated. When I began to crave salsa again, we celebrated at my favorite Mexican restaurant. It was like the brass ring, something within my reach.

Taking charge of my hair loss, though, was a fork in the road. To wig, or not to wig. I chose to wig. I found a hairstylist who was willing to shave my head in the privacy of my own home and trim my wig to suit my face. Some women look cute in hats and scarves, but I felt like Uncle Fester of the Adams Family.

There were, of course, dark tunnels of depression that seemed endless. But when I began to keep a journal, God revealed a normal ebb and flow that followed each treatment. When I felt better physically, my outlook improved. And when I felt drained, I recognized my aimless channel surfing on the couch for what it was—a temporary lull. Eventually, I'd be up to speed again.

Getting my life back on track when the ride began its final descent was a challenge. It came together when I learned to pace myself, which meant relaxing my standards on housework and home cooking. God showed me there are worse things than missing a little league game or ordering carryout for Thanksgiving dinner.

Through all the rides during that family vacation, my kids teased me about keeping a grip on my wig. But the day finally came when I had to give up the familiar comfort that had maintained my dignity for so many months. Saying good-bye to my wig meant the end of perpetual good hair days, and the beginning of experiments with kinky hair. That milestone was the final corkscrew in my ride.

When my ride came to a complete stop, I hoped it was one I'd never have to take again. But if I have to queue up for another, I think I'll raise my arms this time, knowing my strength and dignity is in my precious Lord, and that He will be in the front seat, taking the brunt of the impact for me.

In that crazy photo, I'm soaked to the skin with wig askew. My dear family—with me all the way—is equally soaked and disheveled. But our faces are joyous. Together, we'd been through another sort of ride, and the end of that one is truly the happiest place on earth.

Divorce Is Not an Option, but Murder Is

Amanda Rankin

*We felt we were doomed to die and saw how powerless we
were to help ourselves; but that was good, for then we put
everything into the hands of God, who alone could save us.*
—2 Corinthians 1:9a TLB

Life as I knew it stopped on April 15, 1994. Before that day, my
husband and I lived fast-paced lives. For twenty-four years, Tony's
sales jobs took us all over the country—from selling cameras to the
White House and to *National Geographic* in Washington, DC, to putting on press photographer's shows in California.

We traveled on our frequent flyer miles, visited friends everywhere,
and had a great marriage. I was spoiled, used to having everything I
wanted, and very grateful for my life. We had no children, so all of
our time and money was spent on ourselves and the things we wanted
to do.

I had a wonderful time running our Arabian horse farm, while Tony
traveled during the week. On weekends we had "honey do" projects
together, and barbecues on Saturday nights. Life was happy and social. In fact, life was *grand!*

Then one morning we were having a bowl of cereal and reading the paper together when Tony gave a slight cough. When I looked up, he was sitting and staring into space. His cereal bowl had tipped and was spilling milk onto the sofa and under his leg.

"Tony, are you all right?" I asked.

After a long pause, he responded slowly with a quiet "Yes."

I wasn't convinced. Moments later, I noticed Tony standing in a daze, with the left side of his face drooping, his mouth turned down on one side. I knew he'd had a stroke.

As I called an ambulance, Tony thumped to the floor every time he tried to stand. I convinced him to stay on the floor until the paramedics arrived.

He spent the next eight days in ICU, flat on his back, while they searched to find the reason for his stroke. Then he was sent to a rehabilitation hospital for therapy.

That first week was the most horrible week of my life. My precious "I can do anything" husband, who built a horse farm for me and was so good at anything he put his hands to, was reduced to a pale, thin, drooling man who had to be tied into the wheelchair so he wouldn't fall out.

The shock was almost too much to bear. Would he be like this for the rest of his life? I felt like it wasn't real, as if I were caught in some strange, surreal play. This just couldn't be happening to us!

For my sanity's sake, I had to believe that God would miraculously heal Tony. It was too painful to think of any other option. Everything became a gray haze for the next four months as I focused on Tony alone. During his month in the rehab hospital, I squeezed into the bed with him and stayed with him. We took naps together. We talked. I covered two walls of his room with his get-well cards. I kept thinking that this was surely an adventure that would soon be over.

We went to therapy together. With every step he took, holding onto rails and guided by his therapist, I mentally took it with him. To learn spatial concepts all over again, he placed plastic rings over cones, and to help his speech he practiced silly rhymes with a therapist. And I was there, living every moment with him.

For the first few months, Tony improved significantly. He advanced from the wheelchair to walking on his own—although he dragged his left leg. He learned how to put on shirts with his right arm only, and how to get up when he fell. When his recovery slowed, I dragged him off to alternative medicine clinics, where he improved a bit more.

I still fully believed Tony would be miraculously healed, and we'd give God the glory. I continually repeated what I thought were Job's words in the Old Testament, "Though He slay me, yet will I praise Him." We refused to give up.

By that autumn, the reality set in. Our income was reduced to disability insurance and Social Security. Tony had stopped improving; his left arm was still paralyzed and his left leg still dragged. Worse, his mental powers were almost gone. He couldn't follow a conversation without getting lost, and his keen wit had disappeared.

I went back to reading Job, and found that the passage I'd been quoting actually said, "Though He slay me, yet will I trust Him" (Job 13:15 NKJV). That was more like it! "Trust" was easier to say than "praise," because "praise" wasn't what I felt. But I did trust God to get us through. Besides, what alternative did I have? Where else was I going to turn?

The thought of living with this man for the rest of my life was intolerable at times. Nothing about him seemed familiar. He was a shell of the man I once knew. He slept, or sat staring into space for hours, and there was no communication between us. It was as if he were brain dead.

For two years, I could barely leave Tony alone in the house for a minute. He'd leave the water running, the refrigerator door open, or the gas flame flaring on the stovetop. When he wasn't wreaking havoc, he was in bed with the covers pulled over his head, sleeping and depressed. I wanted to just run away, to leave my marriage. But I knew God didn't allow that option. My motto for several years was, "Divorce is not an option, but murder is!" No, I couldn't leave him.

And so the months turned into years. My walk with the Lord became deeper and deeper as I sought His very present help in my time of trouble. I more earnestly sought, through the Prince of Peace, the "peace that passes all understanding." And for the first time in my life, my heart became that of a servant. The gift of intercession was received, and I encountered a God more wonderful, more exciting, and more extraordinary than I'd ever known—and I never would have known if we'd continued the self-gratifying life that we had before Tony's stroke.

We now live in a retirement village where Tony volunteers for everything, takes our standard poodle to the nursing home every day, and everyone loves him. And I have become an author and speaker. Our web site, ahelpfulhand.com, has ministered to many hurting people who've suddenly found themselves with a paralyzed member of the family and are struggling to know what to do next.

And Tony and I are once again very in love, walking with the Lord. By seeking His help and His presence, by trusting in Him, we have been delivered into not only a rich and satisfying life—we have been delivered into peaceful life.

Grandma Wore High Tops

Lisa Copen

Stand your ground . . . for shoes, put on the peace that comes from the Good News, so that you will be fully prepared.

—Ephesians 6:14–15 NLT

I've never seen such bone deterioration in someone your age." The podiatrist's voice was gloomy after looking at my feet. Two years of rheumatoid arthritis was having an impact on my ability to walk.

My childhood memories of Grandma include how she walked with great difficulty, while Grandpa made her daily tasks harder by disconnecting the dryer and lights to "save electricity." Each year, my mom would take her to the foot specialist, who'd design and order her special shoes. They weren't pretty shoes, and I felt sorry for her. Her heavy footwear resembled combat boots—large and clunky—and the rough laces snagged her polyester pants. Regardless, she was always excited about new shoes and hopeful that they'd make life easier.

It took Grandma fifteen minutes to loosen the laces with her arthritic hands; she'd carefully pull them off her swollen feet, remove two pairs of sport socks, and then endless bandages. Without her boots she could barely stand. Her feet were so broken down she walked on the inside of her ankle bones, which rested flush with the floor. When she removed her shoes in front of me, I felt embarrassed for her and tried not to stare at her swollen and red, callused, and deformed feet. My little painted toenails seemed frivolous.

As technology improved, Grandma's "army boots" were discarded. When my mom brought Grandma home from the foot specialist, she smiled and said, "Guess what kind of shoes Grandma gets to wear from now on?"

"What?" My little sister and I couldn't imagine her wearing anything but the boots.

"High tops!" Grandma shouted and laughed.

"High tops?" We giggled. "You're going to wear high tops? Like basketball players? Will you be able to run and jump now?" We thought it was the coolest thing we'd ever seen. How many people have grandmas that wear the same shoe as Michael Jordan?

From then on, Grandma's high-top sneakers came with special insoles and were especially designed for her pants suit outfits. The famous swish was her ever-present accessory. Yet, I always wondered how she lived so unselfconsciously. Her appearance didn't seem to bother her in the least. I couldn't imagine wearing high tops with everything! I was grateful when my mom told me I was the lucky kid since I didn't have those "family feet" like Grandma's side of the family.

At the age of twenty-four, however, I began to get a severe shooting pain in my feet that made it nearly impossible to walk. Within three months, as the rest of my body began to flare, and cortisone shots stopped working, I was diagnosed with severe rheumatoid arthritis. Limping into work, wearing white tennis shoes (and cute socks and nylons), I could feel the burning stares of managers, who imagined I'd misunderstood the dress code. Explanations were futile.

Now, after eleven years of chronic illness, my feet are beginning to look like Grandma's. I notice how bad they are when I see their reflection in the mirror. The only shoes I can get my swollen, deformed feet into are sandals; I often bandage each toe to delay blisters. My podiatrist recently shared his concern. "Surgery is just a matter of when, not if. Walk as long as possible and just try to be grateful for every step you can still take."

I've worn tennis shoes and ballet-style slippers with suits and pantyhose and have tried to ignore the whispers of those around me. As a former fashionable gal who preferred a bit of a heel with jeans, exchanging heels for high tops continues to be emotionally difficult.

Sometimes I take slow walks down the shoe aisle and I fight back the tears with everything in me. I'm tired of feeling sloppy. I'm tired of not wearing real shoes. I want to be like I was before my illness. God continues to work on my pride.

One day some well-meaning evangelists appeared at my grandmother's door, and when she wouldn't let them in, they flung a sarcastic challenge at her.

"If your God is so good, why hasn't He healed your feet?"

"I've never asked Him to," she calmly replied. "I've just asked Him to let me walk one more day . . . and He's answered that prayer."

Grandma's "high-top legacy" has been my foundation for living with chronic illness. She passed away just before I began a ministry for the chronically ill. Had she been here, she would've walked door-to-door—despite any pain—to share it with others. For decades she got up every morning and laced those heavy, tough, leather boots, and later high tops, and continued to thank God, simply because she could walk one more day—and that Grandpa hadn't yet disconnected the washing machine.

Like her, I hope to live an enduring message of faith in the midst of failures; to strive to be holy, even when times are horrible; to put on high tops with my little black dress and let people laugh. It's a legacy filled with discomfort I wouldn't have chosen, but a gift which I've learned to embrace—sport socks and all. Along with my shoes, I simply put on peace—and let my toenails shine!

Poor, Poor, Pitiful Me!

Jeff Friend

For our light affliction, which is but for a moment, is work-
ing for us a far more exceeding and eternal weight of glory.
—2 Corinthians 4:17 NKJV

I don't care who calls on the phone or stops by to see me," I instructed my wife, Nancy. "I don't want to talk to anybody and I sure don't want to see anybody! And I mean anybody!"

I'd just returned from a hyperbaric treatment at the hospital, and the pain from the large wound on my leg was intense. Over the last three years I'd already endured five surgeries and now the hyperbaric treatment was preparing me for another operation. The treatments consisted of wearing an aviator's mask while sitting for two and a half hours every day in a pressurized chamber that looks like a miniature submarine. It was extremely uncomfortable and generally just aggravated my wound.

So as I settled into my recliner, I was not in the mood for conversation. I was depressed and in pain, and I just wanted to feel sorry for myself for awhile. I had a right to feel miserable, didn't I? I have the right to sit and be grumpy—and nobody had better try and stop me!

Within thirty minutes, the phone rang. "Remember what I said!" I shouted as Nancy picked up the phone.

After saying "hello," she mouthed the caller's identity to me. It was a retired pastor who'd been a close family friend for years, and a man I greatly admired.

"I'm sorry, but he's really not up to speaking to anybody right now," she said.

She then spoke softly to him for a few minutes, and although I couldn't hear what she said, I was sure she was telling him that I was in the middle of a pity party. When she hung up the phone, I felt proud that my plan was working so well. Nobody would cheer me up if I had anything to say about it.

Yet, the more I stewed, the worse I felt about refusing to talk to him. To distract myself from my guilty feelings, I turned on the television. I flipped to the Christian channel, and there was evangelist Dave Roever giving his testimony. Dave lost an ear and was grossly disfigured during the Vietnam War, yet he was telling how fortunate he'd been and how good God had been to him. It was an incredible and moving story of God's love. Now I was really starting to feel bad. My plan of misery was beginning to unravel.

Finally Dave Roever's talk was over and the next program started. Now David Ring, an evangelist stricken with multiple sclerosis, was explaining his life story and the many obstacles he had to overcome. Then he made a statement that simply froze me.

"What I look forward to the most when I get to heaven is being able to drink a glass of water without spilling it all over myself." The simple act of eating was an effort for him because he lacked control over his body. What incredible struggles this man had to face every day of his life, and here I sat pouting about my problems.

Within an hour, there was a knock at our front door. My wife raced to the door, thinking I was about to tell her to make the person go away. But now that I'd been thinking over what I'd heard, my little pity party was breaking up.

"Who is it?" I asked.

"It's Pastor Randy," she replied as she led him in.

Oh no! The man of God is right in my house. Okay, God, I give up. You win. First a phone call, then the evangelists, and now my pastor shows up. I know when I'm whipped. I get the message!

I told my pastor what had happened in the last couple of hours. He listened quietly and attentively as I rambled on. We talked a little longer, and as he prayed with me before he left, all my anger and self-pity faded away.

I thought I'd needed to withdraw from everyone and feel miserable for a while. Poor, poor pitiful me. But God knew what I really needed—words and acts of encouragement, reassurances that whatever situation I might face, He would be with me, that many people faced bigger challenges than mine.

Over the next three and a half years, I had seven more surgeries on my leg, but I never again felt the despair I did that day. God proved to me that there's no need to get wrapped up in self-pity—not when I can trust Him and get wrapped up in His love instead.

Taking Up Space
or Giving Grace

Evelyn W. Davison

I am sure that God, who began the good work within you,
will continue his work until it is finally finished on that
day when Christ Jesus comes back again.

—Philippians 1:6 NLT

In this part of the country, flash floods get little notice. Around Austin, near Texas Hill Country, storms sometimes come and go quickly. Other times they linger for weeks.

A recent nighttime storm dumped four inches of rain. I got up early the next morning, and as usual, rushed to get out of the house. I opened the garage door, and revved my engine, anticipating beating the morning traffic. As I backed out, I glanced over my shoulder and slammed on my brakes. Our neighbor's garbage receptacle, with its lid open, was blocking our driveway. Traffic was building, and I didn't have time to deal with their trash bin, but I had no choice. I threw the car into neutral and got out to deal with the nasty thing.

I closed the lid, tilted it on its wheels, and gave it a hard shove to get it out of the street. But then the water inside the bin splashed back up into the closed lid. The lid popped open and hit me in the head, causing me to lose control and fall head first into the bin. I was stuck with my head in the barrel and my feet flailing just above the rim, drowning in four inches of nasty rain water and stinky garbage. A passerby must have thought I was quite a sight as he pulled me from the barrel. I tired to ignore my head wound and regain my composure, acting as if I frequently spent time upside down in water-filled garbage bins. But it was clear my injuries were greater than I thought. Along with my head wound, I'd done some major damage to my hand. It needed immediate surgery.

My husband, Van, worried that the folks who witnessed the "crazy video moment" thought he was throwing a wife away. Even the surgeon was hesitant to give an oral report at his medical meeting for fear no one would believe him.

Yet reality set in as doctors tried to save my hand. They quickly found themselves trying to save my life from a pseudomonas infection that mutated and became antibiotic resistant.

I slowly healed, but I was far from my comfort zone as I plunged into rehab. Rather than being surrounded by my loving family and friendly coworkers, I found myself with a lot of sad, sorrowful, broken people. But after several weeks, things began to change as I made new friends. One was the rehab director, Stella.

The first time Stella sat down to work with me she said, "I am glad I get to help you. You know, I have been watching you."

"Really?" I responded. "Why?"

"From the first day you came into rehab, even though you were hurting, I noticed you were different. What is it that makes you different?"

I smiled and asked her what she thought it was.

"I don't know. You aren't like the hundreds of people I see come through here," she said. "You're different, but you also make a difference."

I thought for a moment and finally said, "The difference you see is *choice*. I choose every morning how I'm going to use my day. My choice is to take joy, cheer, and love with me wherever I go. If anyone comes into my space, the Lord wants me to give them grace."

Her eyes grew teary, but that didn't stop her from peppering me with more questions. Soon, we were the center of the "rehab rodeo" as others perked up and listened.

One day, Doctor Bob was running late, and everyone was grouchy. After a while, I said to everyone there, "When Doctor Bob comes in, let's all clap." Most everyone glanced at their hands and then back at me. "Whoops!" I said. "That won't work." No one could clap. None of us could, including me, because we all had wounded hands. So I said, "How about we just stomp our feet instead?"

Arriving later, Doctor Bob was surprised to see a room full of hurting people stomping their feet. Coming directly to me, he gave me a hug and whispered in my ear, "You are something."

If given a choice, I wouldn't have chosen to nearly drown in a trash bin and to have hours upon hours of painful therapy. But accidents happen, and if we let Him, God will use the unexpected for His purpose. Three times a week, I spent three or four hours in a room where pain was unavoidable. I chose to enter that place with a smile in hopes I could brighten someone's day and show others that God works, even in the most miserable of circumstances.

How will you spend this day? In your place, will you take up space or give grace? It's your choice, and when you choose to be different, you can make a difference!

The Rubber Band Master

Karen J. Olson

*So do not fear, for I am with you; do not be dismayed, for
I am your God. I will strengthen you and help you; I will
uphold you with my righteous right hand.*

—Isaiah 41:10 NIV

I've hit a new low in the fight against excess weight. I quit smoking about eight years ago and replaced my cigarette habit with an eating habit. Better, according to my internist; frustrating, according to the mirror.

Late one night, I'd deviated from my usual routine walks, treadmills, or Leslie Sansone videos and got sucked into an infomercial for a weight loss device—the magnificent fail-proof Rubber Band Master. A woman who looked like Barbara Eden of *I Dream of Jeannie* kept huffing into the camera, "Prove me wrong! It's guaranteed!"

It sounded like a dare to me.

I thought it over, but not for too long. I had only four minutes left to place a call in order to get the special low, low price . . . three easy payments of $19.95 (plus shipping and handling). *But*—and this was the kicker—they'd pay the first installment if I ordered within the next three-and-a-half minutes!

I got my purse and fished out a credit card. As I held my platinum Visa, my breathing rate escalated like I'd been jumping around with

Richard Simmons's *Sweating to the Oldies*—the mantra of my weight loss failures. I briefly wondered if I was giving my credit card number to crooks and identity thieves.

The television screen flashed an 800 number, and I was ready for it. I began to dial . . .

"But wait!" the Genie look-a-like said.

I paused with my finger over the number 8.

"If you call now, I'll send you a complimentary tip guide, *plus* a handy carrying pouch. But you must call *now*."

That was it . . . opportunity was knocking. I dialed the number.

"Hello, this is Janelle! Welcome to the weight loss bonanza of the twenty-first century!"

"Hi, Janelle," I said in a professional, don't-mess-with-me voice. "I'm calling to order the magnificent weight loss machine . . . you know, the one I can do sitting in my recliner, watching my favorite show." *So much for any attempt at intelligence or dignity.*

"Wonderful! What a great choice! And your name?"

Now we were getting somewhere. Janelle thought it was perfectly fine that I expected to lose weight sitting in my recliner. Perhaps she was sitting at her desk with that rubber band wonder, becoming inches and pounds smaller even as we spoke. I was in the throes of complete delusion by now.

The funny thing is, I *knew* this was all a crock of beans, that I was probably buying a large rubber band stuffed into a zip lock baggie posing as a carrying case. But I had no control. They'd appealed to a baser instinct—my vanity. Like a home shopping junkie, I willingly, eagerly gave my credit card number to a complete stranger.

I sat through sales pitches for weight loss vitamins, books, and videos. I told Janelle—now a close, personal friend—I could save her some time with her sales pitches because I was only going to buy the original item. *No one is taking advantage of me!* Besides we were wasting crucial time. I could see the clock ticking on the television screen.

I interrupted Janelle's spiel. "Am I still going to get the Rubber Band Master for only three payments of $19.95?" I was worried I'd miss out on the special price because of her blathering.

"Oh yes!" she said with authority. "You will, but I have to ask these questions!"

Even my negative responses were covered in her script contingencies. We laughed together and went through her "to do" list like two girlfriends having coffee.

Finally, we reached the part where she spoke at length about the Rubber Band Master. She was preaching to the choir as they say. I was on board. I was all over it. I was there.

Now all that remained was the shipping information. But wait. "I know you want to start right away!" Janelle said. "So I'm allowed to offer our best customers the option of sending your Rubber Band Master via priority shipping for a slight additional charge!"

Cool.

Then she asked if I had a friend who'd like a Rubber Band Master (at a substantially reduced price). I wanted to know why my friend's cost would be so much cheaper. Janelle couldn't answer that. Apparently it wasn't in her script.

A vulnerable feeling I'd rather not experience again gave me pause—but I shoved it away and continued in denial. I just knew this wonderful Rubber Band Master would work for me. Janelle told me so just before we said good-bye.

Feeling a little foolish, I called a friend to tell her of my purchase. She told me about the hundred dollars worth of beanie babies she ordered late one night, and the time she ordered a Chinese jump rope for exercising, that fit on a door handle. I phoned another friend who'd just ordered a juicer off E-bay. I felt so much better now that I had a couple of codependents.

My Rubber Band Master arrived with the promised videos, book, and handy carrying pouch. It looked exactly as it had on television, but I must confess to feeling somewhat disappointed. Why? What was the problem? It had seemed so wonderful and shiny on the infomercial. In person, without the TV hype, it was just a big rubber band.

Wouldn't you know it. I got sucked in—again—by the glitter and glamour of the material world. It seems like I fill my life with so many things—so much stuff, appointments, and obligations—that I barely have time to breath. Then I sit back and wonder why I feel so bereft, so alone, and so spiritually unfulfilled.

I paused with the Rubber Band Master instruction book in hand and picked up a different Book. When I read God's instructions for life, I feel the well of my soul fill with His love and purpose. I reprioritize so that my Lord and my family come first. I become moored—anchored in my faith. I not only receive spiritual benefits, the health benefits are immeasurable. Plus, I get free tech support twenty-four hours a day, seven days a week.

Wake Up, Sleeping Beauty!

Cynthia Komlo

Lord, help me to realize how brief my time on earth will be. Help me to know that I am here for but a moment more.

—Psalm 39:4 TLB

"No! Leave me alone!" I snarled at God. It was 3:00 A.M. I was asleep, as most reasonable adults are at that hour—until God sounded His alarm.

Wake up, Cynthia! Wake up!

I was annoyed. Couldn't God have waited until sunrise? No-ooo!

Wake up!

"What?" I blurted. My husband continued to sleep in spite of my bellow.

Then deep from within my heart I heard, *It's time for you to go back to school for the skills and training for what I've called you to do.*

Excuse me, God? Skills and training? For what? What have You called me to do? I thought I was already doing it! I'm a wife, a mom, and a professional volunteer. Isn't that enough? Sure, I remember how I once promised. "My life is Yours, Lord," but . . . school? No thank you. Anyway, my childhood dream of a college degree died twenty years ago. Remember?

I glanced at my husband. God bless him! He's a good provider for me and our kids. Thankful, I burrowed deeper under the covers, ready to slip back into sweet slumber. "Good night, Lord."

But again the message rang loud in my thoughts. *It's time for you to go back to school for the skills and training for what I've called you to do.* I moaned, "This can't be for real."

As an insomniac counts sheep, I, too, began to count—only I counted excuses, explaining to God why returning to college was a bad idea.

1. I hate math.
2. I'm too old.
3. I don't want to be away from my family.
4. I don't have the money.
5. I haven't gone to school in twenty years.
6. What school?
7. What degree?
8. Need I mention that I have a vision handicap that would make school really tough?
9. What about transportation? Remember, I can't drive a car because of my low vision.
10. I'm not looking for change. I'm happy just the way things are.

The next thing I knew I was awake, and it was morning. Surely, the call to college was just a nightmare—probably some guilt left over from my teens.

I'd tried college when I was seventeen years old, but was forced to quit after one semester because my low vision made it impossible to compete in a sighted world. Computer technology was not available like it is today.

The morning after my dream, and after my family had left for work and school, I spun through the house for a quick tidy up. Afterward, I settled down for my morning prayer, but with one final distraction. The newspaper.

I scanned the news and, to my horror, there it was—flashing like a road sign! FINISH WHAT YOU STARTED. GO BACK TO COLLEGE.

The half-page university advertisement called upon adults to continue their education.

"No!" I hollered. But negotiating was not an option. How could I deny the call? How could I turn my back and say *no* when it seemed clear that the Lord was showing me how to clear my hurdles. "Okay, Lord," I said, submitting to His will, "but promise to help me get through math."

God kept His promise. Without even searching, I soon discovered a friend, a single mom, who wanted to earn her college degree. Why was I surprised when I learned she excelled at math? Details fell into place as I jumped over more hurdles. My friend and I carpooled together, became study partners, and with diligence, we both graduated from college with honors.

Somehow, though, I knew there was more training for me to do.

As life unfolded, my health unexpectedly deteriorated. I'd developed an aortic aneurysm. In other words, the main artery to my heart, like a worn out car tire, was going to blow. I learned the life expectancy for someone with my connective tissue disorder was forty years old. I was thirty-nine.

So at the age of thirty-nine I had open-heart surgery in hopes I'd gain more time on this earth. God extended His grace and extended my life. Heart surgery was a gift, but it also answered another prayer. While in my suffering, I heard God calling me for more training.

One year after my open-heart surgery, I've continued my training by putting one foot in front of the other. I'm working on my Masters in Pastoral Studies. Today, I'm a hospital chaplain, and I write about healing. Although I still have poor eyesight, my spiritual vision is clear. God has worked all things together for His good purpose.

Looking back, I'm grateful that God rattled me from my sleep at three in the morning. I've often wondered who I'd be today if I'd continued to hit the snooze button. What if I'd used my poor eyesight— or something else—as an idol so that I could ignore God? I could stay comfy and asleep. What would I be doing today if I hadn't rolled up my sleeves and followed Jesus when He said, *Come?*

If I'd stayed a Sleeping Beauty, I would have missed God's blessings—those He has given to me and those I am to give to others.

Even if we live to be a hundred, our time on earth is brief, each breath a gift. I told God, "I'm Yours," and it's a promise I mean to keep. We all have a special call. I got mine at 3:00 A.M., and I'm grateful I didn't sleep through the alarm.

Part 5

Family/Parenting

Father Knows Best

Linda LaMar Jewell

*If you don't know what you're doing, pray to the Father.
He loves to help. You'll get his help, and won't be conde-
scended to when you ask for it.*

—James 1:5 THE MESSAGE

While growing up, I was involved in 4-H. While I could bake a dessert and cook an individual side dish, I was seldom in charge of putting an entire meal on the table. My mom was queen of the kitchen and my dad king of the grill. They were happy, and I didn't see the need to interfere in their royal duties. In a pinch, I could fix a simple meal by warming up a can of tomato soup and grilling cheese sandwiches.

In my early college years, I often whipped up single-woman fare for dinner—popcorn, oatmeal, or cheese and crackers.

My cooking responsibilities took a quantum leap, though, when I married. My husband and I were college students on a tight budget, leaving little room for fancy fare or wasted food.

After weeks of soup and sandwiches, we longed for a substantial dinner. We talked over the possibilities and settled on steak, mashed potatoes, and gravy. We saved our money and splurged on round steak we found on sale, picked up a few potatoes, and took our bag of groceries home with smiles on our faces. My husband went to his Friday afternoon classes and I stayed home, where I put on my apron and began preparing our evening meal.

I turned on our miniature oven to "Low," put the steak in a cake pan, and slid it in the oven to bake.

Next, I turned my attention to the potatoes. As a newlywed, I didn't have a potato peeler, but I did have a paring knife. After I finished peeling them, the once big beautiful potatoes looked like albino radishes. Yet I was proud I'd gotten this far. I rinsed the little spuds off, plopped them in a pan with water, and placed them on the top burner. Turning the knob to "High," I dreamed of my ultimate comfort food—fluffy mounds of mashed potatoes.

While the steak and potatoes cooked, I hummed a happy tune while I swept the floor, cleaned the counters, and set our tiny gray-topped table. I wandered outside to pick some flowers, chatted with the landlady, and returned to arrange the dainty cosmos in a jelly jar. Everything was going smoothly, and I congratulated myself. I wanted my husband to be singing my praises tonight.

After waiting an appropriate amount of time, I opened the oven, anticipating the smell of a thick, juicy steak. My steak didn't smell like my dad's steak. It wasn't plump like my dad's steaks usually were, but flat and unappealing. Maybe it just needed more time.

I returned the steak to the oven and tackled the potatoes. Because I didn't have a potato masher or a ricer, I settled on a table fork and painstakingly mashed the potatoes. No matter where I attacked with the fork, other lumps were lurking nearby. I finally decided to leave well enough alone.

Since I'd spent much more time than I'd intended on the potatoes, I turned my attention back to the steak. Although its appearance hadn't improved, I took it out of the oven and drained the drippings for gravy. I knew that when Mom made gravy she used milk, flour, salt and pepper so I added some milk, enough flour to make it thick, and a couple of extra shakes of salt and pepper for good measure.

My husband was later than expected coming home, so I kept the meal warm in the oven. When he arrived, we pulled out the table so we could both sit down, and I served the steak, mashed potatoes, and gravy with a flourish.

It was a memorable meal in mostly gray tones—the only color on the table being the magenta and pink cosmos. The steak was tougher than whang leather, the potatoes lumpy (years before lumpy mashed potatoes were the rage), and the gravy was so thick we had trouble pulling the spoon from the bowl.

We were both disappointed in the meal we'd longed for. My husband was wise enough not to say anything as I scraped the potatoes and gravy into the trash. I then hacked the steak into chunks and placed them in a marinade of stewed tomatoes and sliced onions to recycle as Swiss steak the next night.

Blinking back my tears, I called my dad to ask what I'd done wrong.

"You said you baked the steak?"

"Yes."

"I've always grilled mine. Only certain steaks can be baked and yours wasn't one of them. Tell me about the potatoes."

"They were lumpy and tasted horrible. I don't understand what happened. As soon as they boiled, I mashed them."

"What did you use to mash them?"

"A fork."

"Next time buy, beg, or borrow a potato masher. Okay. We've fixed those tiny problems. What about the gravy?"

"It felt sticky. Like a pot of glue!"

"How much flour did you use?"

"A cup."

I heard Dad choke. When he caught his breath, he said, "That would have thickened a washtub of gravy. Next time, call me if you're unsure or if you have questions. That's what dads are for."

Why didn't I think to call on my father? I needn't have plodded along blindly, making poor decisions on my own. I had a loving father to lead me and instruct me.

Like an earthly father concerned over his child, we have a heavenly Father, a perfect father, standing by to help us in our daily walk. There's no need to bear our burdens alone. Our Father in heaven is eager to give us the support we desire. No matter the problem, God is able, He is willing, and He will never lead us astray.

God's love will sustain us through the roughest times. Trust me, I know. He sustained my husband and I through the years it took me to learn to cook.

Fighting Fire with Water

Patricia Lorenz

*Turn from all known sin and spend your time in doing
good. Try to live in peace with everyone; work hard at it.*

—Psalm 34:14 TLB

It seemed like gremlins had invaded our home. It had rained every
day that week. My three older children snapped at each other and at
me for no reason. The youngest, Andrew, age four, had decided that
temper tantrums were the best way to get attention. Even my husband
and I were hardly speaking. He was at work now, but for the past three
weekends he'd been away on business and now was planning a solo
trip to St. Louis to visit his ninety-three-year-old father.

I was feeling lonely without a spouse to talk to, crabby because of
the squabbles among the children, and desolate because of the rain. I
felt trapped in the house.

Toward the end of that depressing week, I read in the church bulle-
tin that our parish was having a communal reconciliation service. I'd
never been to one, so I decided to go, more to get out of the house
than from any desire to do something spiritually elevating.

When I arrived at church that evening, my mood was as gloomy as
the weather. After a few prayers, Father Marty led the congregation
through a communal, soul-searching examination of conscience. He
talked about each commandment and about the ways we might have
broken God's laws.

I bowed my head and personally asked the Lord for forgiveness for the many times I'd been impatient with the children, for giving in to depression, for not trying harder to find time for my husband and I to sit down and talk.

Well, I thought, *that wasn't so hard. I'll just try to ignore all the grief my family gives me.* Maybe things would get better at home after all.

Then Father Marty gave us a double whammy. "To truly forgive, each time someone hurts you, snubs you, is unkind to you, acts out, or puts you down this week, give that person a compliment that same day."

Give that person a compliment? Impossible! I began to wonder if Father Marty had his head in the clouds. How can I compliment someone who hurts me or makes my life miserable? Complimenting them would just encourage them to continue to be awful. Why can't I just ignore the hurt and try to go on from there?

Since I was new to this communal reconciliation business, I decided I'd better follow along—to the letter of the law. The next morning I left my husband a note: "Thanks for fixing the chair. You did a nice job. Want to go for a walk tonight?"

The next time Andrew threw a temper tantrum, I picked him off the floor, told him I loved him and read him a story.

When my teenage daughters got mouthy, I diffused them with, "You girls sure are good baby-sitters. I've had compliments this week from two people you baby-sit for. They told me how good you are with their children."

Then Michael, because he couldn't have his best friends in for a sleepover that weekend, stomped off to his room and slammed the door. Later I tiptoed in with a steaming mug of hot chocolate and a few cookies. "I got a call from your English teacher today, Michael. She said you're really doing a great job in her class. I also wanted to tell you again how much I enjoyed your band concert. You're quite the percussionist, son."

To my surprise, when my husband got home from work, he put his arm around me, gave me a big kiss, and suggested we go out for a fish fry the following night. When Andrew and I finished reading the storybook, he jumped off my lap and asked if he could help me set the table for supper. Both Jeanne and Julia showed up in the kitchen to help with meal preparations. We talked, laughed, and even did a few impromptu exercises together when a fast song came on the radio. After dinner, Michael offered to sort the laundry and help with the folding.

All in all, I had to admit it—Father Marty had hit on something big. Most of us naturally want to lash out, to fight fire with fire. But how much better to "fight fire with water." How much sweeter would life be if, when someone dumps manure in our paths, we plant roses instead of slog through the muck; if, when someone treats us like dirt, we treat them with utmost kindness and love. Sure, it's against human nature, but when we do, we'll be amazed at what happens.

If I want to be loved and respected, I must first be lovable and respectable. It's a simple concept, really, and it sure sends the gremlins running!

Important Things to Do

Tonya Ruiz

*You shall love the LORD your God with all your heart, with
all your soul, with all your strength. And these words which
I command you today shall be in your heart. You shall
teach them diligently to your children, and shall talk of
them when you sit in your house, when you walk by the
way, when you lie down, and when you rise up.*

—Deuteronomy 6:5–7 NKJV

I'd expected my life to be like a Walt Disney fairy tale. I was supposed
to live happily ever after in some enchanted land. Instead, my life
turned out more like the plot from *Groundhog Day*. That's the movie
in which Bill Murray awakes at 6:00 A.M. to an old clock radio playing,
"I've Got You, Babe," and relives the same day over and over again.

That was my life, except without Sonny and Cher. My oldest daughter was six when I gave birth for the fourth and final time. The dishes
were endless, and the mountain of laundry was high enough for ski-
ing. My husband tried to help, but he was overwhelmed too. Each day
I would barely get caught up, only to have my routine start all over
again the next morning.

My littlest, Jeremy, attached himself to me like a baby gorilla.
Zachary, at three, struggled with potty training and was inclined to
put small items up his nose. The girls, at five and six, went from chaos

to crisis. One day, it would rain Fruit Loops in the living room, the next day the kitchen floor would be slathered with lotion and turned into an ice rink. I didn't dare take a shower if my husband wasn't home for fear my little darlings might burn the house down. As my mother frequently said about my children, "They're not bad; there are just so many of them."

Bedtime was always difficult. One night, worn out from the endless complaints of "There's a monster in my sock drawer," and "I'm thirsty," I finally got them all to sleep. It wasn't long before I heard giggles. Will they ever just go to bed so I can have some peace and quiet?

As I carried the clean laundry down the hall to put it away, Zachary appeared with a book clutched in his little hands. "Mommy," he said sweetly, "will you read me this bedtime story?"

At three, he couldn't possibly realize how many important things I needed to do before I could go to bed myself. "Just one," I warned him.

While I read halfheartedly, Zachary kept interrupting. He was my child of a zillion questions.

"What did you say?" I asked him with an impatient sigh.

"How did he do that?" Zachary repeated.

I scanned what I'd been reading and said, "Jesus made the fish and bread loaves multiply until all the people had been fed."

Zachary stood up on the bed, waving his arms and squealing. "Mom, that was a miracle!"

Talk about an "Ah-ha!" moment. I'd been so consumed with all my daily tasks, I'd taken my eyes off the Lord and become overwhelmed with my circumstances. Even though my pastor often taught, "Your children are gifts from God," I was forgetting to open the gifts, to spend time with them, and love them. I'd become like Martha from the Bible—so busy serving I wasn't spending any time at the feet of Jesus. And I wasn't teaching my children to either. I was so consumed with the miracle of getting to the bottom of the laundry pile, I was missing the opportunity to teach my children about the miracles of God.

Although my circumstances didn't change, my attitude did. I prayed that God would help me to make better choices, use my words wisely, and be the mother my children needed. Like Bill Murray's character at the end of the movie, I, too, woke up to a new day.

One day, a few months later, my sister came to visit and walked from room to room.

"What are you doing?" I asked.

"I just love to see how messy you are because it makes me feel better about myself," she said. "Your house would give Martha Stewart a panic attack."

Yes, my house is a mess, but I have more important things to do—like go on picnics, make play-dough food, and read Bible stories. Besides, I definitely don't want to be a Martha . . . of either kind.

Leading Our Children

Tim Burns

Mercy and truth preserve the king, and his throne is upheld by mercy.

—Proverbs 20:28 KJV

I learned a lesson at the side of my son's bed one evening. For the past two decades, my hands have been filled with the trials and tests of raising five children. Beginning in 1983, my wife and I were elbow deep in diapers for ten years. We refereed squabbles over everything from stuffed animals to roller blades, and complimented our kids on the beauty of their crayon scribblings to the coolness of their new outfits on the first day of high school.

During these often tumultuous years, we read many books on child rearing. Dr. Dobson became a regular visitor in our home. He was present on the bookshelf and on the car radio as I searched for guidelines on how to set loving, yet firm, boundaries for our kids. Yet all the books I read didn't teach me the most important lesson—how to balance consequences for misbehavior with loving acceptance.

Josh is the strong-willed, firstborn child in our family. From his first breath, he vocalized his ideas about how things should go, and he wasn't afraid to push the boundaries. When he was just six years old, he was already "looking for love in all the wrong places." In his defense, it's often hard for kids in a large family to get all the attention they want. Josh, it seemed, was willing to settle at times for the attention he gained by misbehaving.

One evening, Josh pushed his mom's patience past the breaking point, and I was called in to "escort your son" to an early bedtime. Mom was frazzled, and Josh was a bit worse for wear too. He knew he was in trouble as I guided him to the stairs, and then followed him into his room. Kim and I believed that, in cases of deliberate defiance and willful disobedience, losing privileges was the appropriate consequence. As Josh sat on the edge of his bed, he braced himself for what he might lose this time.

I glanced at him and realized Kim and I had been taking away toys and/or privileges for the past few days now. While Josh's behavior hadn't gotten worse, it hadn't improved. As I paused, mulling over what might make a positive impact on my recalcitrant son, a Scripture came to mind: "Mercy and truth preserve the king, and his throne is upheld by mercy."

Josh had experienced enough truth. He knew he was behaving badly but, at that moment, he didn't know that he was loved just as he was. His campaign of terrorism over the past few days had created strife between his siblings, his mom, and himself, but Josh's misbehavior was the fruit, and not the root, of the problem. He needed to know that he was important, and valuable. So as I told him how much I loved him, and that I forgave him for the way he'd been behaving, his entire body noticeably uncoiled. He'd been sitting stiff and rigid, steeling himself against the consequences. But my unconditional love taught him that he could do better. God's love, flowing through me to my son, taught me the truth of God's wisdom.

Yes, kids need boundaries. They need to know that there are consequences when the boundaries are crossed. They also need to know that regardless of their behavior, they are loved and lovable. Without forgiveness and mercy, love would have a hard time entering anyone's life, and none of us would ever learn its meaning. We're all sinners; we all fail from time to time. But this reality should never overshadow another reality—it is love by which God draws us to Him. And it's fortunate for all of us that "love covers a multitude of sins."

Butterfly Summers:
The Art of Letting Go

Patricia Evans

*But you need to stick it out, staying with God's plan so
you'll be there for the promised completion.*
—Hebrews 10:36 THE MESSAGE

Edith loved silk. The mother of Terry, my childhood girlfriend, Edith said that silk was "spun gold." She was, in fact, so fascinated with silk that she let Terry and I "raise silk" in the sunny entryway of her home.

To this day, I don't know if Edith simply wasn't aware that one actually needed silkworms to produce silk, or if she thought *all* cocoons were made of silk. Regardless, Edith taught Terry and me much more that summer than an appreciation of silk; she taught us lessons for life that I still use today. I wonder if that was her intent all along.

Our "silk worms" were actually caterpillars, and caterpillars turn into beautiful butterflies. Terry and I were fascinated with the cocoons, and we watched our caterpillars spin and spin for what seemed like a lifetime, until finally their cocoon of white threads encased their bodies. Then suddenly they stopped moving and did nothing—at least as far as eight-year-olds could see.

But Edith knew better. She knew this was their most active time, a time of metamorphosis, a time of great change and growth that would propel them into their new lives. In order to curb our impatience, Edith would say things like, "Good things come to those who wait," and "All in due time." But the one that holds the most meaning even to this day was, "All in God's timing." Finally, at the end of two long weeks, something began to happen in the cocoons: they started to move.

The creatures inside appeared to be struggling to get out of their sticky little prisons. They poked and wriggled, trying to escape. Feeling sorry for the poor little things, I reached into the box and began to pull off the end of one of the cocoons.

Edith never raised her voice, but just then she let me know that she was capable of ear-shattering decibels. "Leave them alone! You are going to kill the butterfly!"

I protested almost as loudly. "I'm only trying to help!"

Edith's tone softened, and she explained, as if conducting a lecture: "Helping at this critical, struggling life-stage of a butterfly is not beneficial, but actually severely damaging, even to the point of death."

What Edith understood—and I did not—was that if the cocoon is opened too soon or too quickly, the butterflies emerge before their time, and their legs, which are used to push the body out, are weakened. The butterfly needs the strength of its leg muscles to pump air and blood through the body and wings in order to fly. I can still hear Edith's words of wisdom, "It is God's timing, dear. He knows the exact moment for and the exact reason of each event in the universe. After all, He created the universe, and the caterpillars and butterflies are His." I had to keep my hands off.

Recently, I had to keep my hands off again; only this time the cocoon held my teenage son. It's so difficult to watch my child struggle, and my first response was to jump in and help him open his cocoon. But as with the butterfly, if I'd opened the cocoon too soon or did the work for him, I'd have run the risk of causing additional harm. He had to do the work himself, to strengthen his own muscles, so he could spread his wings and fly.

God made the caterpillar and provided the means for it to change from a creature that "creepeth" into a beautiful winged butterfly. Who am I to open the cocoon before its time, before God's time?

I wanted to help my son. And in the past, I did help. But I was trusting in myself. I'd helped open my son's cocoon, but it was too early. I'd trusted in my own understanding and, his legs being too weak to pump air and blood to his wings, he fell. But when I kept my hands off, when I completely let go, trusting only in God to open my son's cocoon, his legs were strong enough to pump the blood to his wings and he could soar for God's glory.

I learned many lessons that butterfly summer. The most significant lesson, though, was to have patience. God's timing is always perfect, and just as the butterfly didn't require my help in opening the cocoon, neither does God. It takes total faith and trust to accept beyond what the eye can see. Edith knew this when she yelled at me not to touch the cocoon; God knows this when He closes a door or sets up a roadblock along the journey of life.

Opening the cocoon too soon, helping God out when He didn't need my help, prevented God from doing His work in my prodigal son. As a result I was delayed in seeing the glory of God's hand in my son's life. Today, not only is he flying like a beautiful butterfly, he is soaring like an eagle!

Raisin' Great Kids

Raelene Searle

These things I have spoken to you so that My joy may be in you, and that your joy may be made full.
—John 15:11 NASB

"How come she doesn't like being a mommy?" said Aaron, my four-year-old son. He was pointing to the mother of one of his church friends.

"What makes you think she doesn't like being a mommy?" I asked.

"Her face is always wrinkled up, and she's always mad," he said.

"Well, maybe she's tired or maybe we always see her when her kids are being naughty."

"Wrinkled mommy faces aren't happy faces," Aaron said, and he trotted off to his Sunday school class.

Years later, this conversation came to mind when my seventeen-year-old daughter, Megan, and I were having a conversation about mothers.

I was the administrator of a ministry to mothers with children of all ages. I'd been preparing for the meeting, and I asked Megan to help me come up with an idea for the "table treasure"—a small giveaway for each woman as a reminder of the meeting's theme for that day and the key verse.

Megan asked me what the topic was, and I told her, "Raisin' great kids."

"That's easy, Mom. Give them a little box of raisins."

"Raisins?" I asked, a little confused.

Before I could explain that "raisin'" was the slang for "raising," she said, "Yeah, and attach a tag to the box that says, 'Don't let your kids suck the life out of you.'"

Ah. Amazing observation of a teenager.

Then it hit me—raisins are the wrinkled up "faces" of grapes! My mind raced with all kinds of questions. Had I appeared as a "wrinkled up raisin" while raising my kids? How many days were spent shriveled up with the life sucked out of me because I wasn't choosing to enjoy motherhood? How many times did I suck the life out of my children through irrational anger or obsessive cleaning?

I wanted to know—I had to know—was she referring to me? No, I wouldn't ask. I had to believe I'd been the perfect mom. But curiosity overwhelmed me. Willing to risk having my bubble burst, I asked. The result was one of those cherished mother/daughter moments that will always be etched in my heart.

She opened up about her own parenting fears. Her concerns were raised by having watched some of the moms of the kids she baby-sat. She said she always saw these women frazzled and frustrated. She wanted to believe parenting could be rewarding, but how could she if she saw so many unhappy parents?

To my great relief, she felt that I'd been a good mom. Maybe parenting wasn't as bad as she thought.

My seventeen-year-old daughter had opened up to me, her mother, and treated me like a friend! Lord, could this moment please never end?

After our talk, I thought about when my attitude toward parenting had changed. I was now (figuratively) a plump, full grape, but I knew I hadn't started off with the right mind-set.

It amazed me how much time and energy I'd spent on the things that seemed so important. Being superwoman was a goal that always seemed out of reach. Yet I tried to be the perfect mom, the perfect cook, the perfect housekeeper, and the perfect wife.

But in my attempts to attain the June Cleaver image, I was becoming more and more unhappy. "Lord, what am I doing wrong? Why doesn't the 'Leave It to Beaver' script work for my life?" No time to evaluate—too much to do. So I just kept plugging along, still trying to attain perfection as a mom.

My kids could barely walk when I'd outfitted shelves in their closets with beautifully labeled bins in nice neat rows. In the bins were their sorted toys (Legos, Lincoln logs, Barbie). I somehow believed that they'd comply with my rule: "Only one bin out at a time, and when all those items are nicely put away, then you can take out another bin and play with those toys." Boy did I set myself up for frustration.

First, what child plays with one thing at a time? Secondly, what child's brain works with such organization? Something catches their attention and off they go, forgetting the mess left in their wakes. After some time of listening to myself yell with the wrinkled raisin face, I finally realized the problem was mine. My attempts to attain perfectionism only led to having the joy of parenting sucked right out of me.

About the time Megan and Aaron were both in school, I began to regain my sanity and my joy. I was enjoying my own hobbies, now that I had a little more free time. Because it seemed silly to clean up every time I had to stop to take care of something, I left a mess. No problem—I was going to come right back to it. Then God showed me something profound. Okay, it was actually simple. He showed me that, even though the kids don't have the same idea of a clean house in mind, the idea of playing is the same as mine for my hobbies: "I'm coming right back to it."

I immediately began to give up extreme cleaning expectations. Oh, the toys still had to be picked up, but not the instant the kids moved on to something else. And life seemed to take on a whole new sense of fun for all of us.

I soon realized that when I sought my purpose in mothering and the joy that makes being a mom more fulfilling, I was more happy, more likely to display a plump, sweet, joyful grape—connected to the Vine—instead of the disconnected, unhappy raisin. I began to focus on the promise of Jesus in John 15:11.

Now I was wondering what my children saw in those early years. Would they have called me a grape or a raisin?

Through our heart-to-heart talk, Megan answered the question, releasing me from any feelings of guilt and failure. I never was a perfect mom, but I loved staying home and being there for my children. And now, as adults, they've expressed their appreciation for those years together.

Raisins aren't really bad—most kids love to eat them—and mommies who act like raisins are still loved. But I know I'd rather be a plump, joyful grape, seeking to find the daily activities of parenting a blessing—not a burden.

Enjoy being a plump grape and keep the wrinkled raisin face away until those wonderful older years. Then, when people look at you, they'll see your wrinkles are well-earned laugh lines from having enjoyed being a mommy.

Spoiled

Lanita Bradley Boyd

But give great joy to all who wish me well. Let them shout with delight, "Great is the Lord who enjoys helping his child!"

—Psalm 35:27 TLB

I finally heard the car horn honking from the driveway. "Mother! Daddy!" I threw open the door and ran to greet them. I was so excited to see my parents after several months away from them. Although married for six years, this was my first Christmas away from my family. I'd clung to the fact that they were coming to our house to celebrate the week after Christmas. I ran for the open arms I'd grown accustomed to as a child, only to find them full of packages and food containers. Food containers?

Mother grinned and marched passed me, heading for our tiny kitchen. "I thought we might as well bring a load as we came in," she called back over her shoulder.

Daddy quickly followed, burdened with grocery bags, deposited them on the counter, and gave me that postponed hug.

Mother made room in the refrigerator for her purchases and turned to hug me too. "My, your refrigerator is full. I could hardly get my grated coconut in there."

"I stocked up because you were coming," I reminded her.

"Oh, we brought plenty," she responded. Behind her, Daddy smiled and rolled his eyes. She turned toward him and added, "And dear, you'd better get the cooler in right away."

Cooler? Like the plethora of food you've already dumped in my organized kitchen isn't enough? Soon Mom was unpacking barbecued spareribs, sausage, cornmeal, leftover jam cake, chocolate cake, boiled custard, and a container of dried peaches—in addition to the grated coconut. She'd even brought prebaked layers for one of her famous coconut cakes. It only needed the coconut frosting.

Despite being in the cooler, the freshly-grated coconut did not travel well. It had spoiled during the journey from south to north. Regardless of the overwhelming amount of food, this called for a trip to the supermarket. Although this store had met our needs admirably for three years, it failed to measure up to Mother's expectations when it had neither fresh nor frozen coconut.

"I guess Yankees just don't cook like we Southerners do!" she said with condescension in her voice. Mother at last agreed to substitute canned coconut but was almost in tears upon discovering that I didn't have light Karo syrup on hand or a double boiler in which to cook the frosting.

We finally sat down to dinner, and I looked at my table in dismay. My carefully planned Christmas menu was hardly recognizable due to the addition of her cornbread and spareribs. While Steve asked the blessing, I said my own separate prayer: "Lord, help me through this. Help me be kind and patient. I know she means well, but I really need Your help to get through this."

Meanwhile, my delicious macadamia nut pie crouched in the corner of the crowded refrigerator—rejected by all diners in favor of coconut, jam, or chocolate cake with boiled custard. As she served the cakes, Mother fumed, "Why didn't we think to get vanilla ice cream at the store?"

"Because it doesn't go with macadamia nut pie," I murmured. At age twenty-six, I was again muttering under my breath, instantly reverted to fourteen by her mere presence.

Without missing a beat, Mother continued on. "This is great. You can just save your pie for another time." Firmly, she pushed me to my chair as she cleared the table, and then served the cake.

What choice was there? Steve and I would have been rude to refuse her cake, and Daddy wouldn't think of it. Besides, since he'd never tasted macadamia nut pie, he would probably "just as soon not start now," considering his usual attitude about food. Once he'd learned to eat pizza and tacos, he considered the broadening of his tastes complete.

I'd still make it a banner evening with my big announcement. As we relaxed with dessert, I cleared my throat and smiled. "We have a special announcement to make," I began. I was met with silence and an encouraging smile from Steve, so I continued. "We're going to have baby in August!"

"Well, that certainly is a surprise," Daddy said mildly.

"Hmmmm . . . if it's that far off, I hope you aren't going to tell anyone right away," Mother advised. "A pregnancy seems to last forever, even if you wait until you are showing to publicly announce it." Then, as if feeling obligated, she said, "That's really exciting news. Imagine—us, grandparents!" At age forty-eight—and looking even younger—she didn't seem ready to embrace the concept.

"Well, we certainly won't be guilty of spoiling this child," Mother said. "Nothing is worse than a spoiled child."

No hugs, kisses, no shouts of joy. No broad grins or delighted chuckles. The sick feeling in the pit of my stomach was more than the usual pregnancy nausea.

Later came the hugs and kisses and the hearty response, but by then it was too late to be meaningful. Later came the revelation that experience had taught Mother—childbirth could be dangerous, and she was overwhelmed with concern for my safety.

Steve, Daddy, and I had some long pleasant conversations the next day, but none of us saw much of Mother. She'd found three baskets of clothes that hadn't been ironed. That evening, Mother again took over the dinner preparation. Poor macadamia nut pie, passed over once more, but this time in favor of Mother's wonderful fried peach pies. Nor were my spinach and avocado put into a salad as Mother made her special coleslaw instead.

Again, I prayed, "Lord, I love this woman, but she drives me crazy! Why can't she just sit with us—just once? When we're at her house, I know she's always busy taking care of everyone, but here she should be able to relax. Patience. I need it now!"

I have no idea what time Mother got up that last morning. I do know by seven o'clock she'd already cooked sausage, eggs, fried apples, hash browns, coffee, and homemade biscuits. Steve wanted to ask where the cinnamon rolls were, but I convinced him that his sarcasm would be lost on her. She would have left in the middle of breakfast to start them. At that breakfast, where I'd only been allowed to set the table, I got up to get the cream for Daddy's coffee.

"Now you just sit down and I'll get it," Mother crooned.

"If I want to get the cream," I retorted none too sweetly, "I'll get the cream!"

"Atta girl," Daddy grinned.

Mom then related a cute little story from *Reader's Digest* about a woman who was adorably irritable during pregnancy. I sat there, gritting my teeth.

After breakfast, with much good-byeing and waving, my parents took their leave. Finally the door closed, and I locked it behind them. They were gone at last—or so I thought. Hearing the doorknob rattle, I unlocked the door. Had my parents forgotten something?

A hand thrust some money beyond the door. "Buy yourself some red delicious apples with this," she said. "I meant to get you some while I was here, but never did." With that, she was gone.

I fell on the couch, sobbing tears of frustration that had been mounting for two days. I imagined Mother talking to Daddy at length about how we "really didn't seem very grateful" for all they did. Probably adding that I was a bit spoiled.

That was thirty years ago. The baby announced during that visit is now a father himself. When he and my wonderful daughter-in-law told us of the great news of their pregnancy, the Lord sent me a vision of how *not* to respond. Normally a laid-back person, I'd have responded with a quiet smile and a calm, "That's wonderful." Instead, I leapt to my feet—not easy when you're sitting on boulders in the middle of a mountain stream—and hugged them both, showing outwardly the extreme inward love and pride I feel in them and for them.

So, *that's* it, Lord. You give us experiences and memories to help us do better when it's our turn. And I can promise you—I will totally spoil this child!

When the Night Patrol Roamed

Karen H. Whiting

My grace is sufficient for you, for my power is made perfect in weakness.

—2 Corinthians 12:9 NIV

They secretly formed "The Night Patrol." When my four oldest children were all under six, it appeared they'd joined forces to check on my devotion to them during the night.

As dutiful as a military patrol, they roamed the home territory, intent on completing their mission—"See if Mom loves us more than sleep." Every night, each child woke once or twice, spaced to wake me hourly. After each rousing, it took me at least half an hour to fall asleep again.

My plans to make bedtime run more smoothly were no match for toddlers. During the day, outdoor play—aimed at tiring them—zapped me but energized them. I used nightlights so they could go to the bathroom on their own, tucked favorite stuffed animals in with each to calm fears, and provided cups of water near them.

Not only did that fail, the military seemed to be in cahoots with the children. My husband was a military man, and we lived in housing above the main furnace. Our toasty quarters ensured the need for children to drink plenty and use the bathroom often. When not away on orders, my husband tried helping, but because of his sixteen-hour workdays, he slept through everything.

I usually collapsed about eleven-thirty, and the night patrol began maneuvers at midnight. James stood the first watch. I called him my silent alarm as he didn't talk, cry, or even make noise walking. He tiptoed to my bedside and breathed heavily. The feel of his breath across my face stirred me. I stretched out my arm and found the top of his head. "Is that you James?" My hand bobbed up and down for yes and pivoted side to side for no. Unless he handed me his empty water cup, I drilled him, "Do you need a diaper change? Are you scared? Do you need a drink?" I continued until a question brought an up and down response, and then I arose and helped him. Sometimes, on his second trek to the room, his breathing failed to stir me and he fell asleep on the floor. This caused the next night watchman to trip over him, producing yelps and cries!

Generally, my bouncer arrived next. Michael never walked; he charged and bounced. His energy bubbled over, toppling anything in his path and shaking the floor beneath his little feet. When he charged down the thirty-foot hallway to my bedroom, I dreamt of animal stampedes. Then he'd bounce next to me and tap my chest. With the strength of a young Samson, Michael's taps felt like a sledgehammer. At three years old, Michael grunted rather than talked. I had trouble telling a "ggrrr" from a "grrrumph" or understanding what each meant. I quizzed him in a groggy voice until I learned his need, and if I took too long he'd pound on my chest in frustration. When I hit on the right need, he'd make a happy "woof, woof, woof." Whether it was thirst, hungry tummy, or other problem, I dragged myself out of bed and took care of him.

In the next hour, Darlyn cried and shook her crib. If her cry didn't rouse me, her roommate Becky, my oldest, carried her and plopped her on my chest, loudly declaring, "Darlyn needs you." If merely hungry, she nestled her way into nursing and we both settled down. If the scent of another problem drifted on the night air, then I mustered up again and stumbled toward the changing table. Some mornings I discovered that I'd put on her disposable diaper inside-out or taped it to a leg. The pins for cloth diapers would have been lethal in my sleep-deprived state.

In the wee hours Becky arrived. Becky loved to talk, and if I didn't respond, she screamed, "Mother" and repeated her dissertation. Usually, we were out of juice. By this time, I was too bleary eyed to make juice properly, so Becky prompted me with shouts: "Mom, take the lid off the juice can or it won't pour out. Turn off the water now! Mom, get a glass before you pour my juice!" She tried to help, dragging over a stool, standing on it, and saying, "I've got the pitcher. I'll catch the juice." She'd hand me the spoon for stirring, and when she finished drinking, she held my hand and led me back to bed. She tucked me in and said, "Mom you look tired. I think you stayed up too late." Then she'd kiss me and return to her bed.

Morning finally arrived with Becky singing, "It's a brand-new day, Mom!" I greeted her with groans. Undaunted by my reaction, Becky threw open the drapes and gave me her morning weather report. Then the others tottered in with grins and laughs that showed my love passed the test.

Daily I prayed for help and for God to send angels to keep my children asleep. Instead, God kept reminding me that His grace is sufficient and His power is made perfect in weakness.

Finally, I yelled out, "It's my sleep, not your grace, that I want to be enough! Just a few straight hours."

One night seemed worse than most, and with only a few minutes left to sleep, I prayed that whatever sleep I received would be as good as eight hours, and I let God be in control. When Becky woke me, I felt like I'd slept all night. I thought we'd all overslept, yet I'd only slept for fifteen minutes. I felt refreshed all day. From that day on, the sleep received has been sufficient, despite night patrols, the addition of another night-owl child, followed by staying awake through the dating years.

As my children grow and marry, I look forward to snuggling in bed all night and, with glee, imagine them coping with their own night patrollers.

Where's My Teeth?

Patsy Dooley

Therefore we do not lose heart. Though outwardly we are wasting away, yet inwardly we are being renewed day by day. For our light and momentary troubles are achieving for us an eternal glory that far outweighs them all. So we fix our eyes not on what is seen, but on what is unseen. For what is seen is temporary, but what is unseen is eternal.
—2 Corinthians 4:16–18 NIV

I couldn't know how my life was about to change. I stood at the front door of my elderly parents' home on Christmas Eve, but they weren't expecting me. I wanted to make it memorable so, dressed from head to toe as Santa Claus, I knocked on the door and let out a hearty "HO, HO, HO!"

The door immediately swung open and I found myself embraced in my daddy's arms. I have no idea how he knew it was me. Guess I just wasn't as good with "Ho, Ho, Ho!" as I thought. What gripped my heart was that my Daddy began to cry. He clung to me and cried for what seemed an eternity. I had never seen my daddy cry. I believe I wouldn't have known the weeping in his soul had I not surprised him.

My mama had Alzheimer's, and Daddy was her caregiver. I realized on that Christmas Eve how desperate he was for help. So I began to make plans to move to Texas, and God's stamp of approval was burned into my heart when the house right next door to them went up for sale. After I moved to Iowa Park, Texas, in April of 1998, I experienced lots of changes. What had been a life of multiple opportunities, many friends, and much freedom, became a life of going to work, returning to Mama and Daddy's to have dinner, sitting with Mama during the evenings, fixing her hair, rubbing her feet, trimming her nails, and giving Daddy a break.

I'd moved often in my life, always sorry to leave, always anxious to see what lay ahead. At age sixty, I wasn't prepared for the impact this move would have on me. I had no time to make the adjustment before plunging into the care of my mama and my daddy. Life became so structured, so routine, so disheartening as I watched my mama slowly slip into her own private world of delusions, unable to comprehend what she saw and heard.

Mama's favorite pastime was putting things in places where no one could find them, causing Daddy much frustration. I felt like we were playing hide and seek like we did when my sister and I were children. This time Mama had lost her partial plate. We looked everywhere—in her purse, in her chest-of-drawers, in cupboards. That partial plate was not to be found. We had a wedding to attend, and Mom had to have her teeth!

Only one thing to do—Daddy made a special appointment with the dentist. On the way, Mama picked up her purse, opened it, and pulled out a handkerchief. As she unfolded it, she looked at Daddy and said, "Now which tooth did the doctor need to fix?" Daddy looked over, and in that handkerchief was every tooth the dentist had ever extracted from Mama's mouth—including her partial plate. At that moment Daddy didn't see the humor in the situation. As the family gathered for the wedding, however, Daddy shared the story, and we laughed so hard our sides hurt, even Daddy's. Glancing at Mama, I'd have sworn there was a look of pride and mischief in her eyes.

Every evening, we'd sit at the dinner table, and Mama and Daddy would begin to talk. A while back, Mama had put her hearing aid in Daddy's denture water, so anyone talking to her had to practically shriek. She never clearly understood what Daddy was saying. Still, they tried to communicate. Teasing has always been a part of our table conversation, and Daddy played it for all it was worth. Mama could sense Daddy was teasing her, so she'd continue these disjointed conversations simply because she loved the game. I wished I'd had a tape recorder. Their conversations would have rivaled Abbott and Costello's "Who's on First?" What a fortune we could have made!

Mama loved to go to church, but like her mama before her, she wouldn't sing. She felt she couldn't carry a tune in a bucket, so we'd never heard her utter a single note. One Sunday we rushed out the door and we were approaching the church. When Mama got out of the car, we realized she'd managed to wiggle into two more dresses over the one I'd helped her pick out, plus a slip that hung below all three. Her socks had slipped down around her ankles, drawing attention to shoes that now didn't match her three outfits! I could see that Daddy was frustrated, but it was too late.

We entered the church just as the singing began. Daddy, Mama, and I found our way into a pew near the back, and Daddy and I began to sing. Both of us abruptly stopped. Between us, Mama had begun to sing. Tears streamed down our faces while we listened to her joyfully sing every verse of every song. Mama, who tried so hard but couldn't remember names or faces, remembered every word of the old hymns. Suddenly, what she was wearing no longer mattered.

For a long time I felt that I'd given up so much, but in reality I was being given so much more. While I experienced heart-wrenching pain knowing that Mama was ill and would never be the same, God gave me glimpses of His tenderness and care. Alzheimer's is a hard thing to watch, yet I saw God's peace in Mama as she gave up trying to hang on to things—things like remembering names, or looking her best. Instead, she lived the life that had been given to her. And she did it with laughter and singing, letting God lead her in His care.

Part 6

Prayer

Forbidden Fruit

Lori Wildenberg

But each one is tempted when, by his own evil desire, he is dragged away and enticed.

—James 1:14 NIV

Okay, I'll admit it; I picked an easy one. The congregation was challenged by the pastor to fast for forty days during Lent. I went along with the idea, but chose to give up something that wouldn't be too stressful or sacrificial. My plan was to fast chocolate for forty days.

"Why don't you just fast all sweets?" my husband said.

"That would be way too taxing." A frown crossed his face. He was thinking I was missing the point, so I added, "That would make me too crabby." The frown disappeared and he nodded. I knew he'd support my well-thought-through decision.

The first few chocolate-free days were terrible. I discovered I actually craved a piece of chocolate around two in the afternoon. No other sweet satisfied my desire, and I found myself on the hunt for chocolate.

"I'll just look at it. That will help," I consoled myself, and opened various cupboards, peering at the chocolate. Irritability was the result of that plan, and I needed supernatural intervention.

God was way ahead of me, and seized these forty days to work on my unfaithful and lazy heart. I decided to pray when I was obsessing over my chocolate abstinence. Prayer was the answer, just saying *no* wasn't enough. After a few days, God took away the afternoon craving.

But He didn't take away *all* the craving. At the end of week one, I decided to physically move the chocolate to a higher level in the kitchen. "Out of sight, out of mind," I reasoned.

I moved the chocolate up to a cupboard where I'd need a chair to get at it. It was a good plan, or so I thought, until my daughter—while searching for something—found the candy instead. Knowing how much I enjoyed that type of candy bar, my child announced, "Look Mom, here's your favorite. A Symphony Bar."

I couldn't look. Too much temptation. I had to pray.

God was making me more humble by the day. This fast was not going to be successful without His help. After a few more days, all my desire for chocolate melted away. God is faithful.

Although the temptation from within me was conquered, the temptation was present externally. Outside sources were dangling the chocolate carrot in front of me. At unexpected times, people offered it to me.

While I was parked in my friend's driveway one afternoon, she bolted out of her home exclaiming, "I baked a chocolate cake. Take this home. We can't eat it all." She rarely bakes, and suddenly she was shoving half a devil's food cake, complete with chocolate frosting, through my open window!

The following morning while out to breakfast with a friend, I described my fasting experiences and the events of the previous afternoon. As we were having a good laugh over the cake incident, the waitress walked by and casually dropped a handful of Hershey's Kisses on the table! Stunned, we looked at one another and shook our heads.

Chocolate was *everywhere.* Even at a class held at church, M & Ms were on all of the tables, just waiting to be devoured. Following the class, chocolate chip cookies and chocolate frosted brownies were served for dessert.

"Come on! That's dirty pool. This no-chocolate thing is hard!" I screamed silently.

God taught me a lot during my forty-day fast. Temptation—any temptation for any forbidden fruit—comes from two places. My first enemy is my own weakness, and giving in creates a craving for more forbidden fruit. The second is outside sources hitting on those weaknesses. The desire, then, originates in me, and sin results from giving in, thereby increasing that desire to a need. Not giving in to the internal temptation in the first place will prevent the sin.

Most importantly, I've learned I can do absolutely nothing without God's help. And most particularly, without God or His strength I cannot give up chocolate!

The Bicycle Prayer

Jennifer Moore Cason

If you believe, you will receive whatever you ask for in prayer.

—Matthew 21:22 NIV

It was a beautiful, gold ten-speed bicycle—better than the hand-me-down owned by my best friend in seventh grade. I was thoroughly convinced if I prayed long enough and hard enough, God would allow me to win it.

As I look back, much of my childhood was overwhelmingly forgettable. The youngest of three in a single-parent family (such families weren't common back then), I grew up in a tiny southwest Kansas farming community. Rural life may seem like it should have been idyllic, but in a small town everyone knew that my mother struggled to make ends meet on a part-time salary and public assistance. For a twelve-year-old, there was nothing worse. Even so—although most of my classmates had more and nicer clothing and toys than I—the difference in our economic status wasn't particularly conspicuous. Except in one area—every twelve-year-old I knew had a bicycle . . . except me.

My brother had been blessed with a bicycle when he was about my age: a brand-new, shiny gold one with a banana seat and those high "chopper-style" handlebars. It was a Christmas gift he promptly totaled (and broke a leg in the process). Needless to say, neither my sister nor I got a chance to repeat history.

But the winter I was twelve, I happened upon a contest in a magazine. It looked like my chance to even the playing field with my contemporaries. Among the fabulous array of prizes were five, golden-hued ten-speed bicycles—the coolest of cool bikes in my hometown in 1974. It was a sweepstakes, so all I had to do was mail in a completed form and I, too, could be a winner.

What a deal! I wouldn't have to ask for the bike for Christmas. I already knew Mom's finances wouldn't stretch that far anyway. And getting the goodies didn't depend on how popular I was (which I wasn't), how pretty I was (which I wasn't), or whose child I was. Besides, I was convinced that I had God on my side.

Between November 1974 and January 1975 (the drawing deadline) I prayed religiously for that bicycle. At every opportunity I showered God with petitions: *Please God! This is my only chance! Please let me win that bicycle! You know I don't have what the other kids have—it's only fair for me to win this time. Please, God!* Nothing else in my whole life had been so important. As the drawing neared, the prayers became more incessant: *Please God! Please God! Please! I* need *that bicycle so I can get across town to my friend's house and to the swimming pool. Please God!*

As you might guess, January came and went, and no certified letter arrived, advising me of delivery arrangements for my new gold bicycle. I heard nothing more about the contest, and finally, by the end of February, it became obvious—even to me—that God had denied my earnest supplications. Once again, it seemed, He had shut the door on this poor little girl—not even my Creator cared enough about me to grant me that one small request that had meant so much.

I'd like to say I've put that particular disappointment behind me and went on to become a successful woman who can have any bicycle she wants. While the second half of that statement has been true for some time, the first half hasn't—not until I began a serious study of prayer and how it's worked in my life.

The bicycle prayer was only one of a long string of what I thought had been perfectly prayed (and just as perfectly ignored) pleas for help. I was angry with God for not giving me what I believed I deserved. So angry, in fact, that it took me almost thirty years to realize my fervent prayers had actually been answered.

No, God didn't suddenly drop a gold ten-speed out of the sky and onto my doorstep as I'd dictated. But I've since discovered that God is not a vend-o-matic: I can't just insert an incantation, turn some crank, and gather up my personally-designed miracle. God works through His own ways, in His own time. Five months after that long-ago contest, God delivered a ten-speed bicycle to me. It wasn't gold, it wasn't brand-new, but it was more than enough to take me to my best friend's house and to the swimming pool many, many times over the years.

Most important, God gave me the opportunity to earn that bicycle. The golden ten-speed I coveted and begged for was a prize in a contest sponsored by a tobacco company. In 1974, none of us realized that the tobacco company plying me with prizes was also poisoning my mother, who smoked cigarettes, but I believe that God knew it.

Instead, the bicycle I ultimately owned was one I bought myself with money I'd saved from baby-sitting. But I was so caught up in the "injustice" that God wouldn't grant me my petition in accordance with my instructions, I totally missed the fact that my prayer had indeed been answered—and pretty quickly, too, considering our earthly sense of time means nothing to our Eternal Father.

I've come to see the wisdom in God's refusal to allow my directions to limit His giving. In fact, as I search my memory, I see many instances in which, as with the bicycle, God has answered my prayers, but not in the ways I'd dictated. Prayers work best when they are simple requests without how-to instructions. God doesn't need them—and when it comes to prayer, no longer do I.

The Wrong Prayer

Debi King

But earnestly desire the greater gifts. And I show you a still more excellent way.

—1 Corinthians 12:31 NASB

I know I should have never prayed that prayer. What was I thinking? I'd asked for my weekend at a women's retreat to be uneventful. My prayer had been simple: "Dear Lord, please let me not have any issues in my life. I want to go to the women's retreat and just enjoy the time. I want to listen to the speaker without breaking down in tears, and sing and worship You for Your goodness to me. Lord, thank You for the way things are in my life right now. Amen."

Sounds good, right? Things were good in my life. My husband had a great job and a good ministry; he ran the facilities department at our very large church. My life was getting on track—kids were doing well, I was figuring out how to do the stepmom thing. I was getting along better with my ex-husband, and my new marriage was great. I was working in some new ministries at the church, and women were coming to *me* for counsel and advice on issues in their lives—a miracle in itself. Things were good. God was blessing me up one side and down the other. I was happy and content. So what could possibly be wrong with that prayer?

I went to the women's retreat. The speaker was good—funny, wise, full of great words and encouragement for the *other* women. I, of course, didn't need what she was saying, because my life was good. I had no issues. The praise and worship time was great, like always. I enjoyed singing praises to my God and thanking Him for the answered prayer.

By the second day, I was bored. I called my husband and smiled as I talked and told him that the speaker was good, the food was excellent—I love not having to wash dishes for the weekend. Worship time was powerful, but I was bored. He laughed! I think I called home about five times that weekend.

Sunday morning was our last time to meet together and hear the speaker. As she went on about how God worked miracles in her life and grew her through her many experiences, suddenly I panicked! I heard what she was saying and what God was saying through her to *me!* She was telling a story about how her life had become "perfect." She had a great marriage, an awesome ministry, her children and grandchildren had all moved close to her, she had the house of her dreams, and the life she'd worked hard to obtain. She felt that she'd finally *arrived!*

And then God threw them a curve. He called them to pick up and move from their beautiful little, perfect community in sunny California to gloomy Washington. She knew nobody in Washington, and it was cold and dark there. She couldn't understand why God was moving her, but reluctantly she obeyed and went.

She shared how, through her obedience, she was stretched, how she grew, and how she came to honor God in a whole new way. I shivered in my seat. I'd prayed the wrong prayer.

God can't grow me if I just sit and be content. Certainly I'm content with the things God has already given me, but I'm talking about contentment in my relationship and service to *Him.* He wants to stretch me. I certainly have not *arrived* yet. I have so much growing to do, and without growing pains it will never happen.

Now, my prayer is new: "Where do You want me to grow, Lord? How are You going to change and mold me to become even more like You? I'm ready, Lord. I'm here and willing to serve You right where I am, and willing to go wherever You lead. Cause me to be ready for anything that *You* ask. Amen."

So now I sit and wait, half scared (a healthy fear of the Lord, I suppose) and half excited with anticipation. "What next, Lord?"

Part 7
Moving/Houses

Even Atlanta

Deb Haggerty

*Father, if it is Your will, take this cup away from Me;
nevertheless, not My will, but Yours, be done.*
—Luke 22:42 NKJV

Life was good. I enjoyed my relationship with my husband and family. I enjoyed my work. I was walking closely with the Lord. There was just one little problem.

My husband was talking about moving back to Atlanta, where we'd each lived with previous spouses. He reasoned that he'd see both his children more frequently and that they could live together—part-time with us and part-time with their mother—instead of one with us and the other with her.

Atlanta held so many unhappy memories for me. Emotionally, I stomped my foot: "I do not want to go back to Atlanta."

I sought a moment with God. "Thank You for all You have done for me, Lord—all the many blessings You have showered on me. I want so much to walk in Your will. I will do anything; go anywhere—whatever You want me to do."

Very quietly, yet very clearly, I heard Him say to me, "Even Atlanta, Deb? Even Atlanta?"

I was speechless. I stopped praying.

Even Atlanta?

Did I really trust Him that much? Did I really want to be totally in His will if it meant moving there?

Finally, I could respond. "If it's Your will, Lord, that we move to Atlanta, I'm willing to go. I trust You with my life and my family."

Later that night, as my husband and I talked, I told him that I was willing to go back to Atlanta if he felt that was best for the family.

He never brought it up again.

What he and the Lord both wanted was my willingness. I had to be willing to follow my husband as head of our family; I had to be willing to follow God's leading—even to the ends of the earth. Even to Atlanta.

Spinning Gold into Hay

Donna Jones

If any man builds on this foundation using gold, silver, costly stones, wood, hay or straw, his work will be shown for what it is, because the Day will bring it to light. It will be revealed with fire, and the fire will test the quality of each man's work.

—1 Corinthians 3:12–13 NIV

I had such good intentions. I really did.

At just twenty-nine, I was the new senior pastor's wife in a church in need of healing from past hurts. With the goal of providing the women with a sense of belonging, acceptance, and love, I volunteered to host a Saturday morning coffee at our home.

Hosting the event was not the problem. The complication was that we'd moved into our "fixer-upper" home just two months earlier. Three weeks after that, I gave birth to our second child. Both circumstances made my good intentions a bit more difficult to carry out.

With newborn on one hip and a paintbrush in my hand, I set out to transform our "diamond in the rough." While I may have had a screw or two loose, I was on a mission. I plunged into home redecorating with a vengeance—convinced I'd get it all done by the big event. Somehow, between the nursing and the naps, I managed to paint bedrooms and strip wallpaper. I ordered window treatments, new carpet, and hardwood flooring.

Amazing progress was made, and every room was meticulously redone—except for the kitchen. There, I peeled off the old wallpaper—which left a brown residue. My wallpaper for the kitchen was being specially ordered, but I, an avowed housecleaning nut, could live with ugly walls for a few days. With some of the work done and the orders placed, I was now at six weeks before the big event.

Five weeks and counting, and the wallpaper still hadn't arrived. I called the wallpaper company to check on the status of my order, and was told that my pattern was on back order—due in a week or two. Feeling disappointed, but not yet panicked, I hung up the phone and resigned myself to waiting.

The days ticked by, and each morning I looked at the mess on the kitchen wall. I tried to avoid becoming depressed by telling myself I could keep a positive attitude for a few more days. After all, I'm a flexible kind of gal.

Three weeks to go. I called again. This time I was assured I'd receive my order in ten working days or less. Frustrated and beginning to feel a bit stressed, I hung up—desperately wanting to believe the "a-bit-too-eager-to-please" young wallpaper rep.

Ten business days later, exhausted, overworked, postpartum, hormonal, and a wreck, I called the wallpaper company. By now, I'd had it with delays. The poor customer service agent who had the misfortune to get my call didn't know what hit him. I ranted. I raved. I refused to accept any more phony promises.

"Do you realize in *five days* I'll have one hundred women in my home?" I wailed. "I have brown glue the color of baby-poop all over my kitchen walls!"

I convinced myself I had a right to be upset. Five days. Glue on walls. Baby-poop brown. Totally unacceptable. Yes, I was a pastor's wife, the senior pastor's wife no less. Sure I wanted the women to feel I was approachable, normal, even one of the gals. But having them see my kitchen in utter disrepair was . . . well . . . unthinkable.

Later that day, I recounted my decorating woes to my best friend. I felt totally justified as I explained my little outburst. After all, I'd been patient. I'd been given the run around. Knowing I was right caused her words to hit me even harder.

"Oh," she said kindly, "you began planning this event with an attitude of gold, silver, and precious stones. Now it's become wood, hay, and straw."

I sat back in my chair with my mouth hanging open. No one had ever been so brutally honest with me. And no one had ever been so right. Only a true friend would have the guts to knock me back to where God wanted me to be.

I'd begun this project with a pure heart, desperately wanting to please the Lord, to glorify Him, to communicate His love. I'd fallen into the trap of wanting to please man and glorify myself. Communicating love was the last thing on my mind while talking to the woefully incompetent wallpaper company.

Eleven years have come and gone since my decorating distress—since my friend shared her truthful, yet painful observation. That Saturday morning outreach was an undisputed success. Women came, laughed, talked, and bonded. They even oohed and aahed over our home—as I'd hoped they would. The kitchen looked beautiful and only my best friend knew the last bit of wallpaper went up at 1:30 A.M.—by a very kindhearted and hardworking wallpaper hanger who took pity on me and my plight.

But the biggest success was not in the completion of my home decorating, or even the bonding, love, and acceptance felt in my home on that day. No, the biggest success was the change in my heart. I went from self-focused to other-focused; from me-centered to God-centered. Oh, what a success that was!

I started out with such good intentions. I really did. And in spite of myself, I ended there too.

High Heels or High Tops

Daphne V. Smith

Therefore, if anyone is in Christ, he is a new creation; the old has gone, the new has come!
—2 Corinthians 5:17 NIV

I grew up in *North* Dallas. I emphasize North to convey a certain attitude that's commonly associated with the area. There's an unspoken standard that's expected of women. But I'm not putting down the "dress your best even to go to the grocery store" mind-set. In fact, for years, I embraced it.

As a young mother, I got involved in the cosmetic industry. Wanting to supplement our household income and be around grown-ups were my reasons for doing so. It seemed like a natural transition; I'd been a model as a child, been in the diamond industry as an adult, and I'd always wanted to make a statement with my appearance. I loved high heels and high fashion.

All that changed, though, after I left Dallas. Due to a career change, my husband moved our family to Arkansas. Arkansas! Of all the places in the world to be transferred.

I was born and raised in the United State of Texas. You can't imagine the stories of hillbillies and razorbacks I'd heard while growing up. Did they have a mall where we were moving? Had they even heard of "shop 'til you drop"? Other than overalls, what did Arkansans wear?

Once we got to Arkansas, I was deeply thankful that, indeed, there was a mall. Granted, it was forty-five minutes away from our home, and at the time it only had three department stores. And much to my surprise, it took several weeks of living there before I actually saw anyone wearing overalls—and that person had a full set of teeth and was wearing shoes.

But the greatest thing Arkansas had to offer me was the state motto—the natural state. For the first time in my life, I truly experienced all four seasons, not just observed them in the store windows of the concrete jungle. I saw, felt, and smelled the natural beauty in the trees and hills.

While I surveyed that beauty, I began a closer walk with God. I found myself actually slowing down long enough to appreciate my surroundings—and to hear that still small voice within. Before, while living in the big city, I was too busy to hear anything. I was so consumed with keeping up, I was quickly burning out.

I've lived in Arkansas for more than eight years now. Many seasons have come and gone and I can now call Arkansas home. Don't get me wrong—I'm still very proud to consider myself a Texan. I'm also in many ways a high maintenance woman. But to me, home is a place where I don't have to dress to impress. Home is a place where my inward beauty is far more important than my outer beauty.

Ultimately, it won't be the designer label that matters or measures my life. I'm now in a place, where regardless of high heels or high tops, I know I'm loved.

I Don't Want to Go!

Betty Southard

Look here, you people who say, "Today or tomorrow we are going to such and such a town, stay there a year, and open up a profitable business." How do you know what is going to happen tomorrow?

—James 4:13–14 TLB

God's country! That's what I felt about Oregon, my birthplace. Majestic mountains, verdant forests, rushing rivers, rolling hills, fertile farmlands, beautiful beaches, even the desert areas were alive with interesting foliage. All of our family and friends lived there. Our home church was the one in which my mother had been raised and where my father's family had been members for years. My grandparents were still an integral part of this church family.

I loved Oregon, my church, my friends, and my family. As my grandpa always said, "It's God's country, why would anyone want to live anywhere else?"

I threw that very question in my husband's face. He'd come home and announced that U-Haul, his place of employment, was relocating to Tempe, Arizona.

Have you ever been to Arizona, particularly back in the late 1960s? Tempe was a dry little town, brown everywhere, and no sign of green grass or beautiful big fir trees. Everywhere I looked, all I saw was brown,

brown, brown or shades of brown. I don't like brown! The houses had no character, the yards were rock instead of grass, street after street looked the same—flat and uninteresting.

Over all my protests, Fred and I sold the wonderful, dream home we'd just built in Oregon, packed all our belongings in a U-Haul truck (yes, working for that company we had to move ourselves), and headed out in late January to relocate in Tempe.

To my eyes, the landscape got barer, drier, and uglier as we drove closer and closer to Tempe. January 31, the night of our tenth wedding anniversary, we headed into town. As we literally bumped our way down Grand Avenue (the roads were old, no freeways at that time) and crossed the bridge (over a dry riverbed) into Tempe, Fred made the unfortunate choice to remark that we had set the goal of spending our tenth anniversary in Hawaii. He plastered a smile on his face and said, "Look, honey. Palm trees."

I wanted to hang him from one of those palm trees.

I frankly felt as though God had abandoned me and sent me from the beautiful, cool, green heaven of Oregon to that other place of torture. I fought God—and Fred—every step of the way. I didn't want to be in a hot, dry, and friendless place. I was lonely, unhappy, and determined not to follow the directions his boss had given each employee. We were instructed to buy a home *in* Tempe, *without* a swimming pool. We were also told that we were not to return to Oregon for a year.

I went back five times that first year. I searched everywhere *but* Tempe for our new home. I finally found the right one, in Tempe after all, but it *did* have a swimming pool. It turned out to be just a few blocks from Grace Community Church, which had just opened its doors. We'd already visited several churches in the area when a babysitter invited us to visit Grace. I sat in the service on Palm Sunday when God very clearly spoke to me. "This is why I moved you to Tempe."

There, in what I'd thought was a God-forsaken place, I met God in a fresh new way. There, in that church I was first mentored in ministry. And there, I learned the excitement of leading others to a personal relationship with Christ. We grew with that church, and the faith of our three daughters was laid upon a firm foundation. I made new friends and discovered the benefits of being moved beyond my comfort zone.

I learned to really study the Bible—and, finally, to teach it. I learned the secrets of growing a dynamic women's ministry. I even learned to appreciate the beauty of the desert. Arizona was exactly where I wanted to stay for the rest of my life.

I'd found my niche. We had friends, family—my sister relocated there—and a wonderful church. Ah, yes, Arizona was the place for me.

Once again, Fred announced he'd received a better job offer in California.

California? Why would anyone want to live in that crowded, crazy state?

But, move we did, and once again, in spite of lessons I'd learned years earlier, I went kicking, screaming, and complaining. And once again, God proved that there were new horizons to conquer and fresh lessons to learn. This move allowed me to attend Fuller Seminary and receive my Master's Degree in Theology. And in California I became a partner with the Littauers and the CLASS ministry.

I'm happily settled in California, with friends, family, and a wonderful church. I love it here. What wonderful opportunities living in California has brought to my family and me. We all live here now. Why would anyone want to live anywhere else?

Don't worry. I know who holds the future, and He has been trustworthy so far. And perhaps I've learned, at last, to trust Him for my tomorrows, wherever they may be.

His Name Shall Be Wonderful

Kirk Hine

But they that wait upon the LORD shall renew their strength;
they shall mount up with wings like eagles; they shall run,
and not be weary; and they shall walk, and not faint.
—Isaiah 40:31 KJV

After twenty years of globetrotting, it was time to retire from the U.S. Navy. I was a Chief Petty Officer, having served honorably on ships, submarines, and naval aircraft, and at several overseas bases in Europe. My final assignment had been at the National Security Agency in Fort Meade, Maryland, located midway between Washington, DC, and Baltimore. Neither my wife, Judi, nor I had any strong connections to this area, and we'd always wanted, upon retirement, to move to a place of our own choosing, rather than the Navy's.

The places we talked most about were Colorado and Michigan. Both of us leaned a little stronger on the side of Colorado. For those of you who've ever been "Rocky Mountain High," you know why.

But with the date of my retirement looming large, and with no firm plan for relocating in mind, we felt it best to stay put, at least for the time being. We weren't sure how long we'd stay in the area, but we could make plans without the added dual pressures of moving out of base housing and finding a job. And so we started our transition into civilian life, first by finding a decent job for me and second, finding a new home.

I scoured the Baltimore-Washington corridor for a "second career" as a training specialist. I had a fair amount of academic and practical experience in the training field, and I was comfortable that I could succeed in this new profession. After only a five-week search, I found a decent training job with a "Beltway Bandit" defense-contracting firm in Herndon, Virginia.

While northern Virginia wasn't "home" to either of us, we knew we needed to settle there. We were used to living in places for relatively short amounts of time—a year here, two years there. So we began house-hunting in northern Virginia to find a new home within a thirty- to forty-five-minute drive of work. We found a house under construction in Leesburg, Virginia, and took active steps to begin its purchase.

At the time we found the house, we moved out of base housing, and Judi, our three kids, and I lived out of suitcases for two months in a small, one-room cabin in a Christian campground in Maryland. Our household goods were in storage, waiting our orders to deliver them to our final destination.

For those who've never lived in a drafty cabin in Maryland during the month of October, it's an experience you don't soon forget. Although we did enjoy "roughing it," we were far past ready to get resettled.

While things seemed to be coming together, it just didn't feel right. We didn't really have any peace about what was happening to us. And the tug toward Colorado was stronger than ever. We asked the Lord to work His will, and it wasn't long before He told us that He had plans for us elsewhere.

So, placing our faith in Him, we "loaded up the truck and moved to Beverly," in a manner of speaking. I gave my employers two weeks notice—turning down a substantial raise to stay—piled kids, kit and caboodle into the cars, and headed west.

We had no idea what we'd find or how long it would take to find it, but we were trusting God to provide for us as He had so many, many times in the past. Judi and the girls stayed with family in Montana, while I headed straight for Colorado.

We never suspected the separation would last nearly seven months. But it did. I stayed with good friends in Colorado Springs while I searched in earnest for a new job, sending out countless résumés.

As Christmas neared, though, I felt a real need to be with my family. So a couple of days before Christmas I started out to Montana. On a lonely stretch of Wyoming highway, my car skated on a patch of black ice and was thrown into a concrete drainage ditch.

Thankful that I wasn't injured, I wondered, *What, now Lord?* He isn't called wonderful for nothing. In moments, God provided a Good Samaritan, who took me to the nearest town. The following day, my car was towed to Casper, Wyoming. The repair shop there didn't have the parts I needed, and by this time it was again approaching night.

What now, Lord? I wondered. Again, something wonderful. I remembered some friends who'd moved near Casper. I looked in the phone book and, sure enough, my friend's number was listed. They welcomed me into their home for the night, and the next day I rented a car and continued to Montana.

At long last, at four o'clock on Christmas Eve, I was once again with my family. I don't think Christmas ever meant so much to us as it did that year.

After the holidays, I returned to Colorado, and for weeks and months, no decent job came along that could support me and my family. I went on several interviews, and at one point had a job offer, contingent upon a particular contract materializing. It didn't. Without a job, I couldn't bring Judi and the girls down from Montana.

But God answers our prayers as He sees fit, and when it's time—when, as is written in Jeremiah 9:7, He had melted and tried us. He provided a job in the Denver area, one better than I could have hoped for. At the same time, He spoke to Judi, and told her to join me in Colorado, and she drove down the week before I started my new job.

We've lived here for five wonderful years, with wonderful friends, a wonderful church family, a wonderful husband for our oldest daughter, and wonderful prospects. Perhaps I'm overdoing *wonderful*, but it's to make a point. All this came about because we placed our hope and trust in the Lord— the One whose name shall be called Wonderful Counselor.

My So-Called Pseudo-Life

Kim Johnson

*Let us also lay aside every encumbrance and the sin which
so easily entangles us, and let us run with endurance the
race that is set before us, fixing our eyes on Jesus.*
—Hebrews 12:1–2 NASB

I should have been in a good mood. It was a beautiful, early spring Saturday. The sun was shining and the trees were beginning to bud. Soon they'd be green. Yes, I should have been in a good mood—but I wasn't. We were still living in this place. I didn't like it. I didn't like it when we moved here, and nothing was going to make me like it!

We'd moved here two years earlier from a place close to the ocean. There I'd had a best friend, my kids had been happy, and we'd all been extremely content. My husband, however, decided he wanted to return to school for a graduate degree. Worst of all, the school he wanted to attend was two-thousand miles away.

"It won't be so bad," he tried to convince me. "Think of it as an adventure."

Yeah, right! As adventurous as a bee sting. We prayed about it and, just my luck, of course, the Lord apparently was on my husband's side. What could I do? I reluctantly agreed. My passive-aggressive personality type, however, wouldn't leave well enough alone. "I'll make the move, but I'm not going to enjoy it." Grumbling and muttering, I packed, and off we moved—four states away where it was hot, humid, and where we didn't know anyone.

I decided to treat this season as my pseudo-life. Maybe some things were okay, but when anyone asked me, "Do you like it here?" my answer was always an emphatic "No!" The longer we lived there, the more I wished it was over. And the more I wished it to be over, the slower time passed. Since I blamed God for putting me in this position, my prayers became shallow and my quiet times superficial. My "inner child" threw the tantrum of her life!

So, on that beautiful Saturday, my attitude was just as sour as ever. As I came over a small hill, cars were screeching to the side of the road and people scrambled out. A pickup truck with the front end smashed in was across the road, and another car lay on its side with the tires still spinning. Normally, I would have driven slowly by and then continued on my way. But the immediacy of the moment made me pull to the side of the road and jump out of my car too.

People yelled for emergency help and others looked in the crushed vehicles. I was drawn to the car on its side. A young woman, obviously pregnant, was unconscious, half in and half out of the car door window. There was some blood that seemed to be coming from her nose, her chin rested on her chest, and her breathing was labored.

Time slowed to a crawl as I watched her breathing become harder and harder. I felt if I just moved her head back, she could breathe, so I reached through the window. But someone pulled me back. They didn't think I should touch her.

"Wait for the paramedics," someone murmured.

So . . . I just stood there.

The emergency personnel seemed slow to arrive, and it was agonizing to watch the young woman. Suddenly, her body shuddered and her chest stopped moving. Then the paramedics arrived and rushed over. They called for an air ambulance and went to work on her, but in my heart I feared it was futile. I couldn't move as I watched them extract her from the vehicle and put her in the helicopter. I stood there long after it was out of sight, then climbed into my car.

It was odd to know that my body was functioning, because my mind was numb. I completed my errand, but not before bursting into tears in the checkout line. The cashier didn't know whether to take my money or call security. All the way home I sobbed. Why had this affected me so deeply?

This was a depth of pain I hadn't experienced for a while. Here I was, marking time, until my husband graduated, still two years away. What if *I* had an accident on my way home? What guarantees did I have that I'd make it through the next few minutes, let alone the next two years?

The answer exploded in my heart. *None! Let us run with endurance the race that is set before us.*

How could I have been so selfish? My trivial complaints crumbled in a heap of self-reproach. Where I was at that moment in time— where we were living—was exactly where God wanted me to be, and I needed to trust Him and accept it.

I'd wasted nearly two years, but I was determined that the next two would be productive. Even having to eat humble pie wasn't so bad— at least it didn't have calories! My whole attitude changed and living there took on a whole new look. Time started flying by. I became involved and started enjoying things about my life that I had once refused to even acknowledge. Before I knew it, my husband had graduated.

Best of all, we actually moved back to the same area as our ocean home. God knew that was going to happen all along.

Since that time, the seasons of my life have brought continual change. Some changes have been great and others have been painful. But never again have I resented what has come my way. The inconveniences I've experienced will never compare to what Jesus endured on my behalf. So as I run the race that's set before me, the least I can do is keep my eyes in the right place—upon Him.

Mine or God's?

Lynne Cooper Sitton

For where your treasure is, there your heart will be also.
—Matthew 6:21 NIV

I winced as I watched the movers. They were manhandling priceless family antiques, furniture, and other fragile items previous generations had lovingly preserved. These heirlooms had been handed down to us to enjoy and to pass on to our children. Just one problem: we got transferred a lot. This time from New England to Florida.

Every time we moved, I'd remind myself that I wasn't the real owner of these lovely things. In prayer, I'd handed the family treasures to the Lord.

But I'd also watched rough handling and bad packing ruin thousands of dollars of irreplaceable items. When some disinterested packer layered canned goods on top of my crystal goblets, the outcome wasn't God's fault. Those experiences, multiplied by twenty-five years of moves with the U.S. Coast Guard, made me less than optimistic that we'd incur no losses this time.

My stomach dipped as I observed two gorillas start to lift my antique gate-leg table by the top. "Hey!" I interrupted them. "Please lift that piece by the underside. The screws will pull out if you carry it that way."

One guy shot me a look that said, "Will you please leave us alone," but he changed his hold on the table. By the time they loaded the van, the movers were delighted to part company with me. I fought tears as I vacuumed the last rooms, thinking that I'd find unpleasant surprises in those boxes when they arrived at the other end.

"The other end" was a house in Coral Springs, Florida, which to my dismay, wasn't anywhere near Miami. Its location meant an hour-plus daily commute for my husband and twelve miles to our younger son's new Christian school. The house was pleasant enough, just too far away from Miami and from my dear college friend who lived just south of the city. All my hopes of building a closer relationship evaporated.

Truth be known, I felt like a fragile crystal goblet with a cracked stem. Our older son had opted to remain in Rhode Island to finish his senior year in high school and apply to colleges. My nest was beginning to empty. Within the previous year, I'd also suffered two major surgeries, the onset of asthma, and the unexpected death of my father. God had endured more than a few tears and ranting about the weight of my trials and His perfect timing. Couldn't He *at least* allow me the proximity of one close friend in Miami?

True to form, the move generated some major repairs to damaged antiques. Through bitter experience, though, we'd learned to obtain certified antique appraisals for insurance purposes. So the damage always pierced my heart more than my purse. But part of my own heritage disappeared with each vanishing antique. I couldn't just go buy another 1813 grandfather clock.

When I discovered a particularly dear memento in splinters, I cried out, "Lord, I'm trying hard to simply enjoy these family treasures. But if You want, I'll give them to other family members and buy furniture at Wal-Mart. The movers can trash that stuff, and I won't care."

God knew the true yearnings of my heart. He heard my cry, "Lord, I can't take any more losses now! You had it in Your power to protect my life and my belongings, and You haven't spared me. Like Job, I feel overwhelmed by tragedy and loss. Where is the refuge You promised?"

A year later, the Lord answered my question when Hurricane Andrew smashed south Florida. Before the storm, I'd invited my friend and her extended family to hunker down behind the storm shutters in our home, away from their coastal houses. "Worst case," I joked over the phone, "we'll all camp out in the dark for a few days."

Little did we know their visit would become a month-long stay.

Nine guests and two dogs arrived on my doorstep Sunday night with treasured photos, computers, scrap books, and important family documents. Within hours of that arrival, Coral Springs was blasted with ninety-mile-per-hour winds, but we never lost electricity or water service. Miami and south Florida didn't fair so well. The news broadcasts revealed massive devastation in my friends' neighborhood . . . *exactly where I had wanted to live.*

Wandering into my living room, I felt guilty, yet thankful. The Lord's perfect plan had placed us north and west of Miami. He *had* protected our priceless heirlooms while many families lost everything. I certainly didn't *deserve* to be spared. Through tears, my gaze rested on my grandmother's piano, my great-great-grandfather's Chippendale mirror, and my great-grandmother's Victorian parlor suite. God's mercy had set apart our home as a sanctuary for two families, whose homes and belongings had fallen victim to a hurricane. While they recovered from *their* severe losses, I—with a new perspective—could weep with my friends as they went through their "deep places."

I thanked God for refusing me the one thing that I wanted: to live in Miami. I wanted human comfort because I felt abandoned. But He spared my home and used it for a refuge. He reminded me that the most important things in life are not *things*—no matter how dear they are.

Out of the Ditch
and into His Will

Neva Donald

Trust in the LORD *with all your heart and lean not on your own understanding; in all your ways acknowledge him and he will make your paths straight.*
—Proverbs 3:5–6 NIV

The new year of 2001 dawned full of excitement and promise. My husband had finally retired from a contracting career, and I was ready to move forward with my speaking and writing ministry. We'd made financial provisions for our retirement, and had our future plans in place. We were content and, at times, that's a dangerous place to be.

We'd sold a business some years ago and were getting monthly interest payments. Then in June, the notice came that the business we'd sold was in trouble. As of July 2001, we'd no longer be getting any income from that at all. Even the principal was in jeopardy.

We fumed, we fretted, we stewed, and then we prayed—in that order, I'm afraid. Since our other modest investment money was not available for a few years, we knew we'd have to replace the interest income. Just about this same time, we'd made the decision to move near our son, Greg, and our daughter-in-law on the east coast of Florida. We'd already made an appointment, in fact, with a realtor to scout for a home.

When we arrived at Greg's the last day of June, we told him about our dilemma. I told him that I was going to go back to work to supplement our income, and that I'd already scouted the market, sending out applications and résumés. On this same trip, I had several job prospects to consider. Yet, one by one, they evaporated. Either the position had been filled or they'd hired from within.

Believing this surprise was no surprise to God, we went ahead and looked for houses. After at least twelve homes and two days of looking, our realtor took us to "one last place to consider." She hadn't previewed it, and she was as surprised as we to see such a lovely home backing up to a private preserve, and just down the street from the recreation center and pool. The price was unbelievably good compared to others we'd just seen and, even better, it was empty.

Should we put in an offer? With our changed financial situation and another home yet to sell, could we afford to make the offer? I wanted to find a job—after all the years I'd been so well provided for, it was my turn to work. We decided to sleep on it and, finally, to pray earnestly over the many decisions we had to make.

As we discussed this with our son, Greg casually asked why I didn't consider going back to teaching. Actually, I had thought about just that, but it had been years since I taught.

Greg said, "I'll drive you down to the school board offices and you can see what you need to do to get recertified and if they have any jobs."

That made sense.

The next day, Greg, my husband, and I started out on our quest. About a mile from his house, Greg turned down the driveway of a church, the one he and his family attended. Since they were in the middle of adding another building for their school, he thought his dad would like to take a look at the construction.

When we stopped, Greg waved to the pastor, who was out looking at the day's progress, which included digging a ditch for new plumbing. After introductions, the pastor showed us the latest phase of the project.

Suddenly, he stopped in his tracks, turned abruptly to Greg and said, "I don't know how we'll be ready for school this year. We have all our teachers except one, and I have no idea how we'll find one at this late date."

"What grade are you looking for?" asked Greg.

"Oh, it's not that easy. We need a high school English teacher. That will be difficult to find."

Meanwhile, I stood mute while I watched and listened to the conversation.

"My mother used to teach high school English. She has a degree from Bob Jones University in Speech Education and English."

Without missing a beat, the pastor looked heavenward and breathed, "Thank You, Lord!"

The school administrator happened to be on the property too. He met with us and he scheduled a time to meet with me the next day. I was dumbstruck at the very obvious way God had intervened that day, when we finally allowed Him to take care of the problem.

We continued on to the local school board as planned. Guess what? They had every position in the county filled. They didn't even seem interested in me! And why would they—I was needed somewhere else.

Let me tell you how involved God is in the details. The nice house we liked so well was within four miles of "my" school. After my interview the next day, we did put an offer on the house and it was accepted. The house, we found out, had been on the market for over four months. No one could understand why it hadn't been sold sooner; it was in a very desirable location where houses usually sold within two weeks. We knew why. God had this home planned for us.

One other small problem still needed attention. We had to sell our house in Georgia, but with the events of the past week, do you think we even worried about that? We polished it up, hired a building inspector to evaluate it, held two open houses ourselves, and sold the house to the second couple who looked at it.

Both houses, the one in Florida and the one in Georgia, closed within days of each other. Since I'd already started teaching, my sweet husband had the task of packing up and moving our belongings.

The pastor, as amazed by the working of God as we were, announced to his congregation that the school had found the last teacher needed. He shared with them the story of discovering the English teacher in a ditch that July day.

I was surprised, too, at how easy it was to get back into the classroom after so many years away. Kids are still kids; English is still English, and we are all having an amazing journey together, discovering the truths that are as relevant today as they ever were.

I still write and do some speaking in our area. When God is ready to use me again, I'm available. Meanwhile, I have some very important young people who need to learn about Shakespeare, short stories, sonnets, and spelling.

I'm still awed by the way God worked in our situation. Awed, but not surprised. Once we let God take control of our decisions, He will clear the obstacles, smooth the way, and enabled us to go forward.

A Prayer Meeting for My House

Judy Wallace

God, make a fresh start in me, shape a Genesis week from the chaos of my life.

—Psalm 51:10 THE MESSAGE

All I'd wanted was a larger master bath. That was it. I guess I should have been satisfied with what I had. After all, one commode, two sinks and a shower should be sufficient for any couple, right? But it was a little tight with Tommy and me both in there at the same time. So we put feet to my dreams of a larger dressing area and a whirlpool tub.

It began with a visit to the architect—a personal friend from high school. After two hours of mostly reminiscing, we walked out of his office with three small sketches and one large bill.

"I can do this myself," Tommy stated flatly.

I knew he was right. After all, he'd designed our original house plans, and I'd been pleased. Plus, because of his Phlegmatic/Melancholy Personality, I knew that everything would be done perfectly; I also knew it would be done v-e-e-e-r-y slowly.

The professional sketches indicated that we add on to our existing floor plan. Since our son was in college and our daughter was a senior in high school, Tommy felt we'd be better served to use the existing floor space and simply "rearrange" some of the rooms.

Before we could begin tearing down and repositioning walls, we had to take care of the foundation problems. (Our house had started settling the year it was built.) For three days, large equipment moved into my yard, jacking up our house to place steel beams underneath.

With the settling came cracked windows. Each one was replaced, and new siding and a roof were added for good measure. The jostling outside had left floors uneven on the inside so a concrete truck was brought in, and after the carpet was pulled back, fresh concrete was poured inside my house to level the floors. That was year one, and I still had the same, small master bath.

"Since we have things torn up," my husband decided, "we might as well redo the upstairs too." When we first designed the house we'd put in a floored attic for storage. "That area," Tommy stated, "would make a great bedroom for one of the kids some day." As soon as Jill heard that, she set her hopes of being the one to have that very room.

So began the next phase. We tore out a wall and used that space to add a stairway, then tore out the ceiling for a sitting room at the top of the stairs, and made three openings in the roof for dormers. Enlarging the entrance of the living room and dining room gave the house a more open feel. We also added a sunroom near some huge trees that we loved.

Three years into the project my house was a disarray of torn out drywall and exposed wall studs. Furniture and boxes were moved from one place to another as each room fell under the hammer of my determined husband. In disgust, I told my friends, "My house looks like it has thrown up!" To top it off, I still didn't have my master bath.

I wish I could say I remained calm, cool, and collected through it all. I wish I could say I patiently endured each and every aspect of each stage in the remodeling. I wish I could tell you I lovingly supported my husband in every decision and in the time frame within which he chose to work. I wish I could—but I can't.

I was frustrated, angry, hurt, tired, and felt as torn apart as my home. I was sick and tired of living among boards and boxes. I was sick and tired of not being able to come home and relax or entertain guests. Mostly, I was sick and tired of being sick and tired, and I was definitely *not* happy with my husband.

During one of our ladies Bible classes I finally broke down and asked them simply to pray for my house. It seemed silly to ask for a remodeling-job prayer, but not one of them laughed. They knew what I was going through, and for a full hour, each of them took turns praying for me, my husband, and my house.

That was three years ago. Jill has her new room; she moved into it two days before her wedding. We're still not completely finished, but I do finally have my beautiful, new master bath, complete with whirlpool tub and a larger dressing area.

I also have something else—a remodeled spirit. The prayer and support from the ladies at my church didn't cause my husband to work any faster, but it did help create a new work in me. My house may have been in chaos, the work unfinished, but I could see progress, and I'd leave the time frame in God's hands. In a similar way, my chaotic spirit now has a shape and purpose. God started on my foundation, tore down some walls, exposed some barriers, and removed some things in my life that had hindered His work through me.

Such a project is, of course, a major undertaking. And even at this phase of the project, there's still some work to be done. I will now, however, leave the time frame in God's hands, because I really like what He has done so far.

The Dynamite List

Mary Maynard

In everything give thanks; for this is God's will for you in Christ Jesus.

—1 Thessalonians 5:18 NASB

Everything except the dynamite was my husband's fault. And I was trying to blame him for that too.

With many years in the construction business under his belt, David had successfully built us three homes. So with a cheerful attitude, I packed boxes for relocation to the small house we'd rent during the construction of our newest home. I also packed boxes for storage, including all my Christmas decorations, in a unit halfway across town. Mentally, I prepared for six months of living without most of my possessions.

I never figured dynamite into the equation. We needed to dynamite because my husband had dug the original hole for our foundation in the middle of a proposed street. When he discovered his error, we had to change our plans, unless I wanted my garage in the middle of Elm Street. He chose the top of a hill for our new position, and the top of that hill was solid rock.

That ground was so hard that, in order to dig the foundation, we had to use dynamite eleven times. I'm not making that number up. The first explosion was lots of fun. We brought the kids out to the property and stood behind trees while chunks of solid rock whizzed past our heads. That first explosion had almost a picnic atmosphere. About the fifth time, it ceased to be fun.

Totally out of character, David made many mistakes throughout the building process. His business was so busy he could barely keep up. With his high stress level, he needed me to comfort and believe in him, but all I could see were his blunders. I was highly inconvenienced, and I blamed him—loudly.

I could only see my pain. Living out of boxes like a nomad, my plans for being in a new home for Christmas were dashed. There would be just the smallest slice of Christmas in our home that year, and there was not a drop of Christmas in my heart. And it was all David's fault.

Before this chain of events, I would have said I had the greatest husband in the world. Suddenly I couldn't see it. Anger choked me, and I felt like I could hardly function. I deserved to live better than this. I wasn't going to have a "real" Christmas, and I started talking to all my friends about the awfulness of David and how he was messing up my perfect life.

My friends felt sorry for me—for about five minutes. Then they eloquently and in rich detail pointed out my selfishness and general ugliness. I'd dug myself into a black hole—one I hadn't needed dynamite to dig—and I wasn't sure how to climb out.

I knew Scripture calls us to be thankful "in everything," so I decided to make a list of what I could be thankful for. I sat down and started typing: "Things I'm grateful for . . ."

1. God. I had to believe that if He was asking me to be thankful in everything, then dynamite was part of the everything. I wrote out, "He is in control, not me." Not the munitions subcontractor, or the stubborn rock, or even David controlled where I lived. Only God. Could I thank Him? Yes. I typed it as a statement of faith.

2. David. I generally give him a ninety-three percent. He's a fabulous guy, not perfect, but definitely an A, and certainly more than I deserve. I'd become so focused on the seven percent that was

bugging me, I couldn't see the many things about him that I was thankful for. I typed in a list of David's qualities that I appreciated.

Focusing on my "right" to have a comfortable and wonderful life had produced ungratefulness in my life. I needed to be thankful that God used something slightly uncomfortable to show me my heart. I could thank Him for not leaving me in the middle of the street, headed toward bitterness, but for moving me in the direction of becoming more like Him—the top of the hill.

I made several copies of my list and handed them to my friends. The next time I started to complain, they could just point to whichever statement best showed where I needed to repent. I put a copy on the clipboard I always carry, and I had to read it every day during those months to even have a prayerful attitude. Those words became my mission statement.

To this day, I carry the list with me. I don't read it every day, but when I feel my selfishness rising up, I can quickly find it. Being mad didn't make me happy; it made me feel awful. Loving David when he most needed encouragement felt much better. Deciding I was not the center of the universe and being thankful toward God was like the maple syrup of gratitude instead of the acid of anger.

We now live in that beautiful home on the rock. I'm convinced the eleven rounds of dynamite were only a word picture. God used it to show me that what really needed dynamite was my heart.

My husband may have made a mistake in the beginning. But he was right in the end. After all, the wise man always builds his house upon the Rock.

Wasting Away and Knee-Deep in Sewage

Martin Babb

She looks well to the ways of her household, and does not eat the bread of idleness.

—Proverbs 31:27 NRSV

I'm convinced that an old Chinese Proverb goes something like this: "When sewer backs up into den, best place for husband to be is Memphis."

The plausibility of that proverb hit me in the nostrils a couple of years ago. I'd returned home from a senior-adult trip to Memphis, Tennessee, at 10:45 on a Saturday night. I'm a minister of education, responsible for senior adult ministry in my church. Normally, when I come home that time of night, my wife just greets me with a sleepy "hello." This time, though, I'm certain that I heard the theme from "Jaws," playing in the background.

She was awake and greeted me with a Hannibal Lechter stare that could knock down a moose. Her teeth were clenched and her voice less than angelic: *"Ask me about my day!"*

It was one of those "teachable moments" in marriage communication. I realized almost immediately that if I didn't ask her about her day she'd reach into my throat and pull out my tonsils. No husband, unless he's brain dead, could ignore such a request. I asked.

And I received. She told me that she and our son, David, had spent most of the day wading through water and waste in our garage. During our conversation I learned more about sewage than I cared to know. Sewage backup, like hairstyling, is something I'd only read about but never experienced. She said it started as a groaning and gurgling sound coming from the kitchen sink. Unless it's the subject of a Stephen King novel, a kitchen sink ought not to groan and gurgle—although our sink once voiced some concern over the disposing of a leftover tuna casserole.

Then came the tandem burping of the tub and toilet. Except in fraternity houses, the sound of burping most definitely ought not come from tubs and toilets. Even though Beverly is a schoolteacher and David is a teenager, this was their first experience with belching porcelain. That in itself would have been just cause for concern, but David got one final clue that something wasn't right. When he went into the garage he found one of our Chihuahuas surfing on a Styrofoam board. This was unusual because that particular Chihuahua always surfs on a plastic board.

Well, when the going gets tough, Beverly goes to Wal-Mart. When she returned she was armed with pliers and enough duct tape to wrap three Sumo wrestlers. With the help of our neighbor, they made the proper adjustments to a loose connection and everything was soon back to normal.

When Beverly finished telling me her tale we had a good laugh. It was easy for me to laugh because I hadn't been through it, and I had some rather colorful images of her and David playing in our temporary pond. It was easy for me to smile, too, because the physical damage to the garage and basement was minimal.

While I listened to her story and looked around, I was once again reminded of how incredible she is and how much I take her for granted. She teaches music full-time in our local school system, helps lead a children's choir at church, volunteers to decorate any time the church holds a special event, sings in the choir, plays the piano, and is a loving confidante to our children. On top of that, she's married to a minister. When I get discouraged about something someone said at church, she's there to lift me up. I've *wasted* too many opportunities to tell her how much I appreciate her.

The writer of Proverbs, in the thirty-first chapter, shared some characterstics of capable wives. *"She looks well to the ways of her household."* That description fits Beverly . . . and sometimes she does it standing knee-deep in sewage.

Yesterday, Today . . . and Tomorrow

Peggy Levesque

You will keep in perfect peace him whose mind is stead-
fast, because he trusts in you.

—Isaiah 26:3 NIV

I admit it. I'd been a person who's most comfortable knowing the game plan. My security depended on being able to see how my basic needs would be met—that I knew where I was going. I'm pretty sure that's why God brought me together with my husband. Albert, especially in our earlier years, changed direction more often than a football in play. We lived in the fast lane.

At one point, Albert was partner and sales manager of a company that sold livestock-feeding systems in upstate New York. For more than a year he'd been on the road at least two weeks out of every month. In addition, I'd been away from home one week a month, frequently with my husband, fulfilling business obligations. Too often we had to leave our two junior-high-school-aged sons and toddler daughter with a sitter. Because I felt that the children weren't getting enough of us, I exhausted myself trying to make it up to them and at the same time meet the demands of travel.

I didn't complain to my husband because I knew he was doing the best he could, and I didn't want to add to his burden. But something had to change. "Lord," I prayed, "please get me off this merry-go-round. I can't keep up."

A couple of weeks later, my husband came home unexpectedly from work. "How would you feel if I sold the business to my partner," he asked, "and we moved to Australia?" He had to scrape me up off the floor. Later I registered my objection to what I perceived as God's warped sense of humor. "This wasn't exactly what I had in mind, Lord." I hadn't been looking for *that* much of a change. After more than four years, I was settled in my community. The weather wasn't much to brag about, but we had good friends and a comfortable life. I was secure.

It didn't take long, though, for excitement to set in. Albert accepted that job in Australia, a long-standing dream of his. So we put our house on the market, obtained copies of birth certificates, applied for passports and a visa, and made plans to move overseas.

To everyone's surprise, the house sold in a record twenty-one days in a weak market; most homes took an average of eighteen months to sell. "Things sure happen fast when God is involved," I told my husband.

We had a gigantic "deck" sale and began to pack things for storage. Everything moved along nicely—until the day we were notified that the Australian government would not authorize a work visa. Due to a three-year draught, a new policy had been implemented. Every job was to be posted for six months. If no suitable in-country applicant was found, an out-of-country employee could be hired.

"What are we going to do?" I wailed. "We have no income, soon we'll have no home. We'll be out on the street!"

"Relax," my husband said. He's the optimist in the family. "We have the down payment from the sale of the business."

But that wasn't enough for me. No—I wanted it all . . . job with income, home, and money in the bank. To make matters worse, instead of taking me into his arms to comfort me, my husband patted my arm. I felt like his faithful dog.

The days ticked by, and as the closing date on our house drew nearer and nearer, I worried more and more. We were able to work out an agreement with the buyer to rent until we had somewhere to go. This was some consolation to me, but not much. I railed at God, "How could you bring us this far, Lord, and just leave us here?"

One particularly stressful day, I grabbed a pamphlet I'd received from one of the radio ministries I listened to, and headed upstairs for a long soak in the tub. I felt totally used up. Leaning back, I allowed the hot water and bubbles to ease away some of the tension. Picking up the pamphlet, I began to read, and the first thing I saw was Isaiah 26. Verse three stopped me cold. Here was His promise that I could have the perfect peace I longed for. So why didn't I have it?

Because your mind is not steadfast on Me in trust.

I didn't hear the words out loud, but they hit me with as much force. How many times had I wondered, *How could the Israelites grumble against God in the wilderness?* They should have *known* He would be faithful in their need. Hadn't He revealed His power to them by parting the Red Sea and performing a host of other miracles?

Hasn't He revealed His power and faithfulness to me?

I'd taken my eyes off the working of God's hand in this entire experience and allowed myself to wallow in my human—and very female—need for tangible security. "Please forgive me, Lord," I said through my tears.

That's all He wanted—for me to trust Him with my future, to allow *Him* to be my security. Within three weeks, Albert had a job in another state and I'd picked out my dream house.

As a bonus, my husband's travel schedule was greatly reduced, and I wasn't expected to participate at all in business affairs. Imagine that. We had a resolution to the very problem that had started this adventure in the first place. Our children had their parents back!

Part 8
Church Life

No Big Deal

John Leatherman

And let us consider one another in order to stir up love and good works, not forsaking the assembling of ourselves together, as is the manner of some, but exhorting one another, and so much the more as you see the Day approaching.

—Hebrews 10:24–25 NKJV

I read the Bible verse, decided it didn't apply to me, and forgot about it. When I first read Hebrews 10:24–25 during high school, I thought it said, "Go to church." Well, I went to church, so it didn't apply to me. And I moved on to the next verse.

After graduating high school, though, going to church became hit and miss. I lived in a dormitory during college, twice a year moving stuff to a different location. During one three-month period, in fact, I moved my things from home to an apartment, then back home, then to a dormitory. I saved my empty boxes—if I unpacked them at all—knowing I'd need them for the next move.

This turned out to be good preparation for life after college. Economic conditions and opportunities demanded I not attach myself to one job or even one city. During the first three years following my graduation, I lived in Texas, Colorado, North Carolina, and Tennessee. Through experiences with professional long-distance movers, small-time local haulers, U-Hauls, and benevolent coworkers with pickups, I became a true connoisseur of moving.

Not getting too settled could, in fact, be a metaphor for parts of Christian theology. The Bible says anything in this world is merely temporary. We should live our lives in a state of constant readiness to go wherever God calls us to go next—whether it's another town, another country, or our eternal home.

But this kind of life didn't do much for my spiritual growth. I attended church during that time, but it was hard for me to feel any sense of community with the congregation. Typically, I'd attend the same church a few consecutive weeks, get tired of it, and then find another place to worship. I achieved a record four months at one church in Raleigh, but only because I'd landed a solo in the Christmas pageant.

Why did I do all this worship shopping? At large churches, I vanished into a pool of nameless visitors. At small churches, I felt like an outsider.

Often, I blamed the churches for refusing to reach out to me. I suppose, though, I shared some of the blame. At some of the churches, I might have found a home if I'd only made an effort to do more than just show up. But that would have been work. Sunday is supposed to be a day of rest.

Shallow? Absolutely. But easy. I even justified it by saying, "It's no big deal. Why invest so much of myself when tomorrow I might have to move?"

There were times I wondered why church was even necessary. Hundreds of churches broadcast their services. I could hear sermons and Bible study lessons without having to expose myself to other people who might not accept me. I didn't even have to leave home—and often I needed to be home since I hadn't finished unpacking!

Some Sundays, I tried this route. At first I listened to local churches on the radio. Again, it was easy to justify. I could tell myself, "It's no big deal. I'll listen to their services on the radio this week to decide whether I want to attend their church next week."

I stopped listening to the radio services when I noticed something: these churches always seemed to have only one microphone for the broadcast. And that mike always seemed to be close to the congregation's worst singer.

So I started watching church services on cable TV. I had lots of choices there. Of course, most of them were from churches in other cities and states. I could hardly feel any community with them, but I still managed to justify my decision. "It's no big deal. If I really like this church, maybe I'll try to find a job near it so I can start attending it."

I might have continued that kind of remote worship if not for something that occurred one Sunday morning while I was living in Colorado. I was watching a favorite preacher from somewhere in South Carolina, telling myself how nice it would be to live there, when he introduced his sermon. "I would like to welcome everyone who came today. I also want to welcome our cable TV viewers around the country. But we want to remind you that watching a sermon on television doesn't substitute for face-to-face fellowship with your Christian brothers. We hope you're watching us because you're away from your church home or in the process of finding one."

"It's no big deal," I thought. "I'm sure he says that every week."

At that moment, the screen flickered into static. The cable signal was gone. The cable goes out all the time. But the timing of this particular outage was just a little too coincidental.

Okay, I thought, *that's a big deal.*

Suddenly I knew that when Hebrews 10:24–25 said, ". . . not forsaking the assembling of ourselves together, as is the manner of some," that the "some" included me. I turned off the TV, got my coat, and went to a church.

I won't claim attending church got easier after that day. It didn't. It would be several more years and moves before I felt comfortable in a church family. But I never would have gotten to that point if God hadn't shown me, through a conveniently timed cable outage, that my presence at church was important. More than important, in fact. It was a big deal.

Pride Comes Before a Fall

Sharen Watson

Pride goes before destruction, a haughty spirit before a fall.
—Proverbs 16:18 NIV

I remember it clearly. No doubt about it. It was February 25, 2002. That particular day, I was meeting a friend to discuss the study we were teaching together, a lesson dealing with pride. After we finished, I offered to stay and close up the room we'd been using. Little did I know, the Lord planned to wrap up our study with what we teachers would call a "hands on" lesson.

Believe me, "pride goes before a fall" has taken on a whole new meaning. I tripped over a brand-new crack in the sidewalk. I tried to regain my balance, but to no avail. I went down—fast! I executed one of the worst tumbles of my life at one of the most sacred places in my life—my church! And if falling wasn't bad enough, everything I held in my arms tumbled along with me.

My organized, functional filing system for Women's Bible Study, Women's Retreat, and multiple to-do lists fluttered to earth and scattered around me. And there I was sprawled, amidst the debris of my importance. And of all places, by the window of the children's pastor. Fortunately for me, it was lunch hour . . . at least I think everyone was gone. If by chance they watched this humiliating incident, no one's breathed a word. And if that's the case, I'm appreciative of their effort to keep "our little secret" and preserve my wounded pride.

I took a quick inventory of body parts: elbow, although a little scraped, still bent in the right direction; no head injuries, as far as I can tell; shoulders . . . okay; knees, toes . . .

Wait a minute, back to those knees. I have no idea how I avoided tearing a hole in my slacks, but as I lifted up my pant leg I felt like I was ten years old. I beheld one of the brightest, ooziest, shiniest badges of honor I'd ever seen—one my sons would be proud of. It was quite a nasty surprise.

And then I thought, isn't it just like pride to take you by complete surprise? The minute you load up all your "stuff" and forge ahead with confidence, guess what? The proverbial "crack in the sidewalk" will trip you up.

The whole experience of falling isn't graceful or pretty. Just like the face of pride, it's just plain *ugly!* God makes it clear to us in His Word, He "hate[s] pride and arrogance" (Prov. 8:13 NIV).

So there I was, a woman of forty-something cleaning her own bloody knee. And as I flushed my wounds with warm water and peroxide— cleansing all the impurities—I was reminded of the Lord's process of removing the dross from my life. It wasn't comfortable; it was, in fact, downright painful.

Next came the antibiotic cream—*with* painkiller. Smoothing this ointment over my tender, open wound brought great comfort, relieved the pain, and started the process of healing. In a similar way, when I undergo painful life experiences, I'll always look to the Father to clean my emotional wounds, bring comfort during the times I hurt the most, and lead me toward spiritual growth and wholeness.

Healing takes time. Two years have passed, and I still have reminders of my ungainly descent. The daily sight of those scars convinces me I want to quickly learn my lesson on pride. I do *not* want a retest. It's simply too painful to repeat.

Proof in the Pudding

Lynette Sowell

*Consider the ravens: They do not sow or reap, they have
no storeroom or barn; yet God feeds them. And how much
more valuable you are than birds!*

—Luke 12:24 NIV

I don't see how we'll manage to pay for the groceries." My husband,
C.J., added another item to our shopping list.

"We'll figure something out." I tried to sound more hopeful than I
felt. "We'll make things stretch. I get paid next Thursday."

My husband had taken a leap of faith and started his own business.
As with most new businesses, money was tight at the beginning. We
had less than thirty dollars to spend on a week's worth of groceries for
a family of four. So, with our list in hand, we headed to the grocery
store.

I kept track of our purchases with a small calculator. A bag of chicken
leg quarters, a gallon of milk, some cereal, a box of instant vanilla
pudding, and other food items went into our cart. Our bill escalated;
time to make some hard decisions. What would we buy, and what
would we return to the shelf? Better to do it now, instead of being
embarrassed in front of a cashier and a line full of shoppers. Still, I felt
a tinge of shame as we assessed the items in the cart.

Back onto the shelf went the pudding. We wanted to buy it as a treat for our kids, but we rationalized it could wait until payday. A frivolous item like vanilla pudding shot to the bottom of our priority list along with a bottle of soda, coffee creamer (I'd make do with milk), sugar, seasoning salt, and a new drain plug for the sink. We'd learned to identify true needs from the extra perks we used to buy without a second thought.

C.J.'s scowl spoke volumes. What kind of a father couldn't afford a box of instant pudding for his kids? I tried to encourage him as best I could, but we still left the store with dampened spirits. I struggled not to cry. We reminded each other that God would take care of us. Our needs were met. Our kids weren't going to bed hungry. With that we would have to be content and hang on until brighter days when his business brought in more money. Above all, I wanted C.J. to know that I believed in him. I feared my tears would only discourage him further.

After we returned from the store and unpacked our few bags of groceries, the kids got ready for bed. A knock sounded at the door. We weren't expecting anyone, and we looked at each other with questioning faces.

Shannon, the youth pastor's wife from church, stood on the doorstep. She clutched a cardboard box packed with cans and boxes. "Hey guys, I hope you don't mind, but I brought by some stuff from the food pantry. We can't give out this stuff, and we couldn't see throwing it away."

We knew that our church had a food pantry, but we didn't feel right asking for food. Other people needed help more than we did, and we expected our financial situation to improve soon. We wouldn't, of course, turn down food the pantry couldn't distribute to the public. You'd be amazed at the food people consider a good donation—expired or dented canned goods, even cans with missing labels. I foraged through the box like a dog sniffing out steak. I hoped Shannon didn't see my relief at the sight of more canned vegetables, some bags of rice and pasta, and some dented boxes of macaroni and cheese.

A large round metal can caught my eye. Big as a giant coffee can, I knew it was an institutional size of something—maybe tomato sauce or ketchup or—I picked up the can to check the label.

I began to laugh. "Honey, look at this!" Then I wanted to cry. When C.J. saw the can, a grin spread across his face. The kids came running in pajama feet, wanting to see what was so funny. Our youth pastor's wife wondered about the joke.

"I'm sorry," she began. "It's kind of an odd thing, but we thought the kids would like it."

We had a mammoth can of prepared vanilla pudding, enough to feed a small army. Our heavenly Father indeed remembered us. And although we hadn't asked for assurance of His love He gave it to us anyway. In our time of deepest need, the proof was in the pudding!

Special Rick

Elaine Stone

So let each one give as he purposes in his heart, not grudgingly or of necessity; for God loves a cheerful giver.

—2 Corinthians 9:7 NKJV

The first time we met him, we couldn't help but notice. Rick's unusual ways and unique characteristics earned him the name "Special Rick." We gave him this label courteously and lovingly, not knowing exactly how else to help our three young children understand him. A severe accident in his high school years had caused some brain damage and he was no longer a "normal" guy.

From the first day he drifted into our church, his unusual ways and unique characteristics drew my attention. He always had a story to tell and often talked longer than you wanted to listen. He used a loud voice and seemed to cause commotion everywhere he went. We knew he was there without looking. It seemed he was in attendance every time the doors were open.

Not having a family present, he would often sit with us in church. Although he was in his early twenties, our elementary children were better behaved than him. It seemed that understanding common behavior and routine etiquette was sometimes beyond his patience and attention span. Some of the things he did were so funny it seemed as if he was doing them on purpose—just to test our response. It was difficult not to laugh.

Once, Rick insisted to our fourth grade daughter that she was not singing the hymns correctly and proceeded to loudly explain to her midsong how she could better project and use her voice. For several weeks, he "instructed" her in singing and would give me a report after each service. He told people he was giving her voice lessons and that she was "singing much better."

Although he was different, in most instances he was really refreshing. His simple view of life and his desire to help were easy to detect. He was friendly to all and never met a stranger. Sometimes, he seemed to understand that he was different, and it was in those moments that we saw his frustration. We hurt for him, wishing, as he did, that he could be "normal" again.

One day, I was working at the church. The main doors were closed, because the receptionist was at lunch. I was using the microwave in the kitchen when a delivery came to the kitchen door. Opening the door, I saw Rick pull up. His car was rocking from the sound system he had set at full volume. He bounced up the stairs into the kitchen, and immediately sought my approval of the "tunes" he had left blaring for my benefit. He began to wander farther into the building. I stopped him and asked where he was going. "To the sanctuary," he responded simply. I questioned the wisdom of leaving his car running, and reminded him that since his keys were in the ignition, anyone could walk up and take his car. Rick's eyes became as big as saucers; clearly that thought had never occurred to him. His only thought was to make sure I could hear his "system." At my suggestion he bolted out the door, turned his car off, and returned with keys in hand, dangling them for my approval.

I couldn't help but wonder, as I returned to my office, what had brought Rick to the church in the middle of a weekday and why he was headed for the sanctuary. Shortly after, I heard footsteps on the stairs leading to my office. I sighed. Rick's visits were never short and my work load that day was all-consuming. I prayed for patience. He reached the top of the stairs, and said "Hi" to me before continuing down the hall to the other offices. Soon, I heard his steps returning.

"Where is everyone?" he asked, as he entered my office.

"They're all gone for lunch," I replied.

"Oh, well could you do me a favor?" he asked, and reached for something in his pocket. *So that's why he visited the sanctuary,* I thought, recognizing the corner of an offering envelope.

"I just cashed my paycheck and wanted to drop off my tithe before my shift starts this afternoon, can you take care of it for me?" A few one-dollar bills fell from his pocket, as he handed the envelope to me. "I couldn't give all my money because I need some of it to put gas in my car," he said ashamedly, picking them slowly up.

When the financial secretaries returned from lunch, I carried out the favor as I promised him I would. But "Special Rick," a minimum wage janitor, had already done me a far greater favor. On that day, I witnessed a true gift given out of obedience and loyalty. Unlike most people I know, tithing was not a burden for Rick; it was his joy, his priority. He wasn't even able to wait for the next church service to give his money to God; it was worth a special trip. The humble amount of his offering had no bearing on its significance. I know that God was honored in that moment.

Rick will always be "Special Rick" to me, but the "special" is no longer just an attempt to explain his strange behavior and actions to my children. It is a reminder to my own heart of what God thinks of him. He is indeed "special," a rare child, who offers God the best he has with a joyful and yielding heart. Now, the sight of offering envelopes always brings up important questions for me: *Is my gift honoring to God? Is giving Him my money a priority and a joy?* Knowing Rick has made "normal" look less attractive. My heart desires to be "special" in God's eyes . . . just like Rick.

Strung Along at Center Stage

Craig Sundheimer

*Think of ways to encourage one another to outbursts of love
and good deeds. And let us not neglect our meeting together,
as some people do, but encourage and warn each other.*
                              —Hebrews 10:24–25 NLT

I hoped to become part of this church family. I stood onstage on a
Sunday morning amid the members of the praise band at Cottonwood Church, a brand-new church in Albuquerque, New Mexico. I
was still getting to know my new congregation and wanted to fit in.
Having served as a music minister for more than twenty years in several churches, I'd suddenly left my previous church only a few months
before under difficult circumstances. Now I yearned to belong and to
experience that special bond of fellowship with a new church family.

When I stretched my fingers onto the frets of my guitar, my hands
ached from the arthritic condition that had been diagnosed a few years
earlier. My new doctor had been working to find the right mix of
medications to ease the stiffness in my hands and wrists. It was becoming increasingly clear, however, unless my condition improved,
I'd be unable to continue playing the twelve-string guitar that I'd used
since my college days.

The greater tension of a twelve-string required more hand strength than I was now able to muster. If I were to continue playing guitar in our praise band, I'd have to find a new instrument. I'd discussed the problem with my wife, and we agreed that the best solution would be a new guitar. With our recent move to Albuquerque and establishing a new home, money was tight, so hunting for a bargain became top priority.

I browsed the local music stores and settled on a Yamaha AEX-500 acoustic/electric guitar with a smooth, easy touch that allowed me to play the chords with my limited dexterity. As I anticipated the joy of playing worship music more easily, my heart sank when I looked at the price tag. I wouldn't be able to make the purchase immediately. We simply couldn't afford several hundred dollars for the guitar and amplifier. I decided to place them on layaway with the intention of making payments over the next few months, paying off the guitar first and the amplifier later.

A few days later at our weekly praise band rehearsal, I told Paul, our sound engineer, about the guitar I'd found. I showered him with a detailed description of its smooth acoustic expression, beautiful appearance, the light, easy action, and how my fingers could glide over the strings. My voice rose in pitch and volume as in my excitement I explained to him my plan to purchase the guitar and amp. I provided more information than even Steven Curtis Chapman might have cared about, and certainly with more emotion and enthusiasm than a volunteer "sound guy" needed. He seemed to listen attentively, but I'm sure he was relieved when the other worship team members arrived for rehearsal and our one-sided conversation ended.

The very next day, my family received the sad news that my stepmother had passed away after a lengthy battle with cancer. I called my pastor to inform him that I'd be unable to lead the worship music that week, then my family and I made hasty travel arrangements to Dallas. There, we joined my other family members as we supported my dad and celebrated the life of my stepmom.

After returning home from the difficult, emotional trip, I looked forward to joining my friends on the worship team. Sunday arrived, and as I stood surrounded by the other band members, I shook out my hands to relieve my aching fingers, then strapped on my twelve-string to begin a worship song. Smoothly and reflectively, we progressed through the first verse.

As we came to the end of the verse, the speakers started a squeal that became more and more annoying. Suddenly, the sound went completely dead. I continued playing, hoping Paul would be able to quickly fix the problem from his position at the sound controls at the rear of the auditorium. Despite my attempt to carry on, with the sound fading, the other instrumentalists stopped playing. Frustrated, I looked up to see Paul sprinting down the aisle toward the stage. He cleared the five steps to the stage in one bound, moving directly toward me with a look of concern on his face. While trying to maintain a calm appearance, my mind began to race. *Paul, what are you doing? What's going on?*

He reached out and grabbed the neck of my guitar with one hand and urgently informed me, "Your guitar is overloading the sound system. You need to take it off and give it to me."

I felt confused and more than a bit irritated—this was interrupting the flow of the worship service. Nothing like this had ever happened to me in my twenty-plus years of music ministry. I sensed many pairs of eyes glued on me, and could only imagine that the worshipers must have felt as confused as I. Since Paul seemed ready to yank the guitar off of me, I fumbled with the strap to unhook it.

As the guitar left my hands, I was aware that someone was moving behind me. In the hubbub, I hadn't noticed that Jerome, our lead guitar player, had slipped backstage while Paul held my attention. I turned toward Jerome when he stepped from behind the curtain.

"Here, Craig," he said quietly. "Try *this* guitar." And he handed me a freshly-tuned Yamaha AEX-500.

While I'd been at my dad's the previous Sunday, Paul had informed our congregation of my plan to buy the guitar. Since it would have taken several months for me to complete the layaway, the church took up a special offering, purchased the guitar and amplifier, and surprised me with the gift.

I was stunned, and merely stood on center stage as Jerome helped me strap on the beautiful new guitar. My jaw dropped and the members of the congregation giggled with joy and applauded as they shared my surprise. I moved my left hand onto the fret board to form a chord on the smooth new strings. I wasn't sure what to say or do. The cheering subsided, and I simply picked up where I'd left off a few minutes before, moving into the chord progression leading to the chorus.

The other instrumentalists joined in, and we lifted our voices in a song of thankfulness to the Lord, humbly reflecting on His grace and mercy. The music swelled as more voices joined in the singing, and I closed my eyes, overwhelmed by awe and gratitude as the chorus continued.

I'd made plans all by myself to purchase a new guitar, but this group of fellow worshipers had something else in mind. By presenting me with such a wonderful, unexpected gift, they shared in the blessing as they anticipated the surprise, watched as the event played out, and joined me in a mutual celebration of joy. They offered me their gift of encouragement as they, creatively and unexpectedly, shared their "outburst of love and good deeds."

I knew I'd found a place to belong, a new church family to serve and love—and be loved.

The Wrong Rub

Barb Loftus Boswell

Do not seek revenge or bear a grudge against one of your people, but love your neighbor as yourself. I am the LORD.
—Leviticus 19:18 NIV

It shames me to admit it. The neighbors I find hardest to love are usually decent folk who just "rub me the wrong way." When asked, most times I can't even pinpoint the source of the offensive "rub." I'm quite certain the problem is mine and not theirs; none-the-less, loving these neighbors takes a conscious effort.

Even more than effort, it takes grace. I don't mean that I'm necessarily grace-full. I'm oftentimes painfully lacking in grace. Rather, grace, thank God, comes in spite of me.

A case in point is a woman at my church, Joan. I was introduced to Joan no less than three times, at each of which she admitted that she couldn't recall my name. Having a poor memory for names myself, I pushed my irritation aside. Then I saw Joan walking along the street one day, hand-in-hand with her sons, and heard her pleasantly comment, "Look, boys, there's that lady from church."

That lady from church? *Harumph!* I thought, *I do have a name!* A chip of ugly pride plopped right down on my shoulder.

Several months later, I volunteered to join the monthly trip to a homeless shelter to serve dinner. Although I'd sent casseroles in the past, I'd never gone to the "front line" to serve. My husband wouldn't be home from work early enough to watch the girls, so my daughters, ten and seven years old at that time, were with me. I arrived at our church, girls in tow, after a long day of work. I was tired and regretting the decision to go to the shelter. "Summer is always short-staffed," I was told by the chairwoman of the meals, so my help was greatly appreciated.

Rats! I thought with uncharitable silence, *no getting out of it.* So I prayed to be a useful servant to God and his people—to put my own inconveniences aside. I prayed for a more charitable heart.

We waited for the other volunteers to gather. When the last one pulled into the lot, I saw that it was Joan. Moments later, she was pleasantly saying, "I'll ride with you and your girls." I couldn't help but smile to myself and think, *Okay, God, I see what You're doing.*

On the way to the shelter, an amazing thing happened. Joan and I talked. We started with subjects like our children and living in the same town. Quickly we moved on to our shared love of music and serving God.

The meal turned out to be a blessing in so many ways. My daughters loved serving and asked when we'd be going again. They sweated and worked and politely offered food to each and every person in line. As Joan and I rubbed shoulders, we chatted and joked with each other and with the folks who'd come for dinner. People who had so little to their names wished God's blessing on me.

I saw Jesus' light very clearly that evening.

Later, when Joan and I parted in the church's parking lot, it was with genuine friendship. I'd gone kicking and screaming that night, but I left thankful and awed—and minus one chip of ugly pride.

What's *Your* Name?

Elaine Stone

He said to them, "But who do you say that I am?"
—Matthew 16:15 NKJV

This was a rare evening. And I admit, I didn't expect a huge challenge from God during this service. As a pastor's wife, I had not one obligation or responsibility to perform upon entering the church. Unless you consider it an obligation or responsibility to watch my youngest child perform in the children's musical. This was an opportunity to sit with my husband, not in the choir. "Sit and soak" described my frame of mind as I prepared for one of those "entertaining" evenings at church.

My husband and I chose a front-row balcony seat to give us the best vantage point for viewing our daughter. We didn't want to miss a move she made. A few moments before the service started, a father, mother, and their four-year-old daughter sat next to us. They'd been members in our church about a year, and I knew they, too, had several children in the musical. We shared greetings, and their daughter, Karen, smiled at us with the warmth of the sun.

After the offering plate was passed, Karen walked over and climbed into my husband's lap, giving him a big hug. My husband's fondness for children is well known. He delights in the special friendship he's developed with the children of our church. He visits the hospital when most of them are born and works at becoming their friend each time he sees them. Some run to him for hugs, some want to be thrown in the air, some want candy, and a few have asked for his hand in marriage. God has given him a special connection with the young ones. So it came as no surprise that this young child would climb into his lap.

A few songs later, as Karen was still perched on my husband's lap, her father leaned over and asked her a question. "Karen, do you know his name?" Smiling, she nodded her head yes. Her dad, with laughter in his voice at her sweet demeanor said, "What is it?"

We knew he was testing her memory to see if she could remember the name of one of her pastors. None of us were prepared for her response. Her reply was whisper soft but audible to my husband and me. "His name is Jesus."

We all caught our breath.

My husband immediately said to Karen, "Oh, Karen, I'm not Jesus, but I do love Him with all my heart. My name is Mr. Jim."

She simply smiled and shook her head. Her parents were enjoying a chuckle, so did I for a moment—before my heart was pierced: my "entertaining evening" just became a tremendous challenge.

I thought about the time when Jesus asked His disciples, "Who do people say that I am?" The disciples' responses varied. Finally, Jesus turned the question around and asked "Who do *you* say that I am?" On this evening, I felt like God was again turning around the question and asking my husband and me, "Who do people say *you* are?"

Countless times since that evening those words have replayed in my heart. Who do people say I am? Do they identify me with Christ? Is it obvious to them that I love Jesus? What is my name to people? Even more importantly, who does God that say I am? Who am I after the exterior is stripped away? Is it consistent with who I say I am in Christ, or am I fooling myself? Is my heart consistent with my behavior? Am I living out my spiritual name, Christian—one who follows Christ? Do I resemble Christ?

God can use the smallest, even slightly amusing experiences to speak to our hearts in profound ways. God used a four-year-old to speak to my heart. Karen's words were totally sincere and sweet, but I believe they were words that God ordered to cause self-examination. Ultimately, it's God's opinion about our name that matters, but God wants the whole world to see the difference in His children. He wants us to bear His name and resemble Christ's appearance to a world that needs His redemption.

What's *your* name?

Part 9

Garden/
Outdoors

Fences

Raelene Searle

But the Lord is faithful, and He will strengthen and protect you from the evil one.
　　　　　　　　　　　—2 Thessalonians 3:3 NASB

Gardening was never a dream of mine. It was, in fact, more like a nightmare that I avoided like the plague. I figured I had enough dirt to deal with from my kids. Fresh vegetables? I lived in California, where everything is already fresh and natural. All I had to do was drive down the road to the local grower and get whatever I wanted.

All this changed when my friend Lisa shared her love of gardening with me. An avid gardener, she loved spending hours each day laboring over her fruit trees, vegetable plants, and flowers. Her backyard was a beautiful landscape that could have been mistaken for the yard of a professional gardener.

Her passion soon began to rub off on me. Eventually I asked Lisa to help me plant my own garden. Like her, I wanted to enjoy walking out to my garden and cutting leaves of lettuce for the dinner salad, eating sweet peas right from the pod, and having strawberries on a whim. It turned out to be a lot of fun and very rewarding as I nurtured those little sprouts. I especially enjoyed telling guests that what they were eating came from my very own garden.

I kept my garden for several years with great success. I was able to grow all the lettuce, peas, and strawberries I desired, as well as many other types of plants. But the time came when we had to move. I'd have to start all over again—and this time, Lisa wouldn't be there to help me.

I waited a year after settling into our house before I again began to garden. My husband, Chip, and I worked hard to remember all the things Lisa had taught us—tilling the ground, building mounds, and planting flowers in ruts that would keep unwanted critters away—all the things necessary to have the perfect garden as before.

The garden was coming along well—sprouts shot up everywhere, the flowers grew beautifully. It seemed we would have a great garden.

And then we adopted the newest member of our family—an energetic chocolate Lab named Java. Both my garden and my puppy got along quite well in the beginning, despite the warnings of one of my girlfriends—a veterinarian, mind you—that it wouldn't continue this way for long. I was more optimistic than she, and at first Java was a very good puppy. But, alas, puppy events are unavoidable.

Summer came and we were making preparations for our annual family reunion. I'd arranged for a sitter to come watch the house, including the garden and the puppy, for the four days we'd be gone. Sarah worked during the day and would only be staying at our house during the evenings.

We weren't gone even one full day before it happened.

After arriving at our house the first evening, Sarah called her mother in a panic. Her mother advised her, "Honey, just gather the plants and try to replant them in the ground."

To which Sarah replied, "But mom, there *are* no plants to put back in the ground! Java ate them all!"

Sarah was devastated. She called us in tears, apologizing profusely for "allowing" Java to shred the plants. We assured her that we weren't angry, knowing it wasn't her fault. Java, on the other hand, got the cold shoulder for quite some time.

I couldn't believe that my new puppy and my new garden didn't play well together. Actually, I guess I could. But still, I was devastated. The very first garden that I had created all on my own was ruined. All our hard work, all our labor, all amounted to nothing.

Needless to say, my "I told you so" friend had a great laugh—at least until she realized she wouldn't be sharing in the fruits of my labor.

We had no garden but plenty of room to create a new one. Our first project, however, before replanting was to build a fence around the garden area. The little sprouts would need a wall of protection before they'd be able to grow healthy again, safe and secure from any chocolate Labs looking for a snack.

During the process of building the fence, God began showing me how the "garden" of my home needs the same type of protection. As a mother, I need to be erecting fences around my children and my marriage. Just as the garden needed the white picket fence, so my children need fences around their hearts to guard them from hurtful relationships, inappropriate television shows, and even from some games. Likewise, my marriage also needs fences, to protect the family from temptation, complacency, and selfishness.

"Critters" (not necessarily limited to chocolate Labs) are always prowling about, looking for "gardens" without fences in order to wreak havoc on unsuspecting hearts and minds. We must properly guard ourselves by allowing the Holy Spirit to build fences around our own homes and families—fences with solid, godly foundations, and with gates that even the Evil One cannot shake.

Flowers That Walked and Talked

Bonnie Compton Hanson

Flowers appear on the earth; the season of singing has come.
—Song of Songs 2:12 NIV

What in the world can we do with those awful, awful flowers?" Everyone at our church was asking that. It was easy enough to know which flowers they meant—those that circled our church sign out in front of our building, inviting passersby and neighbors to come worship with us. Or at least, they were supposed to.

Our church membership is quite small, with all the yard work done by volunteers. Years before, one of our women had volunteered to care for this large flowerbed as her own special ministry. She did a magnificent job, several times each year lovingly purchasing and replacing annuals that surrounded the sign with bright colors.

But when she could no longer keep up with this responsibility, we decided to plant dusty millers for easier upkeep. Most people love dusty millers, at least when they're young. Ever faithful, modest, and long-suffering, they grow their little hearts out, season after season, making few demands on their gardeners except for weeding and a trim now and then. They provide a neutral background for vibrant colors, presuming, of course, that any vibrant colors are near them.

In our case, wrong presumption. The church walls were made of stones that were a dull, muddy brown. The grass was green—at least as far as each of the sprinklers reached. The few trees were ordinary and unattractive, especially since the students from the junior high school across the street hung around them—and on and under them.

As for those dusty millers—well "dusty" is exactly how they always looked. Dull, dirty, and discouragingly dusty. Absolutely no spark or pizzazz.

"They look so sad," little Anita told me one Sunday morning after service. "As if we don't care."

"Well, we do care," retorted her younger sister, Patsy. "We need to have flowers there that let people know we love God. Something pretty—like a crayon box full of colors. You know—the kind that's got sixty-four colors in it, not just eight. And none of them broke."

"But with lots of red," added their friend, Megan. "I like red. Everybody likes red. Everybody likes flowers."

So my husband, Don, and I volunteered to buy and plant the flowers, and have them in the ground by the very next Sunday. At our local Home Depot, we were dazzled with the array of annuals. We could choose from petunias to impatiens to marigolds. Finally we settled on a sparkling rainbow of portulaca, commonly known as moss rose. We chose colors of red (lots of red), coral, rose, lemon, gold, fuchsia, and more. Not only are moss roses forgiving when the sprinklers aren't turned on regularly, here in Southern California we can count on them for a long season—all the way to midfall. That way we wouldn't have to replant again until Thanksgiving.

We filled our car with tray after tray of those winsome beauties, and headed for the church. Seeing all the dead foliage, we trimmed back those forlorn millers and spaded and fertilized the ground in a large oval around them. Finally we planted and watered all the flowers, before cleaning up the site. The girls were right. The blooms were absolutely spectacular—red ones and all.

How exciting the next morning to pull into the church driveway and see that spectacular display in full bloom! Patsy's family drove in right behind us.

"Patsy!" I cried. "Take a look at the flowers we planted yesterday!"

She jumped out of the car, clapped her hands and cheered.

Anita nodded. "Everyone loves flowers. Now they'll know we love them. And that God loves them too."

I smiled. "Good girl. God wants everyone to know He loves them."

I left the children outside admiring the flowers and got caught up with some music preparation. When I returned to the foyer, I found it filled with people. And laughter.

"What's up?" I asked casually.

"Oh, some little girls are handing out bouquets to people as they come in," someone told me. "Such precious children. Isn't that a nice thing for them to do?"

It certainly was. "Did they buy the flowers themselves," I asked, "or did someone else bring them and ask the girls to hand them out?"

"I don't know. They didn't say. You'll have to ask them."

I made my way to the front door. From a distance, I was struck with the charm and grace of the little girls as they handed out the colorful bouquets and greeted each worshiper. "Welcome to God's House," they chanted as they curtsied and held out small bunches of flowers. "God loves you and we do too."

Then I took a good look at the little girls—and the flowers. They were moss roses!

"Anita! Patsy! Megan!" I cried. "Did you get these flowers from around the church sign?"

Three angelic smiles greeted me. "Sure, Mrs. Hanson. You said if people see them they'll know God loves them. So we wanted to share God's love with everyone—especially with all these nice people in our church." The expression on my face must have alarmed them. "Is something wrong?" they asked.

Yes and no. Those cheerful little bouquets filled our sanctuary with smiles and color that morning and made a lot of people happy. But the sight made me ill. All that hard work. What had those precious girls done?

The girls' parents helped them understand that flowers don't have to "walk and talk" to deliver their message of love and beauty. They grow best when left in the ground. The delicate blossoms are even more beautiful left on the stems. It's fortunate that moss roses are very forgiving, and eventually they grew back to fill in all the spots that had been picked clean.

Those little girls did have one thing right: flowers are, indeed, a gift to please the eye and refresh the spirit. That gift comes from a generous God and shows us how much He loves us . . . each and every one of us.

Why Bother?

Georgia Shaffer

His righteousness shall be like a budding tree, or like a garden in early spring, full of young plants springing up everywhere.

—Isaiah 61:11 TLB

I planted two dozen broccoli plants yesterday," my mother said, "and five of them disappeared last night." My petite, seventy-three-year-old mother was visibly discouraged. "I guess the rabbits ate them," she sighed.

Hours later, after a trip to the local nursery, she telephoned. "They suggested I buy fox urine. The odor of the urine is supposed to scare away the rabbits."

"The mere thought would scare me away!" I said. "How much does fox urine cost?"

"Fifteen dollars."

"Fifteen dollars? You're kidding! Why would you pay fifteen dollars for urine when you can buy broccoli at the grocery store for about a dollar?"

"Because I like my vegetables garden fresh," she said.

The next morning, my mother stopped by to drop off some fresh red raspberries she'd picked. "I put the urine out last night," she reported. "And this morning I discovered that six more plants had been eaten. I told our neighbor about it, and he suggested that I put a wire fence around the plants." Then she added, "I'm heading to the hardware store now. Do you need anything?"

"No," I shook my head, biting my tongue. *Why doesn't she just consider the broccoli a total loss?*

Later that night, with eighteen dollars worth of wire fence, my mother built an enclosure around the thirteen remaining plants. She worked hard, making it secure so that no opening would allow rodents to crawl under.

The next morning I got another call. "Guess what? There are only five broccoli plants left. Those rabbits must have jumped over the fence."

I rolled my eyes and attempted to make light of the situation. "It sounds like you have an offspring of Peter Rabbit in your garden."

"I just called another garden center," she continued, "and they suggested I get a live trap and try to catch them."

"I really hate to ask . . . but what does a live trap cost?"

"Forty-five dollars."

"Mother!" My humor had suddenly evaporated. "Think how much money you've already spent, and you only have five of the twenty-four plants left. Why don't you just go to the farmer's market? You could buy loads of broccoli for forty-five dollars."

My mother decided not to buy a live trap, but she didn't give up. Each night she covered her broccoli plants with inverted bushel baskets that she already had in her barn.

About two weeks later I realized I'd heard *nothing* about the broccoli plants. "Mother," I asked, "how's your broccoli doing?"

"The baskets work," she said with a smile. "But it's a pain to cover those plants each night. Then in the morning I have to remove the baskets so the broccoli can get some sun."

I thanked God my mother was no longer investing money in her meager broccoli crop.

But it's not only the broccoli plants that have frustrated my mother. She planted red beets from seeds and tenderly cared for them for weeks. Then a month before the harvest, some varmint chewed the tops.

And then in the summer of 1997 the Japanese beetles arrived like an army and ruthlessly attacked her red raspberries. One local nursery advertised "Beetle Battle Station" in red letters. My mother visited that station and bought the material needed for a victorious campaign—lure to bait the beetles and green plastic bags to trap them.

Whoever liked her broccoli apparently thought beetles were also tasty. One morning she found the bags of beetles chewed open and lying on the grass. For weeks, too, my mother had beamed as she shared how her cantaloupes were thriving. Then one evening she brought me a lovely specimen—with a huge hole gnawed out of it.

"Mother, don't you find gardening frustrating?" I asked. "I mean you're constantly battling the insects, the weeds, and the animals. Don't you ever want to give up?"

"There are pleasant surprises, too, Georgia." My mother was always one to focus on the positive. "Remember those five-year-old pumpkin seeds I found in the closet and planted? You should see how large and plentiful those pumpkins are this year. Besides," she added, "I like being outside in the fresh air. And at my age, the exercise is good for me. I enjoy having my *own* fresh vegetables!"

Vegetables aren't my thing; my passion is flowers. Only a few days after that conversation with my mother I headed out to my garden to pick a few roses. No luck. The beetles had eaten the heart out of every rose in my garden. As I turned to walk up the steps to my back door, I noticed the beetles had also nibbled the leaves of my morning glories.

The question I'd asked my mother echoed in my head. *Why bother?* Suddenly I understood. When we truly love and cherish something, we're willing to nurture it and protect it—no matter what the cost.

If we can feel this way about growing broccoli or morning glories, surely we should feel the same about our relationship with God. Our faith, too, faces an army of invaders—everyday business, popular culture, a world that is hostile to the things of God. I want my flowers to bloom and thrive, but I also want to nourish and protect my spirit. I want it to grow into a beautiful garden in which I can walk daily with the Creator of all that bears fruit and seed after its own kind.

After I'd set aside time to nurture *that* garden, I headed to the telephone. "Mother, where's that beetle battle station?"

Part 10

Holidays

A Lavender Thanksgiving

Nanette Thorsen-Snipes

*Give thanks in all circumstances, for this is God's will for
you in Christ Jesus.*

—1 Thessalonians 5:18 NIV

Thanksgiving day. But this day, with the wind whistling outside, I
was less than thankful. I fished another boiled egg from the pan,
and as I shelled it, I felt anger heating my cheeks. My husband had
helped me start the small turkey, then squirreled himself away on the
sofa.

"Do you need any help?" my husband asked as he peered from behind the sports page.

"No," I answered tersely. As I tossed the half-peeled egg into the
pan, I felt the tears building. I picked up the hospital bracelet my daughter had just taken off and threw it into the trash.

Just two days before, I'd rushed my teenaged daughter, Jamie, to
the emergency room. For nine hours, I stood beside her, wondering
what caused the severe pains in her stomach. The emergency room
doctor poked, prodded, and tested my daughter as she doubled over
in pain.

One by one, the doctor ruled out ulcers, kidney problems, stomach
virus, and pelvic infection. About midday, I felt relieved to see our
family doctor. He gingerly felt her abdomen, causing her to shrink

from his hand. I noticed he kept coming back to her right side. Finally, he stepped back. "It's her appendix."

By 9:00 P.M., Jamie had her inflamed appendix removed. While her problem had disappeared on the operating table, mine had just begun.

We'd planned to celebrate Thanksgiving at my oldest son's house. I'd hoped the bustle of holiday activities there would keep me busy. Then I wouldn't remember that Thanksgiving was the time of year my former husband, my boys' father, chose to commit suicide. But now, with my daughter's surgery still fresh, Jamie would be unable to make the trip. The troubling memories would linger at the edge of my mind.

I stood at the kitchen sink, my head pounding. A tear trailed down my face. I dialed my next-door neighbor, Donna. "Do you have any aspirin?" I asked trying to keep my voice from quivering.

"No, but I'll be glad to pick up some for you," she said in a cheerful voice. "I have to go out anyway."

I sighed. "That's all right. I really need to get out." My voice cracked, and I added, "This just isn't a good day for me." I hung up the phone. Nothing had gone right. Thanksgiving? What a joke. I was incapable of being thankful for anything.

I drove alone to the store, my nose still red from crying. I felt so exhausted, so tired. I wondered how I'd ever make this small Thanksgiving come together. By the time I drove back to my house, I felt so weak I just wanted to crawl into bed.

Pulling into the carport, I noticed a little pot of gaily-wrapped lavender flowers beside my back door. Jamie is so well loved, I thought. My daughter's friends had shown up all week with flowers, teddy bears, and videos. I brought the flowers inside and set them on my table.

To my surprise, a simple piece of white paper in the flowerpot had my name on it. "His strength is perfect when our strength is gone," it read. I turned the paper over; it was from my neighbor, Donna. The heaviness in my heart began to lift.

I touched the soft lavender petals thinking how thoughtless I'd been. Right there, I whispered, "Thank You, Lord, for Donna, who cares enough to give me flowers to heal my heart."

When I can't get beyond my own self-pity, I'm grateful that God, in His infinite wisdom, provides a neighborly act of kindness to get me back on the right path.

When I returned to my pan of eggs, my husband stood by my side, shelling an egg. The smell of the roasting turkey filled the room, and my husband placed his arm around me and kissed my cheek. My heart overflowed with thanks.

The Lord is ever present and an ever-present help in trouble. I'm amazed how He reaches out to me, His daughter, through others. How mighty is my Lord, and He is mighty to save. He takes great delight in me and quiets me with His love. He rejoices over me with singing, even when my heart cries.

A Treasure in the Trash

Gayle Team-Smith

Blessed are you who are poor, for yours is the kingdom of God.
Blessed are you who hunger now, for you will be satisfied.
—Luke 6:20–21 NIV

Every year at Christmas, our family adopts a family that's in need. Our town's Hope Center organizes the arrangements and, with the applying families' permission, their names are shared with our community. Along with a name, the Hope Center also gives an information sheet telling how many children are in the family, their ages, sizes, etc. It's something I wanted my children to be part of from the time they were old enough to understand the words, "It is better to give than to receive."

One year in particular made an impact on all our lives and changed our view of those in need. We were excited about our Hope Center family—a grandmother raising her grandson. Our first contact was to be made by phone, and we called, eager to fill their Christmas with wonderful memories.

"Hello," answered a woman's gruff voice.

"Hello," I said with all the Christmas cheer I could muster. "We're your Hope Center helpers and we'd like to bring you groceries, gifts, and Christmas dinner." I asked if she'd like a smoked or oven-baked turkey.

Her response caught me off guard. "I don't like turkey. I want ham."

"Okay, that sounds great. How about stuffing, potatoes, yams—"

"I don't like any of those things," she snapped, and then listed an assortment of strange items she wanted for her Christmas dinner.

I was beginning to feel a bit indignant. After all, look how nice we were being by helping her with her Christmas plans. But it was her dinner, I guess.

Believe it or not, the conversation took a turn for the worse.

"We'd like to get each of you a gift. What's on your wish list this year?"

"You can't afford anything I want, and you certainly can't afford the bicycle my grandson wants."

By now my temperature was rising. Who did she think she was, telling me what we can and can't afford? But I was in way too deep to back out. My voice remained cordial as I jotted down a number of things she seemed to think we could afford. Nothing grand, and frankly I wanted to do just that—nothing grand.

I turned on my Christmas music, determined to get back into the holiday mood. I even asked God to forgive her, remembering Jesus' words on the cross. "Forgive her Father for she knows not what she does." Little did I know how true my prayer was that morning. After several shopping trips, and a generous discount from our area bike shop, we completed her list and even stayed under budget. I was so proud and the kids were beaming.

We loaded up the station wagon, turned on our Christmas carols, and set out to bring this family some Christmas cheer. "Kids, do you see the building we're looking for?" I asked. There were no address numbers or apartment numbers, and I was getting concerned. But I knew I'd followed the directions that she gave me.

About that time we saw something in one of the large dumpsters at the edge of the complex. Whatever it was it was large. Our eyes grew as big as silver dollars when we drove closer and saw a woman's head pop out of the dumpster. Her hands were filled with left over trash. She was obviously salvaging for Christmas gifts.

I rolled down the window and asked, "Do you know where apartment number twenty-two is?"

"Yes," she said. "That's my apartment."

Our jaws practically dropped to the floor. We jumped out of the car and helped her out of the dumpster. She asked us what we wanted, and we told her we were her Hope Center helpers and we had brought her Christmas.

What we saw next changed our lives forever. "You came and brought us Christmas?" Tears welled in her eyes.

We fought back our own tears as we followed the elderly woman to her apartment. The walls were bare and the floors grimy, but we could tell she was doing the best she knew how to care for herself and her grandson. We unloaded the car, and on the final trip, brought up her grandson's new bicycle. She couldn't even speak, and by this time neither could we. Her grocery sacks unpacked and presents wrapped, she hugged us before we left her humble home.

Our ride home was silent. No music, no talking, nothing. Our thoughts and hearts carried us home. Walking through the door, we looked at our beautiful Christmas-filled home with decorations everywhere and a multitude of gifts. Yet none of it inspired us as much as the elderly woman whose life had been so hard and who had given us her greatest gift—a hug.

God touched us that year and we were forever changed. In fact, I found I was now the one seeking the Father's forgiveness for a haughty spirit. We thanked God for giving us the gift of sharing His love with another family. In that tiny, run-down apartment, with its bare walls and grimy floors, God taught us the true meaning of Christmas.

Today, not only can we say with certainty, "It's better to give than to receive," but we can also add, "Every time we give, we always receive."

Christmas Elf

Gail Cawley Showalter

But through love serve one another.
—Galatians 5:13 NASB

"Joy to the World"? The Christmas carol was playing on the car radio, but I didn't feel any joy in my world. It was five days before Christmas—the first Christmas since my divorce and the first one I would spend without my children. They were born like "stair steps"—three babies in thirty-seven months. The older two were now in school but, because I was no longer a stay-at-home mom, I had to place my youngest in daycare. Putting him there had further crushed my broken heart.

Working in the home had been a whirlwind of diapers, teething, and allergies. Working outside the home had become a necessity. I'd been a theatre instructor, but I quickly realized that teaching theatre, which required evening rehearsals, performances, and weekend competitions, would not be practical with my having young children. So I went back to college and became certified to teach English. Just one year after the separation, I was commuting forty minutes to teach in another community.

Thoughts of all the responsibilities of motherhood whirled in my head as I listened to "Joy to the World." It was Friday, and I was on my way to pay the sitter. She's a wonderful woman and one of the few blessings I'd been granted.

But one of my greatest wishes wouldn't be granted this year. My children wouldn't be coming home with me; they'd be staying with their dad until the afternoon of Christmas day. They were at the ages that made Christmas extra special, and their eager, wide-eyed expectations had made Christmas morning fun for me the last few years. I tried hard not to imagine a Christmas morning without their giggles and squeals of delight when they saw the surprises that had mysteriously appeared under the tree overnight.

When I drove my old station wagon into the baby-sitter's driveway, a familiar sleek, black sports car was parked there. My heart sank. It was my husband's lady friend coming for my children. Should I stay or go? Confusion gripped me, but before I could decide, my children came out of the house, climbed into her car and waved, "Bye, Mommy" to me as if I were an acquaintance beside the road. In the blink of an eye, they were gone.

I paid the sitter without a word, and returned to my car. There, despair overpowered me. My tension grew until all the muscles in my neck and back clenched into knots and I began to sob. Soon hot tears poured onto the cold steering wheel. How could this be happening? How could I get through Christmas without them?

"Oh God, please, please, please get me through this."

As I drove home with blurred vision, I remembered my mother's overcoming spirit. She often quoted Art Linkletter: "In love's service, only the saddened qualify." Well, I certainly must be qualified! I'd never known such sadness in all my life. And I was willing to "serve" in any way to remove the pain.

"What can I do, God? What can I do?"

A wonderful idea! Since I've been involved in theatre all my life, I'd be a Christmas elf for children who were not as fortunate as my own. It was easy to put together a Christmas elf costume, a green felt skirt, tights, green elf shoes, a green hat made from gift wrapping, and stage make-up completed the look.

I dialed the number of a local hospital.

"Hello, I was wondering if you had children who are still in the hospital, and if they'd like a visit from a Christmas elf?"

"Yes . . . we have a few. Are you with a group?"

"No, just me."

"Well . . . I guess that would be okay," a pause, and then, "Yes, come on."

Soon I was on my way to the children's ward in my little green station wagon. Surely children there would welcome a visit from a Christmas elf. I'd get to see eyes filled with wonder after all.

An elf's arrival in a hospital, even at Christmas, attracts quite a lot of attention. Heads turned, and some people grinned, but my goal was so intense that my inhibitions had vanished. I wasn't the least bit self-conscious.

A boy's eyes lit up as I walked into the shadowy room.

"Hi, Lance. How are you doing?" I asked with an elfish grin.

He didn't speak at first, not believing his eyes. I handed him a candy cane and a coloring book.

"Say thank you," said an adult voice from a dimly lit corner.

"Thank you," Lance spoke softly.

Tubes and medical devices surrounded Lance, but for those brief moments he could forget the pain, and fantasy prevailed.

"Hi, Damon. Merry Christmas!" I said to the older boy in the next room. "I just came by for a quick visit."

"Are you for real?" he questioned.

"Sure I am," I replied. "It's Christmas you know." He was alone in the room, and I handed him a candy cane. Dark circles under his eyes and needles in his frail arms made it clear that he'd be hospitalized for a while. I sat on the edge of his bed and read *How the Grinch Stole Christmas*.

The last child I saw was a girl. She was very unhappy about being in the hospital, and she made it clear that she didn't get off on elves at Christmas or any other time for that matter. She took the candy and seemed pleased that I treated her with respect, even though I was an elf.

"Christmas is really a birthday celebration, you know?" I said.

She nodded.

"What's your name?" I asked.

"Treva," she said clearly. "That's Reva with a *T* in front for Tough."
I could tell she didn't want to be as tough as she thought she needed
to be. I held her hand and she began to relax a little. A faint smile came
to her lips.

"Well, Treva," I said, "I hope you'll remember to celebrate the birthday party." I left her smiling with an inexpensive little necklace as a
gift.

I didn't linger with any of them. I hoped to provide each child with
a bit of fantasy to tell others about, or just to give them a fond memory.
The element of surprise was the best gift. The expression on their faces
inspired me too.

The spirit of Christmas, the spirit of Christ was coming through.
Christmas—the spirit of love, love in action. It was, in fact, so exhila-
rating that I went on to two other hospitals, without even calling ahead.
Walking in, unannounced, added to the drama for me, as well as for
the nursing staff.

On the way home, I sat at a traffic light in my green wagon and
green costume with my red-painted cheeks and artificial freckles. I
was so wrapped up in the adventure I forgot about my appearance. I
glanced over to the other lane and saw a gentleman in a black suit and
tie, driving a huge black Continental. He was laughing. I looked at
myself through his eyes, and my pain was gone. I'd completely forgotten my sorrow and myself.

Christmas was not about me. It was about the Gift, about Christ. I
could go back to my empty house now and plan for the after-Christmas
celebration. When my children returned, I'd have a spirit of true joy
in my heart—the joy of Christmas—a joy I'd continue to share with
others regardless of my current circumstances.

Mother's Day—Not!

Bonnie Compton Hanson

He settles the barren woman in her home as a happy mother of children. Praise the LORD.

—Psalm 113:9 NIV

Growing up, Mother's Day was my favorite holiday. How we six kids would labor over our homemade cards and gifts and poems for Mom. Then on Mother's Day itself, we'd carefully prepare burnt toast and undercooked eggs to carry on a tray upstairs for her breakfast in bed.

We brought her bouquets, picked from her own carefully-nurtured flowerbeds. We practiced in secret around the piano to surprise her with an off-key arrangement of "No Place Like Home." Then we proudly sat by her and my father in church on Mother's Day, clutching pink carnations handed out by the ushers. At that shining moment, I was supremely confident that my mother was the world's most perfect mother—and that we were the world's most-appreciative and perfect children.

I could hardly wait to grow up and be a mother myself. What I didn't realize was the great difference between a family with girls and one with only boys. That is, until God placed three sons—no daughters—into my own eager arms.

Yes, each Mother's Day I, too, received handmade cards and poems and gifts from little sticky hands. I, too, was surrounded by grinning faces and wiggly legs during Mother's Day services. I, too, enjoyed burnt toast and slightly-scrambled eggs in bed—at least until I had to shake the crumbs out of the sheets and wash the dishes and pans in the kitchen. But, hey, this was Mother's Day, and I was a mother. No greater joy, right?

Then, almost overnight, my toddlers sprouted thick arms and long legs and big attitudes. Before I quite knew what happened, I'd become—besides working full time outside the home—chief cook, washerwoman, and homework taskmaster for three handsome, talented teens.

All too quickly, Mother's Day services at church found them several pews away with their friends, catching up with us afterward for lunch before heading back out with their pals. The world still celebrated Mother's Day. The stores were still filled with hearts, pink roses, marvelous presents, schmaltzy music, and all the rest. I just didn't get the mushy stuff anymore.

And then one year I woke up on the second Sunday morning in May, expecting cards and presents. Instead, I got, "Hi, Mom, what's for breakfast? Can you iron this shirt?"

Okay, they were teenagers. Time management is not their specialty. After church, that's when I could expect the cards and presents and the meal at a nice restaurant.

Instead I got a ride straight home and, "Hey, Mom, what's for lunch?"

I suddenly snapped. "Nothing," I cried. "Nothing at all until someone around here remembers it's Mother's Day." Then I trounced up the stairs, slammed my bedroom door, and dissolved into tears.

Downstairs, there was stunned silence. Then lots of talking. Then silence again. About an hour later, I heard a timid knock on my bedroom door. There stood my four men, their long arms filled with cards and chocolates and roses and a philodendron plant almost as tall as I was. Plus a bucket of the Colonel's best chicken for lunch. My sons were smiling, but looked a little scared.

"Happy Mother's Day!" they all shouted.

And it was. Especially after they'd hugged and kissed me, scarfed down the bucketful of chicken, and headed off for their own agendas—leaving me and God alone to do some deep thinking—me, that is; God, of course, didn't have to.

What I discovered wasn't pretty. Why had I bought into the world's pretty-pink-pouffy commercial view of Mother's Day so completely that I couldn't appreciate the treasures I already had before me—three loving, upright, hardworking sons and their equally loving, upright, hardworking father? No, they didn't always remember to make or buy me gifts. But they were gifts themselves—precious gifts to me from God.

After all, this was not only Mother's Day, but the Father's day, as well—the Lord's Day, the day to honor my heavenly Father. And my door-slamming and all the rest weren't exactly honoring to Him.

Although my own Mother recently passed away at ninety-six, I still love Mother's Day. And now my grown sons and their precious wives and children help me appreciate it even more—not as a day to get, but as a day to give.

Starting with giving thanks that I can truly be "a happy mother of children. Praise the Lord!"

The Year of the Toaster Oven

Patricia Lorenz

*For which is greater, the gift on the altar, or the altar itself
that sanctifies the gift?*

—Matthew 23:19 TLB

There we were, schlepping up and down the aisles of Sam's Club. It was dark outside, snowy, windy, and cold—two days before Christmas. As a single-parent mom, I was exhausted after a long day at work. But Andrew, my high school freshman, insisted we make the trip.

"Come on, Mom, you have to tell me what you want for Christmas. I really want to get you something nice, something you want. Give me some hints," he pleaded.

I harrumphed, noting my headache had intensified, and I muttered, "Why didn't you think about this weeks ago? Couldn't you have walked to the store near our house with one of your friends and picked out something that would be a surprise?" My mood soured further. "I absolutely hate being here two days before Christmas. I have a thousand things on my mind. Mostly, I hate having to pick out my own Christmas present."

Hot tears welled up, but I blinked hard. I wasn't going to cry right there in the middle of the store. I swallowed and continued my tirade, pushing the cart faster as I swerved between pallets of Christmas goodies. "Are you going to wrap it up and expect me to act surprised when I open it in front of everyone?" My voice trailed off when I noticed the forlorn look on my son's face. I took a deep breath as we rounded the book aisle and ambled over to the housewares section.

How could I have been so mean-spirited? I was starting to hate myself. "I'm sorry, Andrew. I'm just tired." I had to make it up to him. "You know what I'd really like?"

"What?" his voice sounded positively exuberant.

"A toaster oven."

"Great! Let's look at 'em," he said as he steered me over to the small appliance section.

Madam Scrooge surfaced again. "Oh no. Look at those prices. I won't let you spend that much, and besides, you can't afford fifty dollars. You don't need to get me a Christmas present. Let's go home."

"Mom, please, I really want to get it for you. I've got the money. I've been saving for months . . . and I want to get you something nice, something you'll use a lot. This is perfect."

"How about if I pay half? It'll be a gift for both of us. You'd enjoy a toaster oven as much as I would, wouldn't you?"

"No!" Frustration clouded his face. "Mom, please, I want to buy it for you. Let me do this, please."

Grudgingly, I put on a happy face as Andrew paid for his purchase with mostly fives and singles. As he carried the big box to the car, I noticed he was walking taller, happier.

At home, I made myself a cup of lemon tea and went into the family room. There, I turned on the Christmas tree lights and flopped into my favorite rocker. Why was I such a crab when it came to gifts? I thought back to before Andrew's father died, to all the Christmases and other gift-giving holidays. Harold bought me the most ridiculous gifts that any human being could imagine. The muumuus sprang to mind. Long after muumuus were fashionable, he'd given me three huge muumuus, in three different ghastly multiprints.

One Christmas he bought the two of us matching sports jackets, maroon with yellow stripes, in an ugly shiny material. His was a man's extralarge-tall, mine a man's large. I looked like a Green Bay Packer across the back, and the sleeves crept down to my knuckles.

I was cooking a special Valentine's Day breakfast when Harold came downstairs with his "I have a surprise for you" grin. He whisked me upstairs to see his latest declaration of love—six hooks that were pink, plastic, life-size replicas of curved index fingers. They were screwed into the walnut paneling in our bedroom, spaced every two feet along the wall. I looked at Harold's face to see if it was a joke. *Oh Lord, please let this be a joke! These plastic fingers do not go with my country antiques! Please, Lord, make this April Fool's Day and not Valentine's Day!*

I kept looking at Harold, and his eyes sparkled. "See, honey, you can hang your bathrobe on this one, your pajamas on that one, your bath towel over there, your clothes on these."

All I could do was nod my head and hold back the tears.

One Christmas seventeen presents with my name on them sat under the tree, thirteen of them from Harold. Our gift opening custom involved taking turns: the four children, then me, then Harold. That year after we'd gone through the cycle four or five times and everyone else's gifts were opened, I still had twelve left to unwrap. I was embarrassed and angry at my husband for being a mail-order-catalog addict. That year, he'd fallen victim to an ad that read, "Get 13 surprise gifts for $2.98 if you order $50 worth of merchandise."

I started to dread every birthday, anniversary, Mother's Day, Christmas, and Valentine's Day. I knew Harold would either buy too many gifts I didn't need and wouldn't use, or he'd spend too much money on something that wasn't my taste. Now here I was, fifteen years later, nearly fifty years old and I was still acting skittish and mean-tempered about this gift-giving thing with Andrew.

I grabbed my Bible and did a quick study on the giving and receiving of gifts. Flipping through my concordance, I looked up *gifts:* "For which is greater, the gift on the altar, or the altar itself that sanctifies the gift?"

Suddenly those Christmas tree lights seemed brighter. The gift itself wasn't the important part of the equation; it was the heart of the giver, the vehicle of the gift, the "altar" so to speak, that made all the difference.

Just then Andrew bounded into the family room with his big box all wrapped and decorated with a shiny bow. As he placed it under the tree, he smiled, "You don't have to act surprised, Mom. I'm just really glad you're going to like it. Hey, I think I'll even like it. I can make all kinds of things in a toaster oven, right?"

"Absolutely! Your favorite Italian bread with cheese on top, open-faced tuna and tomato sandwiches, even leftover pizza."

Andrew's face was as radiant as the Christmas angel on top of the tree.

Before the year of the toaster oven, I'd been too wrapped up in what the gift was, or whether I could use it, or if it fit properly, to pay much attention to the giver. Now all gifts please me, whether they're pink plastic finger hooks or something I have to pick out myself. By the very act of giving, the giver has demonstrated he or she loves me . . . and that is the best gift of all.

Three Red Dresses

Golden Keyes Parsons

For man looks at the outward appearance, but the LORD
looks at the heart.

—1 Samuel 16:7 NASB

Cinnamon, sage, onions, celery, and pumpkin pies. Holidays found
the Parsons' household filled with the traditional fragrances. Our
dinner table always overflowed with an abundance of delicious dishes.
This year our oldest daughter, separated from her husband, had three
children, ages three, two, and an infant. Our middle girl was a sophomore in college, and the youngest a senior in high school.

I struggled to make the holidays festive. We'd directed a wonderful
conference ministry for the last ten years, but the retreat center had been
sold, and we were let go. In the transition, we had to leave our home on
the property as well as our career. This was the second year since our
dismissal that we'd been unable to find profitable employment.

As our daughters were growing up, my husband and I had enjoyed
creating family traditions. We felt they were important building blocks
of security for them, and we guarded mealtimes together jealously.
Our girls knew they were to be there, on time, and ready to share with
the family. Today, when our daughters are asked about their fondest
memories of home and family, our mealtimes are among the first re-
collections they mention.

We played all sorts of silly games, prayed together, observed certain rituals, hung special ornaments on the Christmas tree, and enjoyed traditional dishes. Every Christmas Eve our youngest daughter and my husband gathered firewood and built a fire in the fireplace together. After having to leave our home at the conference grounds, there was no fireplace, so they simply built a fire outside. They continue that custom to this day.

As winter moved toward the holiday season, our family had a major problem fulfilling some of our traditions—one in particular. In our little rental house, we had no stove. I had an electric skillet and a microwave, but no oven in which to cook the traditional turkey. After our oldest daughter and her husband separated, she and her babies moved into a small house across the street from us. She did have a stove. We decided to cook the turkey and dressing and pies in her oven and bring them over in time for dinner. All day, we scurried between the two houses, preparing a holiday feast as best we could.

The two oldest grandchildren ran back and forth, squealing with delight over the festivities. "Poppaw, watch!" they shouted as they swung on the tire swing in the front yard. They seemed oblivious to our frustration over trying to provide a warm, memorable holiday for them.

Still, there was plenty of love, kisses, and hugs for everyone, even though the wounds of my daughter's troubled marriage as well as the loss of our home and career were still raw. The gifts under the Christmas tree were sparse this year, but we managed to have our usual huge tree, and the ornaments and lights glittered as brightly as ever.

I've always enjoyed dressing up for holiday dinners, and when the girls were little, I outfitted them in dresses with matching tights, tying their blonde hair up in bows and frills. As the girls grew older, however, they began to resist and wanted to dress more casually in jeans or sweats. I held out as long as I could, but eventually gave up. I came to see that, in the grand scheme of things, not dressing up for Christmas dinner was a minor issue. We loved each other, we were healthy, and we were together. God had abundantly provided, for which I was grateful. I barely gave the dress-up tradition a passing thought this year.

The time was approaching to get the turkey. My mom, our girls, and the grandchildren stayed at our house preparing the table, filling the drinks—munching on goodies as they worked. As my husband and I went out the door toward my daughter's house, I casually mentioned over my shoulder, "I suppose it wouldn't do any good to ask you girls to dress up, would it?" The girls looked at me and rolled their eyes as I shut the door.

My husband and I basted the turkey a bit more and stayed longer than we'd anticipated, letting the dressing brown up nicely.

Meanwhile, our youngest daughter squealed to everyone in the other house, "Ooo—ooo! I have an idea! Come on." She raced to her closet and brought out three dresses—her red prom dress, another red ball gown she'd worn as the senior girl representing our small town, and still another red gown our coed daughter wore as a nominee for a college beauty pageant.

Jeans and sweats went flying as the girls wriggled into the formal gowns.

"How does this look?" the oldest daughter asked.

"Amber! Better if you'd take off your socks and tennis shoes!"

"Ooops!"

The girls stumbled over each other as they giggled and ransacked the bedroom to find all they needed to complete their outfits. Finally, they got the zippers zipped, hooks hooked, undergarments on or off, whatever the case, and ran to the window to see if we were coming across the street yet.

"Here they come! Now . . . everybody line up!"

The meal was cooked to perfection. My husband and I walked across the street, balancing our Christmas Tom on a tray, while steam rose from the dressing. When we opened the door of our house, there stood our three beautiful grown daughters—arm in arm, all decked out in red evening gowns—laughing and giggling just like they used to do when they were little girls.

"Is this dressy enough for you, Mom?"

My husband and I set the turkey down and burst into laughter as we engaged in a group hug. We then turned to the abundant table to celebrate a festive dinner. That holiday meal is among our family's most singular memories. Even at one of the lowest points in our lives, the love we shared triumphed over the difficult circumstances and pointed us toward what is truly important—faith, love, acceptance, laughter, and family unity.

Valentines and Vacuums

Patricia Evans

For your Father knows what you need before you ask Him.
—Matthew 6:8 NASB

Ahhh, Valentine's Day. It conjures up all kinds of warm thoughts, doesn't it? Roses, chocolate, diamonds, romantic cards, cupids, lace, candy hearts in little pink and white boxes. Hearts, handmade from construction paper adorn our refrigerator doors, admired as if they were created by Michelangelo himself instead of energetic five year olds. Remember the Valentine's cards you exchanged in grade school? And if you didn't get one from the boy you had a crush on, the whole day and the rest of February was ruined.

When my kids were growing up, it became apparent that Valentine's Day was more of a feminine holiday than a masculine one. I ran herd over the boys the night before to get their Valentines done. They scrawled their names on the back without even looking at the front, scribbled a name on the envelope from the list that the teacher provided, threw them in a paper bag and . . . voila! They were done.

With the girls, however, I'd have to buy the cards the second they hit the shelves, which seemed to be before Thanksgiving. Around January first, they'd beg their teacher for a list of names, then spend hours studying each card to be sure they gave just the right message to just the right friend. They'd use markers to embellish them with frills, flowers, and hearts. Everyone seemed a little giddier on Valentine's Day, as if we'd all been struck by Cupid's arrows, but more so for the girls than the boys.

My husband, Jack, is the quiet, romantic type who takes me to wonderful dinners, and after seventeen years, still buys me flowers just because it's Tuesday. But he's also practical, and one February I got even a clearer view of just how differently Valentine's Day is viewed between the sexes. Janis Joplin sang, "You don't always get what you want, but you get what you need," and Scripture says, "Your Father knows what you need before you ask Him."

Life can be crazy at times with jobs, kids, home, carpools, dinner, practices, homework—the list is infinite. In the midst of the chaos, my vacuum cleaner had gone to vacuum heaven—or at least to a recycling center. We had a dog that shed constantly and five kids who stepped in every dirt clod on the planet. Apparently, my children didn't understand the concept of wiping their feet before entering the house; our doormat was the cleanest rug in the house and the vacuum cleaner as essential as toilet paper. As fate would have it, the old vacuum died just before Valentine's Day.

To this day, I still don't know if my romantic husband simply didn't realize it was Valentine's Day, or if his practicality and my desires just happened to coincide. He knew I needed a vacuum cleaner desperately—although I desperately wanted dozens of roses, pounds of chocolate, and lots of lace. Jack suggested we go to Target—I like to pronounce it Tar-*zhay;* it has the sound of a boutique rather than a "one-stop shop for everything" store.

So there we were. While somewhere others sipped champagne or dined on delicacies, we sampled sweepers at Tar-*zhay.* My first thought was, *This isn't very romantic.* Then I thought there must be something along the aisles he'd surprise me with—perhaps at the jewelry counter, or maybe a one-time shipment of decadent chocolate. Shallow as that may be, it was February fourteenth, and I was disappointed. I deserved a good pout.

Yes, I like a clean house, but I was having trouble with my husband's choice of gifts.

Yet, as the weeks passed and I used that vacuum cleaner day after day, I began to realize just how romantic it actually was. This vacuum cleaner wasn't just any ordinary sweeper. In the first place, it cost as much as a week's worth of groceries. No, this vacuum was special. It was a manly vacuum. It wasn't just motorized, it was turbo-charged. With more suction than the earth's gravitational pull, it cut my vacuuming time in half. That meant more time to experience a candlelight dinner, or take a bubble bath, or tickle the kids, or spend a romantic interlude with my husband—or spend more time with God. Who'd have thought a vacuum cleaner would create one of the most romantic gifts that my wonderful, practical husband has ever given me—the gift of time.

The last words of Queen Elizabeth before she died were, "All my possessions for a moment of time." I'm so thankful for the "romantic" gift of my vacuum cleaner on Valentine's Day. Now, every time I vacuum I think about how we may not always get what we want, but we do get what we need from our loving and faithful Father. He knew that I needed—even more than a vacuum cleaner—more time to spend with Him.

Part 11

Career/
Employment

Knee-Deep, but Able

Judy Dippel

Strengthened with all power, according to His glorious might, for the attaining of all steadfastness and patience; joyously.

—Colossians 1:11 NASB

Patience is a virtue, but not one of my strengths. It's a relief to admit that I haven't totally arrived, nor do I have it all together. I wish I did, but I don't.

I've learned that both my strengths and my flaws are mingled in my lifelong process of growth. Maturing brings many rewards, but more frequently stretches me. Praying for patience found me knee-deep in water a few years back. Let me explain.

In my passion for writing, I began to write a women's inspirational book. At the same time, I worked a full-time job. My "paying" job held little challenge. It was, in fact, quite boring, and to top it off the dark office didn't have a window. But complaining only made me feel shallow and small in my unhappiness.

I want to live my dreams, map out my course—in *my* timeline, in *my* way. More than once, however, God has taught me *His* way.

That said, I still tend to "dig in my heels," resisting, as I try to force my heartfelt desires rather than waiting on God's well-timed plan. My habit of talking rather than listening forces God to get my attention rather dramatically.

The problem was one about which my husband reminded me: "We have kids in college and retirement looming ahead." Financial responsibilities prevailed. I prayed that I could have patience in God's perfect timing for my writing. But my days rested in my discontent instead of in the Lord.

I now laugh about what happened next. My stubbornness forced God to teach me patience, and my prayers brought unexpected results. The company's hourly employees went on strike. As salaried employees, I and others assumed operating positions throughout the paper mill.

"Okay," I said. "I can do these physical jobs."

After I passed the training to drive a Hyster, I thought, *This will look impressive on my résumé.* Was this part of my dream? Hardly, but I maintained a positive attitude.

"You don't expect me to drive for twelve-hour shifts!"

"Yes," said my trainer. "Stack the bales—there are always more. And you'll get used to breathing the diesel gas." *Ugh!* Throughout the strike, we were to work twelve-hour shifts for twenty-one days, then have one week off.

Time to write? That disappeared right along with the striking workforce.

I didn't anticipate what came next. My work moved me to the huge, enclosed building that held the block-long paper machine. I wore all the proper safety gear. No exceptions. Steel-toed rubber boots, gloves, ear plugs, safety glasses, hard hat, and regulation ear muffs. *I better have someone snap a picture of me,* I thought. *No one will ever believe this.* I was a sight to behold. *Guess I'll need to overcome my vanity!*

In the stifling, dark, and steamy basement of the paper machine the noise was deafening. I was assigned to hose the pulp that overflowed. In the hot, frighteningly foreign atmosphere of the paper machine, you might say that God *hosed* me with His will.

In the semidark basement, the sweat poured down my face. Wet hair hung underneath my hard hat. The surroundings created fear. Working alone, I encountered clanging metal of every shape and size— all a mystery. I hadn't a clue what these grimy, protruding "things" actually did. Normally I'm up for a challenge, but this harsh environment made me less than keen on learning new skills.

With both hands, I grabbed the huge hose and washed the pulpy water toward the grates in the floor. More water and big chunks of foam fell from above and landed on me.

Dart fast . . . here comes more water. My rubber boots were big, and I tripped and fell with a splash. Knee-deep in the "less than shallow" brown water, the huge, flailing hose threatened to twist free.

I stood, feeling like an alien. I choked, "What am I doing here?" Overwhelmed, I fought back the tears. My nerves jangled from the noise, the heat, and my conscious fear. *I have no business working down here. Every year experienced people are killed in paper mills.*

After days of physical work in the oppressive heat and steam, my resilience wore thin. My fear increased as I imagined myself crumpling alone onto the greasy, dirty floor, covered in water and foam. I told my husband, "Worse case scenario, I'll die in the basement and not be found for days."

Intimidated and feeling unsafe, my anxiety increased. Yet my usual "can do" attitude and pride made me reluctant to admit I was in over my head.

God intervened. Another employee wanted to work my position. She must be crazy!

I traded for the twelve hour night office shift and relished being back at a computer, basking in the familiar, comfortable surroundings.

Weeks later, the strike ended and I returned to my former position. God had shown me in no uncertain terms how to appreciate my dull, windowless office job. I learned an important lesson—*Do not, under any circumstance, pray for patience!*

I'm kidding, of course. God, as our loving Father, must show us through difficult situations that our complaining is selfish and unwarranted. The lesson I learned? I must contend with boredom and no windows. But who cared? I felt secure and good.

Back in my airless cubby hole, as in Colossians 1:11, I felt *strengthened in His glorious might.* In *steadfastness* I took one day at a time. I went to work more content, *patiently waiting* for God to lead me out the door, *patiently trusting* where and when He would open other doors—behind which I might find the fulfillment of my dreams.

Today, I try to appreciate all my experiences. I walk through the doors God opens, but only He knows where they will lead. I pray to wait and *follow patiently.* After all, God is faithful in His leading. I'm in process and continually learning . . . I can only imagine the good places He will take me as I joyously commit to follow. In *Him,* I am able!

A Clear Conscience

Kitty Chappell

Abstain from all appearance of evil.
        —1 Thessalonians 5:22 KJV

I couldn't believe what I'd just heard! "Pardon?"

"I said," the department manager repeated slowly, "you could be terminated for your actions."

Minutes earlier, my supervisor had told me that Mr. Brooks wanted to see me in his office—immediately. When I asked why, she shrugged—yet every eye followed me as I left the room.

Mr. Brooks got right to the point. "Mrs. Chappell, it's been reported that you've been leaving the hospital cafeteria, clocking in on the time clock, reentering the cafeteria and finishing your meal on company time. Your actions are tantamount to stealing from this facility."

Mr. Brooks's accusation was correct. As a slow eater, I disliked having to rush through my evening meals at the community hospital where I worked the evening shift. We had only thirty minutes in which to get our tray, go through the food line, wait in line at the cash register, find a table, gulp our food, and then clock in before rushing back to our departments.

I'd recently started clocking in, and instead of returning to my department, I returned to my table for an extra fifteen minutes. I then compensated for staying the extra time by taking only one of my two daily coffee breaks.

I considered myself a conscientious employee. I even gave time in ways not required. Once I accidentally broke a long tape before it was transcribed, and several unhappy doctors had to redictate their reports. That weekend, I drove to the hospital and worked for several hours without clocking in. No one knew, of course, but I did. And my conscience. It was my way of making up for the trouble I'd caused.

My conscience is clear in every area. How could he sit there and call me a thief?

"Mr. Brooks, I would never steal from anyone," I said, face burning.

"Time is money," he replied, without expression. "When you steal time from your employer, it's the same as stealing money."

"I understand," I stammered, "but I'm not stealing time."

I then explained how I skipped one of my breaks each day to extend my mealtime.

"By law we must provide two breaks a day—and you need those breaks," he explained. "You're not the only one who has just thirty minutes for meals. Either eat faster or talk less. Hereafter, you will take your breaks and you will return to your department after clocking in. Is that understood?"

Eat faster or talk less? Both perfectly sound options for men, but I was a woman. Nevertheless, I agreed, although reluctantly. "Yes, Mr. Brooks."

I fumed as I walked toward my department.

"I wonder who the snitch is that started all of this?" I muttered to myself as I made a quick mental rundown of possible suspects. Probably that unfriendly woman from accounting—shifty eyes always watching me. Or that grumpy guy from Radiology, who apparently had no friends and could abide by Mr. Brooks's eating philosophies quite easily. "Whoever it is, they ought to get a life! Don't they have anything better to do than spy on fellow employees?"

Mostly, I worried about what my coworkers would think. I'd tried hard to "walk my talk" as a Christian. And there I was—a Sunday school teacher—accused of thievery!

Detouring into the ladies lounge, I splashed cold water on my flushed face. As I reached for a paper towel, defensive thoughts popped into my mind: You can't just lie down and do nothing when your reputation is at stake. Your friends believe in you. Let them know how insulted you feel—with a humble but martyred air, of course. Refer to your good work ethics and habits. Remind them how often you volunteer to transcribe difficult tapes that others don't want to do. They'll rally to support you. Especially since they do worse things than you do. It won't change anything, but you owe it to them to fight for your reputation.

Yeah! I was pumped now. How dare anyone accuse me of stealing. After all, my conscience was clear.

Suddenly, my mother's voice popped into my head. "Kitty, the issue isn't *who* is right, but *what* is right. I don't care who started it; I want it stopped right now!"

I groaned. And just like when I was younger, I didn't want to hear anything she had to say.

"Yes, but neither is it right for me to be accused of something I didn't do!"

Leave it to my mom to call in the big guns. God's Spirit stepped in and nudged me. "But you did do it. By not following the rules, you gave a wrong message to others. How do they know you aren't stealing time? They only know what they see. If they see you do something that shouldn't be done, they'll either question your integrity or be tempted to do what they think you're doing. You need to set a good example at all times in all areas."

I wrestled with each line of thinking as I returned to my department. Do I try to protect my image—and my pride—or do I humiliate myself by assuming responsibility for my actions?

When I entered my station, everyone asked, "What happened?" They waited for my answer, every eye upon me. These are my friends, ready to take my side. Don't I owe them something?

"Mr. Brooks accused me of breaking hospital rules because at dinner time I go back into the cafeteria after clocking in."

As expected, my coworkers voiced every objection and presented every justification for my actions that I'd already used. Squaring my shoulders, I resisted the temptation to avoid accountability, and I deflected their loyalty by telling them the truth.

"Mr. Brooks was right. Oh, I didn't think I was actually breaking any rules, just sort of twisting them. I felt justified since I didn't take my second break, but I was wrong. Not only did I break the rules, I gave the wrong impression and caused problems by trying to live above the rules.

"After all," I concluded, "'the issue isn't who is right but what is right.'"

I finally understood what the Holy Spirit meant. When people look at me, they don't see me, they see God. I'm His representative on earth. Whether I like it or not, I'm a role model for those around me. I must do what is right even if it inconveniences me.

At last, my conscience really was clear.

For the Sake of the Call

Jennie Bishop

Humble yourselves, therefore, under God's mighty hand,
that he may lift you up in due time.

—1 Peter 5:6 NIV

I'm going to sell all this junk and take some computer courses!" my husband moaned.

"Again?" I laughed. My husband's love for music had always made our life together simple, yet fun. It never bothered us that we sat on amplifiers in our living room instead of on couches and chairs. And over the years I'd become adept at sweeping under and around a variety of cables and cords.

Whenever money was short, Randy would reevaluate his career choice. Maybe he should become an engineer or a computer programmer. There was no doubt he had a brilliant mind—he aced calculus in high school—but when he wrote and played his music, his listeners felt the presence of God in a powerful way. Since my skills were more marketable, he'd bravely taken on the role of a stay-at-home, home-schooling dad, allowing me to work full time.

But this time Randy's complaint carried a more serious tone. I'd lost my nine-to-five job in a recent downsizing, and our little basement recording studio wasn't bringing in much money. We had two daughters, a one-hundred-year-old house, and a major remodeling project, which had come to a screeching halt.

"Honey," I said, "you know I'd rather live in a hole than have you make great money at a job you hate, just so we can buy a lot of stuff. God means for you to be a musician. Let's just be patient and see what happens."

But even I was beginning to worry. We'd lived the poor musician life for so long, Randy was beginning to wear down.

For the next few months, neither of us had a steady job. Our conservative midwestern town held no openings for a former rock and roller who wanted to lead high-energy worship in a progressive church. Groceries mysteriously appeared at our door, and we bought the cheap brand of diapers. Randy did a recording project here and there, and sat in on worship teams whenever he could. I took freelance writing jobs. And we waited to see what would happen.

Just when our patience was beginning to run thin, a bass player from one of the worship teams told Randy of a job opportunity. His brother was a pastor in Michigan, and his church needed a worship leader.

"They'll have to take me as I am," Randy told me as he prepared his résumé, "I won't be satisfied in a traditional service, and they're a traditional denomination. I don't think there's much hope."

Each day I walked by our aborted remodeling project in the living room. We'd torn down bucket after bucket of plaster and lathe, dreaming of putting up new drywall, but now there was no money.

I am not *going to let this bother me,* I thought, and nailed an old quilt over the doorway.

To our surprise, Randy was invited to make a trip to the church in Michigan. Incredibly, he discovered that their vision was to create a church environment that was totally nontraditional, using modern worship music to make "unchurched" people feel welcome. They fell in love with my husband.

It was amazing how quickly our lives went from "desert" to "oasis"! Suddenly we had a reasonable income, and I was able to stay home with the children. Randy, like a tree whose roots had been bound by a burlap bag, planted himself into the worship leader position and immediately spread his roots. He functioned as if he'd been doing it all his life. In a few short years, he was teaching seminars and leading worship all over the state.

Oh . . . and did I mention that we now live in a ten-year-old home with a basement that houses a modern recording studio? No longer do I greet my guests with a cup of tea and invite them to pull up a cushioned amplifier as a seat. Even though we could still get along on very little if we needed to, we thank God daily for "lifting us up at the right time" and providing us with so many, many benefits—all for the sake of my husband's call.

First Things First

Chuck Noon

Live happily with the woman you love through the fleeting days of life, for the wife God gives you is your best reward down here for all your earthly toil.

—Ecclesiastes 9:9 TLB

My wife, Marita, has followed me in several moves. To the possible detriment of her career, she's come alongside me as I've pursued success. But, while I always had a job, I couldn't quite get ahead. Believing that better opportunities awaited me in Colorado, I took a job, and rented a small apartment.

After weeks of resisting and many, many tears, Marita ultimately tried to make the best of it. Before the move, she'd seen me search for employment, and helped me through my shock of being turned down for a job at Home Depot, even though they'd advertised that they were hiring. I never thought I'd be one of those guys who can't get a job even at Home Depot. Is it any wonder Colorado looked good?

Marita had a tough time with the decision. She couldn't easily move. God had blessed her ministry in Albuquerque with great employees. She had wonderful friends and was very happy. Seeking to keep the marriage alive, Marita drove between Albuquerque and Colorado Springs—five-and-a-half hours—almost every weekend. She was stressed and exhausted, and had three automobile accidents during those six months. Other than in her teen years—she had four accidents in her first year of driving—Marita has had no history of frequent accidents before or since.

One snowy winter evening, while walking my little schnauzer, Harley, and wishing he would hurry up and do his thing, God spoke to me. God has spoken to me in a clear, audible voice only three or four times in my life. So when He speaks, I listen. God told me, "Go home and take care of your wife." I searched the sky. Was this really from God? It wasn't what I wanted to hear, as God's direction seldom is.

Reluctantly, I obeyed and moved back to New Mexico. I took a job I considered to be way beneath my abilities and education, and for a year and a half worked in this humble position. During that time, I read the Bible through, cover to cover, and God went to work where He couldn't before. I didn't look for a better job; I waited for God to select one for me.

Once I put my wife first rather than my career or my search for success, I was offered a job that was impressive and paid more than I'd ever made. Since that time I've been offered many other positions and have had my pick of opportunities. When I sought after my own interests, success eluded me, but when I was willing to put God in the driver's seat and do what was best for my marriage—to love Marita extravagantly—I found the success I'd been searching for. The difference was, I no longer searched alone.

My Not-So-Perfect Plans

Gaylynne Sword

As for God, his way is perfect.
—2 Samuel 22:31 NIV

When I was thirty-four years old I figured out what I wanted to do with my life. I suppose I knew what I wanted to do before that, but when I was thirty-four, my dreams began to look like a reality.

Since graduating from college, I'd worked various jobs, ranging from processing checks in the contribution office for a large Christian organization, to supervising child care workers at our church, and being a secretary at a crisis pregnancy center. I was glad to be a stay-at-home mom for my two beautiful children, Christopher and Kelsey, and worked only part time while they were in preschool. As the kids got older and I got braver, I started pursuing the dream of writing.

Slowly at first, and then quickly, God put the pieces together. He led me to self-publish my first novel and to start a speaking/training ministry for women. I received speaking engagements of various sizes across the country, community groups used my book, and lives were being impacted. All the pieces were falling into place for what I knew was going to be an exciting career.

In January of 2003, I met with some publishers at the Christian Booksellers Association Expo in Indianapolis, and one expressed a keen interest in my work. I walked around the trade-show floor and was amazed when my peers, people I admired, had heard about me. I was flying high.

I returned home, excited about the future. As I waited to hear back from the interested publisher, I worked on my other writing projects, motivated by anticipation. I envisioned book signings and women's conferences, radio and TV shows . . . I was on my way.

But I was feeling tired. Not just up at 5:30 A.M. writing tired, but deep-down-worn-out tired. And my coveted morning coffee turned my stomach. When I felt an aching in my groin, I remembered something from almost eight years earlier. A quick trip to Walgreen's, and back home my purchase confirmed what I couldn't even imagine. Two blue lines appeared on the stick. I was pregnant!

"But God," I whined, "what about *my* plans? I'm done having children. I have a beautiful nine-year-old son and precious seven-year-old daughter. They're in school and able to bathe themselves! I'm supposed to be writing, I'm supposed to be speaking." I picked up a pile of bills. "I'm supposed to be earning enough money to pay off the self-publishing debts I've incurred. *How does this fit into my plan?*"

It doesn't.

"'For I know the plans I have for you,' declares the LORD, 'plans to prosper you and not to harm you, plans to give you hope and a future'" (Jer. 29:11 NIV).

None of us know what the future holds. We're not even promised tomorrow. But even when God throws us for a loop that feels like it's going to strangle us, we can trust that His ways are best. He will work "for the good of those who love him, who have been called according to his purpose" (Rom. 8:28 NIV).

I don't know how He's going to work all this out. I'm still thirty-four and trying to adjust to the new little life growing inside of me. At times I grow scared and confused and full of doubt. At times I cry and wonder how all the obstacles will ever be overcome. But even as I question, I have an abundant sustaining hope in a God that loves me and knows exactly what He's doing.

Just the other night, in one of my weaker moments, my son came to me in tears—worried that something might be wrong with me or the baby. He hugged me and made me promise that everything was okay. My husband, David, and I watched him leave, and then David turned to me and said, "Do you know the worst thing that will happen through all this? We'll stay in our small house, pay off our debts, you'll keep writing your books, and we'll have another child like Christopher and Kelsey."

The tears started to flow. God's plan wasn't what I'd had in mind, but I guess it doesn't sound so bad after all. In fact, it sounds pretty good!

Oxygen!

Chris Karcher

"For I know the plans I have for you," declares the LORD,
"plans to prosper you and not to harm you, plans to give
you hope and a future."

—Jeremiah 29:11 NIV

Trapped underneath a raft, whirling among the rapids! That wasn't where I planned to be when I geared up for a day on the river. But the memory of that event helped me resolve a dilemma.

Some time after the raft incident, I'd been trying to decide if I should leave a lucrative career, pack in the paycheck, and trust my savings account would carry me as I pursued a dream. I began to wonder, though, *Am I crazy?* Living my passion was one thing, but I also like to eat.

Late one night, I searched the Bible for answers. That's when I remembered that mid-June rafting trip.

The river was running high. Dave and I were floating with a group of friends in the most treacherous stretch of whitewater in the Snake River outside of Jackson Hole, Wyoming. Professional photographers would climb down the precipitous mountain slope to the water's edge, hoping the rafters would survive the whitewater and purchase their photos at the end of the trip.

I'd chosen my raft carefully: big! The oarsman was a good friend who rafted professionally and had never flipped a boat. We entered the rapids with momentum and hit the waves head-on. To survive, we passengers only had to hold on; surely, the raft wouldn't flip end to end.

The raft swooped up and over the swells like a rubber roller coaster. I wedged my toes between the rubber tube and the floor of the raft to anchor myself for the jarring ride. As rapids crashed above my head, I seized the aluminum tube on top of the raft. Waves engulfed the boat and I tightened my grip. Up and up we went. My fingernails dug into the palms of my hands. Up, up, and . . . over. Thunderous waves flipped our raft, end to end.

All six of us were thrown beneath the raft, trapped under the churning water. Whether you can swim or not makes little difference at that point. You go where the river hurls you. The flailing arms and legs of the other rafters struck me as we struggled underneath the raft. I found this oddly comforting because it meant I wasn't alone.

Was my current job now like that raft? Was I clinging to it, opting to stay employed because it paid well? Was I afraid to leave my comfort zone?

After we capsized, I thrashed about underneath the raft and pushed upward for air, but my head crashed into the raft. The whitewater spun me back down. Again, I wrestled toward the surface; again, the raft was a barrier between me and fresh air. I tussled. The water churned. Letting go of the raft would have carried some risk. I was wearing a life vest, but might have run into some rocks or been carried away from the others. Finally, I popped out from underneath the raft. Oxygen! I could breathe.

Discovering my passion would require me to leave my comfort zone, but living my passion was like breathing. That was my answer. I had to do it. If I hadn't chosen to leave a lucrative twenty-year career in computer software engineering, my dream would still be burning within me.

My fellow rafters and I landed underneath the raft because we'd felt secure clinging to it, and we didn't want to let go of that security. But what we viewed as security wasn't as safe as we thought. Instead, the thing we clung to was our nemesis. We would've been better off letting go of the raft so we wouldn't have ended up trapped underwater.

By surrendering, by letting go and trusting in God, we can receive the courage to leave our comfort zones and live in accordance with His plan for our lives. The change that God has in store for each of us is good and perfect. It may not be as drastic as a job change; maybe He wishes us to be a Bible teacher or a spiritual mentor. Those, too, are scary prospects to some. But with God, all things are possible.

Now, the line between work and play is blurred. I'm passionate about my work, and because I love it, my "job" doesn't feel like work. By Friday night I sometimes feel a twinge of sorrow because the work-week is over.

God has given me the grace I need to live in accordance with His plans. And I've been richly rewarded. My new sense of meaning and purpose is like a breath of fresh air.

The Rest of the Story

Laurie Copeland

Are not two sparrows sold for a penny? Yet not one of them
will fall to the ground apart from the will of your Father.
And even the very hairs of your head are all numbered. So
don't be afraid; you are worth more than many sparrows.
—Matthew 10:29–31 NIV

It was 5:00 A.M. and my husband had just come in the house. He'd been packing our van before we headed off to an art show where I was an exhibitor. "You'll never guess what just happened," he said.

Neither of us are exactly morning people and the only reason we're up at this unearthly hour is to make the necessary money at the art show. For John to be communicating—coherently—at this time of the morning was cause enough to pique my interest.

"As I was packing the van, I was asking God what we'd do if anyone stole your necklace design."

John was the recipient of a middle management layoff six months before, and my little jewelry business—which I'd started so I could stay home with my daughter—was now paying the bills. My top selling necklace design was our bread and butter during this lean time.

I'd developed a unique design and had it copyrighted. We toured the country, participating in art and craft shows, and I was known for my necklaces. But any artist who understood the medium could copy my design and undersell me. I constantly worried that someone might do just that, and, in fact, it had already happened with five earring designs.

Now John was telling me he'd heard from God. "I had a very strong impression that God was telling me not to worry. He gave the design to you, and if anyone tries to steal it, they won't profit from it."

Although John's conversation with God was interesting, I continued to busy myself with the preparations for the show. When we arrived at the exhibit location, we set up, and then I circled the art show, checking out what was new.

There it was. The copycat necklace I dreaded would appear one day. Its construction was not near the quality, but they'd slashed the price by half and threw in a pair of earrings!

I ran back to our booth in a panic. As I cried, John gently reminded me of God's message. That shut me up and calmed me down—for about eight seconds. "John, you've got to go over there and confront them!" I couldn't do it—I was a basket case. This was our only means of making money, and they had stolen my design and were selling it for less!

John wandered over to their booth and struck up a conversation with the husband and wife team. They'd copied the design from a lady in the mall, who'd been wearing one of my necklaces. When he also found out they were Christians, he told tell them about his early morning conversation with God. The wife seemed a little taken back, but the husband was unshaken, especially with the news that we had the design copyrighted.

"You don't have a leg to stand on," the man said to John.

John asked them to stop making my necklace. (In the arts and crafts business, it's common courtesy to create your own designs—not copy someone else's.) Before John left, they promised to discuss the situation and the next morning would let us know what they'd do. That night, John and I had a regular *prayer meetin'* going on!

The next morning, the couple informed us they would cease to make the exact replica design, but they'd continue to make the ones that were only similar.

We finished that show, wondering what the future held. We knew that someone undercutting us (even with a different design) could be the death of our business and livelihood. John had been desperately pursuing other jobs, but it was a dried up market. Without knowing what the future held, we clung to our faith in God that He would take care of our family.

Often, John and I listen to Paul Harvey's radio show, paying particular interest to the segment he titles, "The Rest of the Story." How many times have we, as Christians, had to trust God, even when we don't know—and may never know—the rest of the story? But on rare occasions, God allows us to know "the rest of the story."

A year later, I was at another show, and a fellow artist—whom I'd never met—came to look at my work. She mentioned that she'd met other artists who'd made necklaces just like mine, and she described to a tee the couple we'd encountered a year ago. They were still selling my necklace design! Then she said something I'll never forget: "You know, it's weird. They told me that they never made money with it; in fact, they *lost* money on the venture."

I'd never wish bad times on anyone, including these two. But I also believe that this bit of artistic justice demonstrated that God has our lives in His hands. He sent John a message the morning we discovered the copycats, and He provided a way for us to keep our finances from going under until John found a job. God showed us that, this design— His design—was a top seller for me. It was a gift. The gift wouldn't fit anyone else who tried it on.

I won't pretend that this period wasn't tough for us. We struggled, even with God's assurances. I failed in my faith at times, but the tears I shed when I heard the rest of the story felt like a spiritual cleansing from my Father God.

It makes me smile to think that sometimes God helps those of us who are faith-challenged by giving us a glimpse into the rest of the story. So when another challenge comes our way, we can once again remind ourselves that He really does have it all under control.

Unless the Lord
Builds the House

Paula Friedrichsen

*Unless the LORD builds the house, its builders labor in vain.
Unless the LORD watches over the city, the watchmen stand
guard in vain. In vain you rise early and stay up late, toil-
ing for food to eat—for he grants sleep to those he loves.
Sons are a heritage from the LORD, children a reward from
him.*

—Psalm 127:1–3 NIV

I've done everything. In addition to staying home to raise my kids
and take care of my house, I've worked part-time jobs at everything
from a daycare center to cleaning houses. But the job I remember the
most taught me a great lesson about staying in the will of God.

It happened about twelve years ago when my son was just a toddler.
At that time we owned a small furniture store and were getting along
fine financially, but I thought it might be nice to bring in a little extra
money. So I went hunting for a very specific type of job; I was interested in working ten to twenty hours per week, and the hours I worked
had to be when my husband was home, so he could keep an eye on
our son.

Within a few days it appeared I'd found the perfect job. It was at a local bakery and coffee shop (yum!) and the hours were perfect. It started at 5:00 A.M. and ended at 9:00 A.M., four days a week. What job could be better for someone who was used to getting up early and loved coffee and muffins?

From the very first day, I could tell the job wasn't a good fit. In the first place, 5:00 A.M. is really, really early. By midday I was physically spent, but still had many more hours of child rearing and housework ahead of me. Also, I'm a people person, so to be stuck in a back room baking muffins at dawn was not an ideal situation for me.

The breaking point came about two weeks into my new job. My husband needed to be at work early, my son was running a high fever, and I was supposed to be at work. I called my boss and told her I couldn't come in. She let me know she didn't need an employee who called in at the last minute leaving her in a bind. We parted ways and, I might add, not in an amicable manner.

After my husband left for work, I got my little one settled down for a "Dimetapp nap." Then I prayed about the whole situation, wondering what went wrong. I laid across my bed, pouring my heart out to God, when a sentence rolled through my mind: "Unless the LORD builds the house." This phrase, apparently from Scripture, was totally unfamiliar to me, so I looked it up in my Bible concordance. I wasn't even sure that I'd find "Unless the LORD builds the house" in the Bible.

Low and behold I *did* find a reference to that Scripture in Psalms. So with great anticipation I flipped to Psalm 127 to see what God would say to me about this "job gone awry."

> Unless the LORD builds the house, its builders labor in vain. Unless the LORD watches over the city, the watchmen stand guard in vain. In vain you rise early and stay up late, toiling for food to eat—for he grants sleep to those he loves. Sons are a heritage from the LORD, children a reward from him. (vv. 1–3)

I laughed and laughed when I read that! God knew all about this situation and all about my desire to earn a little extra money. He had watched me get up at 4:30 A.M., and He had watched me be a crabby mommy in the afternoons because of it. And His word to me was, "Just enjoy your son right now."

It was so simple and yet such a profound lesson for me; when setting off in a new direction—pray about it. I've learned since then to take each decision to God in prayer *first*. And He has been faithful to lead me and guide me every step of the way. I've had more than a few slipups since that time, but I always go back to that original lesson, and again turn my decisions over to God.

Since then, I've had several different part-time jobs that have been blessed by God and beneficial to our family's finances. And I know that many women work full time, with the obvious blessing of God upon their jobs and families. Working outside the home just wasn't His will for that season of *my* life.

For all the major decisions in life—marriage, job, housing, children—I'll take them to God in prayer, because "Unless the Lord builds the house, its builders labor in vain."

Part 12

Friends

Dinner with Sinners

Tonya Ruiz

Now it happened, as Jesus sat at the table in the house, that behold, many tax collectors and sinners came and sat down with Him and His disciples.
—Matthew 9:10 NKJV

I was busy with my quiet suburban life and perfect family—one husband, four children, two frogs, and an aquarium full of assorted fish. Although I homeschooled the children, the amphibians and aquatic animals were on their own. Tomatoes and cucumbers grew in the vegetable garden, and I received many compliments on the calla lilies blooming in the front yard. When the holidays rolled around, my Christmas gifts and cards were homemade. I cut coupons, wore flower-print dresses, cooked pot roast, and kept a clean house. The Stepford Wives had nothing on me.

When I watched our new neighbors move in across the street, I immediately decided we had nothing in common. Different lives, different values, and different worlds. Other than a "Hello" and a handshake, I stayed away, telling myself, "I'm way over quota on friends and neighbors anyway." The new neighbors received no welcome party, not even a plate of chocolate chip cookies from me. Nothing.

After playing with their kids, my son came home and told me that our new neighbors were planning their wedding. "You mean, they're not even married?" I asked. Rolling my eyes, I said to my friend from down the street, "My kids definitely won't be playing at their house."

At the wedding reception, "Welcome to the Hotel California" blared from across the street. "What's happened to our neighborhood?" I asked my husband as I spied out my bedroom blinds.

He shook his head. "You look like Gladys Kravtiz. All you need are binoculars."

"That's a great idea!" I quickly riffled through the drawer looking for mine.

The craziness continued until months later when my doorbell rang and there stood my new neighbor. With a desperate look on her face, she asked, "We're having some family problems; do you know a church where we could find help?"

I was surprised and embarrassed as I stood in a puddle of my self-righteousness. In all my months of condemning and judging, never once did I consider reaching out to them or having them over for dinner. An invitation to church was the farthest thing from my mind. How had it completely slipped my memory that before I was a Christian, I had cohabited with my boyfriends, been a Rolling Stones fan, and gone to more than my share of wild parties?

What if my Christian friends had said, "We can't take you to our church concert because of your colorful language, overdone make-up, and suggestive clothing"?

Shame washed over me. Jesus did not consider Himself better than the tax collectors, prostitutes, or other sinners. Why had I?

Not only did our new neighbors go to our church, but during that year, they both accepted the Lord. We have since bought and moved into the house directly next door to them. We've laughed together and cried together, and they've become our cherished friends.

My neighbors taught me a valuable lesson. I couldn't see past the beer cans to their hearts or hear their desperate cries over the loud music—but the Lord did. Because of them, my vision and hearing have been permanently improved. So I can put away my binoculars for good.

Resentful or Rejoicing

Gayle Roper

Get rid of all bitterness, rage, anger, harsh words, and slander, as well as all types of malicious behavior. Instead, be kind to each other, tenderhearted, forgiving one another, just as God through Christ has forgiven you.

—Ephesians 4:31–32 NLT

When I was twenty-six, I had a hysterectomy. I'd never bear children. I thought I was handling the situation fairly well until six years later when my friend Ruthie became pregnant.

By that time, my husband, Chuck, and I had adopted two wonderful baby boys, and I'd rejoiced with several friends as they had babies. But Ruthie—or rather Ruthie's attitude—jabbed at the scar tissue in my heart.

I'd had friends delighted to be pregnant, and I had no trouble with that. You're supposed to be delighted. I'd had other friends, especially older friends, despair over a pregnancy, and I had no trouble with that either. Sometimes the circumstances around a pregnancy make appreciating the miracle very difficult.

I had trouble with Ruthie because she expressed absolutely no emotion, at least none that I could see. That lack of feeling bothered me—deeply. It was to be a first baby for her and her husband. They were happily married and financially secure. She was healthy. Shouldn't she be over the moon?

A canker began eating at me—although I was careful to keep it hidden from everyone.

"When will you stop working?" I asked Ruthie.

She shrugged. "Probably two weeks before the baby comes."

I nodded. That sounded fine to me. "You can rest up for all those late night feedings," I joked.

But as the months passed, Ruthie did nothing to prepare for the baby's arrival. "I'll do it in the two weeks I'm off," she said.

"But what if the baby comes early?" I asked.

She shrugged. Apparently this baby was definitely going to come on its due date.

The last day of work, two weeks before her due date, Ruthie's co-workers gave her a shower. That night, she went to the hospital and had her son. At that time, the gifts were the only things Ruthie had to welcome her baby.

"It's not right," I muttered to my husband. "It's just not right." My hidden canker was turning into a full-fledged infection of the spirit, and I was unable to keep it to myself any longer.

Ruthie's mother asked me to go shopping with her to purchase some necessary items for the baby's homecoming. We had to buy basically everything—changing table, diapers, blankets, bedding—you name it. Ruthie's husband borrowed a crib and set it up so little Jake would have somewhere to sleep besides a dresser drawer.

"She's done nothing! Nothing!" I groused to my husband. I was careful not to appear so critical in front of others. "It's not right!"

One day, Chuck and I were going somewhere with our boys. Chuck was in the front seat with Chip, and I was in the back seat with Jeff. I started berating Ruthie again. For a few minutes Chuck was quiet. Then he made eye contact with me in the rearview mirror as we waited at a stop light.

"Do you realize you're becoming very bitter and nasty?" he said, his voice conversational and calm. "It isn't becoming, and I hope you do something about it before it's too late."

I was floored. He'd *never* before criticized me like that. I wanted to defend myself, to tell him I was right, that Ruthie was wrong, but I knew immediately I couldn't—for two reasons. He'd spoken in such a nice tone of voice that I'd be the Queen of Petty if I answered back. And, more telling, he was right. I'd become an ugly person. As we continued driving, I thought about Ruthie. What did it matter if she wasn't gushing about the baby? Ruthie, in fact, never gushed about anything. Her husband seemed perfectly content with her phlegmatic behavior. If he was happy, and she was just being herself, what business did I have to criticize?

I knew my discontent was because I couldn't give birth and that I resented her blasé attitude. But it was *my* attitude that was wrong, not hers. Nowhere does Scripture say, "Don't be blasé." But it definitely does say, "Get rid of all bitterness and anger."

Today Ruthie is still my friend, a friendship I doubt would have continued if I'd allowed that Christ-dishonoring bitterness to continue to fester. She still rarely shows her emotions, and that's okay with me. I've learned that loving someone means being kind and forgiving and accepting of differences even when you don't understand. With joy, I've grown closer to Christ's example and, even though she doesn't show it, I'm sure Ruthie's glad about that.

Sally Time

Elaine Britt

*Trust in the LORD with all your heart and lean not on your
own understanding; in all your ways acknowledge him,
and he will make your paths straight.*

—Proverbs 3:5–6 NIV

Miscarriage, infertility, pregnancy, pregnancy, miscarriage. Been
there, done that—in that order. I'm grateful now for two beautiful, healthy children, but the journey to that end takes me down
memory lane. . . .

Part of the infertility process involved progesterone shots during
the first trimester to sustain the pregnancy. They were big, bad, "horse
shots" in the hip, every day for about seventy days in a row—quite an
ordeal. Wisdom dictated choosing a skilled "shot giver" to lower the
level of trauma.

I chose Sally.

Sally met her husband at age thirty-two in the mid-1940s at the
Panama Canal. He was a doctor, she a nurse—both stationed at the
same spot. They met, and it was quickly obvious that wedding bells
would ring—even though they'd each privately vowed otherwise. Many
years of interesting adventures ensued, but no children, so Sally felt a
sense of ownership toward any kids after she'd helped "to get them
here," as she would say.

I'd arrive at her house after work, tired. She'd spend several minutes preparing the syringe, administering the shot, and massaging the area with a hot cloth to minimize bruising. Then we moved to the den and the fun began.

Everyone thought I was so generous, spending my time talking to this fragile, lonely old lady. But, after all, I owed it to her for doing this service, didn't I? To this day, I've had everyone fooled. Despite the age difference between us—almost fifty years—our spirits were kindred in the Lord. Sally had a level of maturity and wisdom, along with a touch of spice and a zest for life, that I haven't seen elsewhere. Our topics of conversation varied widely, and we'd have easily enjoyed several hours a day together instead of one.

Many years ago, Sally had a mastectomy due to cancer, and then lupus—which left her speech impaired. But that didn't slow her down. How entertaining to hear her say, "I just can't go to church luncheons with all those old ladies. All they talk about is how many doctors they go to, how many pills they take, and all their aches and pains. It bores me to tears."

Determined to stay ahead of the game, she told me once, "Those old ladies gripe all the time about having to go to funerals. They won't gripe when I die, because I'm not having one!" She never let age or health get the best of her. Instead, she chose to use her time making computer greeting cards for "old people" in nursing homes, reading, exercising, and getting on with life.

With a two-year-old and a six-month-old, I became pregnant again. Excited, I called Sally and lined up for another round of "shot time." We repeated our routine, falling easily into the rhythm of our former times together. Things ended abruptly when at twelve weeks I miscarried. I tried hard to see Sally, but time didn't permit.

Sensing my anxiety, she told me on the phone one day, "Honey, don't try so hard to get over here. I know all that you have on you. You're in my heart and I know your heart, so relax and take care of those children who I helped get here!"

A period of physical exhaustion and mental depression overshadowed me after the miscarriage. During that time, Sally's cancer recurred. True to character, she didn't call and tell me. Why, she had reasoned, would she want to share something that was such a nuisance to her? By the time I found out, the cancer was well advanced.

In those last days, our visits in the hospital were as positive as her energy level allowed. It was a strain because we both longed to be sitting in her den, each in an old recliner, wrapped in the warmth of her house.

The last time I saw Sally, we both knew it would be our final encounter—God gives us these life hints sometimes. We both knew that I had to leave the room and she this earth. I said to her, "Just remember when you're with Jesus, that I'm terribly jealous!" I meant that sincerely.

Ten years have past and I remember it as if it were yesterday. I'm eternally grateful for lessons learned by observing such a saint of God in action. She modeled unselfishness, faith, love, perseverance— generally a real "God perspective" on life. Knowing her left me with an ongoing challenge to rise to a level of excellence in my life.

A part of my spirit will always be in Sally's den in her old recliner. I see her laughing and dancing in heaven, spreading the zest and spice that is her spirit over everyone there, free from the limitations of her earthly body. I also sense her smiling at me, waving, and watching "her" children grow.

If given a choice, knowing all the pain and heartache attached to those years, I'd do it all again just to possess the cherished memories created in "Sally time."

You Can't Walk Through a Closed Door

Daphne V. Smith

For everyone who asks receives; he who seeks finds; and to him who knocks, the door will be opened.

—Matthew 7:8 NIV

It started off as a wonderful friendship. Upon moving to a new town in a new state, I immediately befriended a dynamite woman named Sue. Sue was bubbly and outgoing, and everyone who came into her presence felt important. Sue had a gift for making others feel accepted, and she warmly welcomed people into her heart and her home. Sue lived her life with an open door.

So, in this new town, in this new state, with this new friend, I started to feel comfortable. When I'm comfortable, I tend to let my guard down, and the "real" me comes out. Part of what drew Sue and I to one another was our opposite—yet complimentary—personalities. While Sue was open, easygoing, and fun loving, I've always been more bottom-line, task-focused, and result-oriented. We made a great team, got a lot done, and had fun doing it.

When a mutual friend of Sue's and mine experienced a dilemma, I immediately knew how to handle it. I intervened, stepping up to the plate and taking over the situation. I ran the show and was happy to do so—until Sue's feelings were hurt. By taking control, I not only stepped on Sue's toes, I walked right over her. This resulted in a huge falling out.

Up to that point, not only were Sue and I friends, but our husbands and children interacted as well. Friday nights would find us at each other's homes ordering pizza. When one of our husbands came home to an empty house, he knew that the gang was over at the other house, and he knew he'd better hurry and join us or miss his fair share of dinner. We even celebrated New Year's Eve together.

But that all changed, and the door to our open lives slammed shut. We no longer spoke to each other. Our husbands went to school functions alone so that Sue and I wouldn't have to run into each other. At business functions, we avoided each other. I can only imagine the strain we put everyone under on the rare occasion we were caught in the same room together.

After a couple of years, I resigned myself—our close association would never return. I figured that I'd "gotten over it," that I could live without Sue and her friendship. I'd forgiven our misunderstanding and moved on—or so I thought.

One day, I was on the phone with my friend Jean. We were discussing a meeting that would take place later that week, one at which Sue would be in attendance. I mentioned how I dreaded the tension I felt whenever Sue was present. "But that's all water under the bridge," I sighed. "I've gotten beyond it now."

Jean called my bluff. "Daphne, if you've really let go of this, you wouldn't talk about it so much. You wouldn't be so bothered by the situation anymore."

The light bulb went on. As soon as we hung up, I prayed. This time I put the situation in God's hands. And this time I really was ready to forgive and to forget—to have a new opportunity that involved a fresh start. That's when the healing began.

Later that same week, at the event Jean and I had discussed, I went into the ladies room. When I entered, I was the only one in there. (This event had over seventy-five women present, and to be the only one in the bathroom is a miracle in itself.) When I came out of my stall, guess who was in there? Yep, Sue. We gave each other a sideways glance while at the sinks.

Then, by the grace of God and Sue's true personality, she said, "Daphne, I'm sorry." Those were the first words exchanged between us in two years.

We quickly shook the water off our hands and ran toward each other for a long overdue embrace. I opened the door for God to do His work and I'm thankful that Sue walked through. To this day, our friendship is stronger because of the most important thing we had always had in common . . . our faith.

Part 13

Older but Wiser

A Field Day with My Face

Lauren Littauer Briggs

For the LORD sees not as man sees; man looks on the out-
ward appearance, but the LORD looks on the heart.
—1 Samuel 16:7 RSV

Vanity, thy name is Woman.
—William Shakespeare

With only one week's notice, I was scheduled to appear on national television. My husband, Randy, happened to be going to
our dermatologist for a scheduled cancer prevention treatment. I asked
him, "While you're there, will you have the doctor switch this lotion
she wants me to use?"

Later, the phone rang, and it was Randy on the other end. "The
doctor needs to know what you want switched," he said. "Here, you
talk to her."

I explained I didn't care for the scent of the lotion she'd given me
for my face and could she change it to a different product. As long as
she was on the phone, and thinking of my upcoming television interview, I asked, "Might there be something you could do, even if it's only
temporary, to minimize some of the wrinkles and lines on my face?
I'm going to be on nationwide TV Thursday and I'd love my face to
look better."

"Have we done a glycolic peel or a laser treatment?"

The names didn't sound familiar, so I answered, "I don't think so."

"Come on down at five-thirty tonight and I'll do a laser treatment," she offered. "That will help with the wrinkles and give you some edema that will last through Thursday."

Having seen the video of a previous television interview I'd done, I knew studio lighting could be harsh and not very complimentary. I welcomed any help I could get.

I arrived at the dermatologist's office at 5:30 P.M. sharp as requested and was escorted to a nurse's station where a thick layer of face numbing cream was applied. I was told to sit on a lone chair down a hallway. I was glad that I'd grabbed a stack of mail-order catalogues from home, and I entertained myself for the next half hour browsing page after page while watching the comings and goings of a frantic medical practice.

After what felt like an eternity, I was brought into an exam room that contained a huge, brand-new machine. My dermatologist finally arrived with an assistant and a staff member from the plastic surgery office upstairs. As I later found out, the gal from upstairs was waiting to have the same procedure done on her—after hours, but I came first. She asked if I'd ever had this done before, and I replied, "I don't think so."

"Oh, you're going to just love it!" she exclaimed. "TV, huh? That's so exciting. Will you be interviewed?"

While the three of them busied themselves in preparation for my "treatment," I explained that I'd be talking about my book on TV. Before long, lead shields were put over my eyes and machinery began to whirr. After an initial test, the procedure began with a *pssshhst* across my face plus a *pheeewwff* constantly blowing cold air on my face.

Did it hurt? No. Was it pleasant? No. Think dentist office. For over twenty minutes, a tool was slowly moved all over my face, followed by separate tools that suctioned away smoke and blew cold air. One of the staff occasionally affirmed that I was doing very well and let me know how much I was going to "just love this!"

The lead eye shields were finally removed, and I sat up. "Will this help these deep lines on either side of my nose?" I asked.

"Well," my dermatologist replied, "there is something else we could do. I could put some 'Super Collagen' in there, which will last two to three months. If you like that, later I could do some 'Radiance' which will last three to five years."

I'm a sissy at heart and abhor pain, but realizing that my face was still numb, I shrugged. "Why not. We're already having a field day with my face!"

My doctor left the room, and while she was gone, the gal from the plastic surgeon's office asked, "Have you ever had your lips done? She does great lips!"

The doctor returned with a syringe and I chose to look away and dream of sandy beaches while she injected the "Super Collagen." All three women were so thrilled with the progress and kept remarking, "You're just going to love this!"

"You really need her to do your lips," the gal from upstairs remarked. "Your lips are very thin."

"Would you like me to do your lips?" asked my dermatologist.

"I guess so," I acquiesced.

"Oh, that's great!" the doctor said.

"You're going to be so happy!" the assistant affirmed.

"You're just going to love this!" they both exclaimed.

Aftercare instructions were provided. I was told to keep this liquefying hydrant on my face at all times, even if it meant applying it ten times a day, until I went on TV.

It was now after 7:00 P.M. and the office felt abandoned. But not to worry—the person who collected the money was still there, waiting for me. Additional products were provided and the calculator whirred. Then I got the greatest shock of all—the cost for this procedure. Not only had I never asked for clarification about the procedure, I never inquired what it would cost. Ten treatments like this and I could have had a face lift! I gulped and offered my credit card, signed the receipt, and hurried out the door.

On the drive home, the liquefying goo definitely liquefied and was oozing down my face and dripping on to my shirt. I arrived home with my face red, swollen, and hot, bleeding from the needles plus a hematoma on my lip. My husband's pained expression let me know I was not ready to be on nationwide TV.

I was to fly across the country early Wednesday morning, arrive on the east coast in enough time to have dinner, and then do my six-minute interview early Thursday morning. Tuesday, while at a nail appointment, my cell phone rang. The voice on the other end identified herself as the assistant producer for the television program and asked, "Is this a good time to talk?"

No one ever asks that question unless that person's going to say something you won't want to hear. Not wanting to postpone bad news, I said, "Sure."

"I really hate to tell you, but they've decided not to use your segment so you don't need to come back."

I attempted to be gracious, in the hopes they'd use me some day in the future.

"I know this is a disappointment to you. You've probably already gone out and purchased a new dress!"

"You have *no idea* what I've been through to get ready for this interview," I muttered as I hung up.

How grateful I am that God looks on my heart! It's reassuring to know that in order to please God I don't have to spend money on my face. I just need to spend time with Him.

By the way, my husband really likes my new face. But that should come as no surprise. Although God looks on the inside, man looks on the outside.

A Really Bad Hair Day

Verna Davis

Gray hair is a crown of splendor; it is attained by a righteous life.

—Proverbs 16:31 NIV

I'd just spent two weeks by the side of my mother's hospital bed. She and I had several long talks about her incurable heart condition and the role reversal it caused. She was now becoming the needy one and I, the caregiver. Both of us were fighting the changes as much as possible. My mother's fight was counterbalanced by her continual praises to God. My fight was with God, for I was plenty angry with Him.

My father had suffered a fatal heart attack, and now this. Didn't God understand that having two parents with heart problems didn't look well on my health résumé? What about my children? Would they suffer from the same genetic bad luck?

I pounded the side of the shower while the water pounded on my head, and screamed my anger and frustration out to God. "Why me, God? I'm the wife of a minister, an inspirational speaker, the writer of a religious column in the local newspaper. Why couldn't this happen to someone else—someone who's not being as effective for the kingdom as I? Why me, God?"

When both the hot water and my tantrum were spent, I looked

into the mirror, examining the red-rimmed eyes and puffy cheeks. That's when I saw a slew of gray hairs that had sprouted overnight. Gray hair? I'm not even fifty yet. God, that's *not* funny!

My mind flashed on an image of my friend Stacy. I adore her hair—blonde with streaks of highlighted color. I knew in that moment, while staring at my dull, dark brown mop streaked with gray, I wanted my hair to look just like Stacy's. I knew she had hers done professionally. "But," I said to myself, "a do-it-yourself kit would work just fine. Remember, you're a pastor's wife on a budget." My husband and daughter were out running errands, so I ran to Wal-Mart and bought Lighter Hair # 4 for less than ten bucks. What a bargain!

Two hours later, I knew I'd made Terrible Mistake # 1. No amount of curling and styling could disguise my new look—that of a brown and yellow striped tabby cat. Maybe I'd messed up during that painful procedure—when I pulled my hair through minuscule holes in the skull cap, using a surgically-sharp steel hook. Or maybe the problem was I hadn't pulled out strands—more like clumps that wound around the end of that hook. Perhaps I should have done a "test" strip like instructed. But I didn't want to waste time on some dumb test. I was in a hurry to get my new look.

So, what to do to cover the yellow stripes? My daughter used a red tint on her hair. She wouldn't miss it if I "borrowed" a box out of her bathroom. I'd been a redhead during a brief time in my thirties and my husband had loved it. Red Flame # 8 should do it. I was grateful no one was home but the dog; he could be persuaded not to spill the beans. For the second time in four hours, I put harsh chemicals on my hair.

Two hours later, I knew I'd made Terrible Mistake #2. No amount of curling and styling could cover up what every kindergartner already knows—red and yellow make orange. Staring back at me from the mirror was a frightening sight—a pumpkin with my face attached! I could have put a brown stem on my head and gone trick-or-treating with anybody willing to be seen with me. Too bad it was January.

I cried. I vowed never to leave the bathroom. I cried some more. The dog came running to investigate. He's a tame, laid-back dog, and he never barks—not even at the meter man. He thinks every stranger is just a friend he hasn't licked yet. But when he saw me, he raised his hackles, bared his teeth, and barked. Ferociously. When I spoke his name, he barked even more.

An hour later, my husband and daughter returned from their errands, and found us there in the bathroom—the dog barking and a woman with orange hair, crying. After they collapsed in laughter, I declared I wasn't going to leave the bathroom looking like a jack-o-lantern.

In a moment of angelic mercy, my daughter dashed out to buy any remedy she could find. She came back with the only thing she thought would cover the red—Dark Sable Brown #17. For the third time in eight hours, I put harsh chemicals on my hair.

The dark brown did nothing for me, but at least it covered the orange, which had covered the yellow stripes, which had covered the gray, which had mingled with . . . um, dark brown. I was back where I'd started—except with frizzies!

The next morning at church, I ignored the startled faces and marched off to find an empty pew. I pulled out my Bible, hoping people would think I was meditating and would leave me alone. I wanted no questions about my frizzed dark brown hair.

I glanced down at the first verse that popped off the page: "Gray hair is a crown of splendor; it is attained by a righteous life."

Oh, God, how could I have been so blind? Although my mother was seriously ill, she was alive and recovering. Certain things in her life would have to change, but she was praising God while I was wallowing in self-pity. Why be so upset about a small cluster of gray hair? Was I not approaching that "certain age"? My life had been full of adventures of obedience, falls from grace, and mountains of mercy.

I'm no longer ashamed of my gray hair, for it's nothing more than a signpost for the life I've lived—days numbered with blessings and righteousness and lessons in maturing. As for that Crown of Splendor, I like the way it feels on my head!

Razing Eyebrows

Marlene Barger

Gray hair is a crown of glory; it is gained by living a godly life.
—Proverbs 16:31 NLT

God spoke to me one day while I plucked my eyebrows. Yep, right there in my bedroom as I perched on the edge of the bed, gripping a magnifying mirror in one hand and tweezers in the other. God can, after all, talk to us anywhere at anytime about anything.

So, what did He want to talk to me about? My eyebrows! And my response to His answer to prayer. While I hadn't prayed specifically about my eyebrows, I had talked to God about my hair. I thought it was contributing to a problem I faced at the time: I attracted too much attention from African bachelors who fancied themselves as my prospective suitors. I was a thirty-something missionary serving in the country of Niger Republic. While half the girls in Niger are married by their sixteenth birthday, I was still within the age-range of a potential bride, albeit a comparatively old bride.

For me, however, marriage was out of the question. I have the gift of singleness, a gift I'd discovered a decade before. I stopped dating as soon as I understood that this is how God would have me live my life. I take my commitment to singleness as seriously as couples take their vows to monogamy. In other words, I wasn't looking for a husband.

"If only I had gray hair," I reasoned, "these fellows would leave me alone. They'd take their affections elsewhere and I could concentrate better on my ministry." So that's what I prayed for—gray hair.

It wasn't long before I noticed those lovely white strands appearing amidst the brown on the top of my head. My crown of glory was becoming visible, and was I ever grateful!

So what was the problem with my eyebrows? While I was happy with the crown glistening atop my head, I was less enchanted by the white streaks in my eyebrows. One by one, I meticulously eliminated them.

Just as I was giving the final tug on yet another white eyebrow, God spoke: "I thought you wanted gray hair."

"I do, Lord," I replied, surprised that He would even bring up the subject.

"Then why are you plucking them out of your eyebrows?"

God really does number the hairs on my head! And He wanted to know why I was yanking out the very ones I'd prayed for. Was I really serious about my request for gray hair? Did I think I could somehow improve on God's provision? Who in her right mind would pray for gray hair and not expect gray eyebrows?

I've been tested by God before and, frankly, this was more like a pop quiz. But it was a quiz deserving of answers. I took this time to reaffirm my commitment both to gray hair and to singleness. God's answers to my prayers are always perfect; they don't need my modifications. And gray eyebrows really do go better with gray hair.

Ten years later, my hair is still not completely gray, but now young African bachelors call me "Aunty" or "Mama." And my singleness is often a starting point for sharing my faith in this mostly-Muslim country. When asked the question, "Why aren't you married?" I tell about this gift, how it allows me to concentrate more on loving and serving God, and why this is important for eternity.

Whether God takes us through times of hard testing or sends us a pop quiz, He's drawing us deeper into our relationship with Him. Becoming closer to God—that's certainly worth a bushel full of gray eyebrows.

Part 14
Travel/Road Trips

Café Olé!

Lilly Allison

Even if I am unskilled in speaking, yet I am not unskilled in knowledge. I know what I am talking about.
—2 Corinthians 11:6 AMP

Paris. The city of lights. The city of love. The city of . . . coffee? Yep. Coffee with milk to be exact. Here I was, speechless, sitting in a picturesque sidewalk café, staring at my coffee.

During my junior year of college, I decided that if I spent the summer in Europe, I'd get fluent and be a better candidate for a bilingual job after graduation. So I convinced a friend to backpack across the continent with me.

We started out in London, and then headed for Belgium. There we stopped at a café in Brussels to eat our first real European meal. The waiter walked up to us and said, "Café Olé." Being timid, I nodded and pointed at things on the menu. We listened to conversations around us as we drank coffee and ate our meal.

The next day, at a different café, once again we were greeted with "Café Olé?" I put it in my memory bank as a potential foreign phrase. My French teacher had said I'd pick up certain phrases, and that I should listen for colloquialisms. Again we ordered, drank coffee, and ate a delicious meal.

I was gaining confidence in my ability to speak with the locals, and started talking more. On the third day, when a third waiter greeted us with "Café Olé," it dawned on me that this must be a colloquialism. So I said it back to him. He smiled. We got our meal, and coffee, which I figured must be a European perk.

I knew that in Italian, "Prego" was a blanket statement for please, sorry, excuse me, etc., so I figured "Café Olé" was the French equivalent. From then on I walked confidently into cafés and said, "Café Olé." They'd smile and nod and say, "Café Olé" with the same enthusiasm that I used and brought me that ever-present coffee. I couldn't wait to tell my French teacher how well I was doing.

As we worked our way across Europe, I started saying "Café Olé" to more people. Everyone seemed to understand it, and people kept giving me coffee. If people ignored me, I dismissed it as their obviously not knowing the latest slang. I even taught the uncultured people in the hostels that this was the latest phrase.

Ten weeks and thirteen countries later, I was using "Café Olé" everywhere. In Paris, I fell off a bus. A man caught me and said, "Fait attencion" (pay attention), and I said, "Café Olé." I said it when I boarded a bus; I said it for good-bye. I was really into that phrase, but I never noticed that only waiters said it back to me. I thought I was so cool, knowing the latest phrase.

During the last week of our trip, we were eating baguettes and jam for meals, and still getting coffee all the time. I was tired of all this coffee and longed for a Coke, but because we were low on funds, we stuck with the ever-present free coffee. The night before we left Paris, we wandered around the *Champs Elysees* then splurged on dinner at a lovely café near the *Seine*. I was reading the menu out loud, and the exact moment the waiter walked up and said "Café Olé," I read, "café au lait" out loud. Coffee with milk? I'd just spent ten weeks saying "coffee with milk" in French?

No wonder I got so much coffee. It wasn't a European perk—I was ordering it. No wonder people looked at me strangely. I was saying "coffee with milk" to everyone. No wonder we were broke. Evidently I'd paid for a lot of coffee. The waiter, having heard me say "café au lait," brought me coffee with milk. I sat there stunned at my stupidity, while my friend figured out what happened and doubled over with laughter.

We left the next day and, on the plane, I realized that even though I'd made a mistake, I had talked to people. Total strangers. I'd been shy and timid, but knowing that little phrase gave me the ability to approach people. I had conversations with people all over Europe, most of whom probably started out thinking I was a crazy American with a coffee addiction.

I also know a little phrase in English that gives me the ability to approach people: "Jesus loves you!" I know that phrase is right, and I know what it means. I may not use all the correct theological terminology while I talk abut Jesus, but I do know what I'm talking about, because I know what Jesus did for me.

In Europe, "Café Olé" gave me confidence to talk to people, even though I didn't really know what I was saying. Jesus gives me inner confidence, a boldness to witness—and I know exactly what I'm saying.

My Noncrisis

Carolyn Brooks

*Don't worry about anything; instead, pray about every-
thing; tell God your needs and don't forget to thank him
for the answers.*

—Philippians 4:6 TLB

Whenever I speak for Christian Women's Clubs, I usually travel by car. On one such occasion, I had a four-hour drive from my home in Bedford, Texas, near Dallas, to speak in Houston. My usual routine is to leave the house hours before any normal human being would think it necessary; my internal time clock dictates that for me to be on time, I must arrive about an hour before I'm scheduled to speak.

Somehow, on this particular occasion, I had yet to leave at my usual time. I felt my blood pressure rising as I became increasingly tense and stressed. About two hours into the trip, I stopped at a convenience store for a rest-room break and to buy a cup of coffee. I sprang out of the car and, since I planned to carry out the cup of coffee, I decided to leave my purse in the trunk. I left the car door open, walked to the rear of the car, unlocked the trunk, and placed my purse inside the trunk. Then, without thinking, I dropped my car keys into my purse and closed the trunk!

I immediately panicked. I'd just locked my keys in the trunk! I ran inside to the cashier, and explained my crisis. I asked her if she knew a local locksmith, and she made a telephone call. "Someone will be here in about ten minutes," she said.

I returned to my car, where I checked my watch every thirty seconds, and constantly swiveled my head in every direction, looking for the locksmith. He soon arrived, and I, with big eyes and much gesturing, explained my crisis to him. He was a big burly guy, with a traditional Texas size cowboy hat and an even bigger Texas drawl.

He scratched his head, and thought for a minute. Then he walked back to his truck. In a few minutes, he hollered to me, "What year is your car?"

I hollered back, "Nineteen-ninety-nine!"

He scratched his head again, and then walked over to my side of the car, leaned inside, and pressed the trunk release.

To my utter amazement, the trunk popped opened! The locksmith looked me square in the eye, and didn't say a word. I immediately said, "Well . . . there you go!"

I'm sure he must have thought something very biblical, like what we find in Luke 8:35: "Be clothed and in your right mind, lady!"

Embarrassed, and feeling obligated to give him a Texas-size tip, I reached into my purse and handed him twenty dollars. He left, and as I sat in my car, my face still red from embarrassment, I said, "Thank You, Lord," and continued on my way.

Isn't it just like us to respond this way? In a crisis, we panic, look to others for help and advice, fret and fidget—and then we pray. Perhaps if I'd prayed first that day, I'd have calmed down, and a solution would have filtered through to my brain. Still, I'm thankful that my blunder cost me only some embarrassment—and twenty dollars!

Freeway Frenzy

Elaine Hardt

God has not given us a spirit of fear, but of power and of love and of a sound mind.

—2 Timothy 1:7 NKJV

The traffic was getting on my nerves. Me, the woman of faith, was becoming a basket case. My husband, Don, and I had set out in June to drive to Spokane, Washington.

For hundreds of miles, Don, with stoic resolve, sat behind the wheel, while I sat beside him and gritted my teeth. At first I suffered in silence, then I began to complain. "I've never seen such rude people and such risky driving."

All along the interstate, people seemed to be in a hurry and in a bad mood. When we left enough room between our vehicle and the one ahead, some joker would pull into the space. Everyone was following too closely, and the whole scene was a freeway frenzy.

I just couldn't close my eyes—or my mouth. I wondered out loud, "Why did we decide to drive?"

Don reminded me, "Because we need a car when we get to Spokane."

True . . . how would we get around the city to see our children and grandchildren? How would we get to the mall for serious shopping with the teens, and do all that other important stuff they'd planned?

We started out each day with a prayer that God would keep us safe and get us to our destination without accident or incident. But as we negotiated the congestion of Salt Lake City, the Lord brought a verse to mind: "God has not given us a spirit of fear, but of power and of love and of a sound mind."

Like a drowning woman, I latched onto that verse and prayed, "Yes, Lord. Do it! Let me live today in Your power, in Your mighty love, and experience the soundness that comes from trusting You."

Glancing up, I saw a gray minivan. A redheaded woman seemed to be yelling at the three kids in the back. The words flew out of my mouth, "I bless you in the Name of Jesus. Lord, help that mom. Have the kids settle down and be agreeable for the rest of her trip."

Instantly, I felt wonderful. A great load of fear had lifted off of my mind. The wonderful revelation of God's grace flooded my heart. I would pronounce the Lord's blessing on every driver on the freeway. Like a generous millionaire, I lavished God's love on innumerable people. The frown lines were replaced by a smile. Right away, I told Don what I was doing, and he agreed. "Keep it up," he said. "We need the Lord's help and protection, and so do they."

Sometimes it seemed like the Lord wanted me to pray in more detail for certain people. For some, I prayed for strength and healing. For others I prayed for a spirit of repentance to come upon them so they would receive Jesus as Savior before it was too late.

We passed a shiny blue Peterbilt that bore an Iowa license and was straining up the mountains in Montana. The Lord impressed me with the idea of praying for the driver's loneliness, along with safety for his family at home. Instead of cringing at how huge his vehicle was and how terrible it would be if he swerved and plowed into us, I was given confidence and a sound mind.

By the time we overtook a white Cadillac limousine out of Idaho Falls, the Lord had even cured me of jealousy. At other times I might have mused on the beautiful home and carefree life I imagined the owners to have. Now, I blessed them: "May you have an awareness of the riches that comes from knowing Christ and a freedom from the entrapment of the world's allurement."

If I'd kept up my whining and worrying I am sure I would've

developed a permanent scowl and my face would have looked like a road map. I might have gotten an ulcer, then who'd test the Mexican food for Don to see if it was too spicy? As it was, my mascara was spared, my smile felt good across my face, and my faith felt stronger inside.

All the way to Spokane I continued with my blessings. Then I kept it up on trips to the mall, the pizza parlor, and all those other important places the teens wanted us to see. And homeward-bound two weeks later—I blessed everyone who came along the highways and roads.

Did God bless each of the people we'd prayed for? I'm positive He did. In John 14:13–14 NIV Jesus says, "And I will do whatever you ask in my name so that the Son may bring glory to the Father. You may ask me for anything in my name and I will do it."

One hot afternoon three weeks later, pulling into our own driveway in Phoenix, we thanked God for a safe trip—all 3,528 miles. Praying for others had saved my sanity, not to mention my marriage. I'd been dispensing blessings, and we'd received some in return. We'd enjoyed our kids, our grandkids, the busy streets of Spokane—and even the mall!

Directionally Challenged

Laurie Copeland

In his heart a man plans his course, but the LORD determines his steps.

—Proverbs 16:9 NIV

Living life directionally challenged is always . . . well . . . interesting. Ask me how many times I've driven around in a parking lot, completely lost. Or the number of times I've walked into the men's room by mistake and didn't notice until I walked out.

My poor husband, the saint, has for twenty years tried to teach me the highways and byways of our hometown. Now he just maps out directions to the grocery store. If I haven't gone there in the last month, I need refreshing. Computers need refreshing, so why not my brain?

Still, at certain times, being geographically challenged can thwart the appearance of being a civilized human being. And I had one of those times not long ago. It happened during one hectic morning. I hadn't yet left my hotel room, and I was already running late. I was supposed to be at a conference where I was to present my idea for a book to an editor. I got dressed only to discover my blouse was missing a button. So much for my planned outfit—a skirt, matching silk blouse, and spiffy yet artsy scarf.

What were my options? This being the last day of the conference, I'd worn all my other clothes. As I scanned the room, my eyes rested upon a heap of something wrinkled on the floor. My traveling clothes would have to do. I didn't have time to iron the outfit—all-cotton lime green pants and blouse with a purple shell.

Ten minutes later, I maneuvered my way out of the elevator, clutching proposals, purse, and that little carry-all-thingy-on-wheels. It's supposed to make carrying all of one's necessities easier, but ends up getting caught in elevator doors. Several three-point turns with my carry-all, and the elevator finally released my wheels and I was off—huffing, puffing, and glowing from perspiration.

The conference had arranged for a shuttle bus to pick up convention attendees and drop them off right at the convention hall's doorstep. But they ran on a tight schedule—if I missed this one, it would be another twenty-minute wait. That wouldn't do, considering my appointment was in fifteen minutes! I bolted out the hotel front door and glanced in the direction I thought the bus should be. It was still there!

As I ran toward the bus, though, it started to roll. I sped up, and sprinted across six lanes of traffic. The wind flapped my green shirt tail wildly behind me and billowed my purple shell in front of me. I must have looked like Barney the Dinosaur.

The bus was in full roll, and like a crazed woman, I ran in front of cars, pulling my cart-on-wheels in one hand and using my other hand to command oncoming traffic to stop. Suddenly, I saw everything as if in slow motion—the riders' open mouths and shocked expressions, the bus driver's confused look, my hand raised to him, commanding him to stop and pick me up. What had gotten into me?

I ran to the door side of the bus, but the driver didn't open the door. He just sat there and looked at me, as if asking, "What could you possibly want?" I motioned for him to open the door, and when he finally did, and I staggered aboard. Except for my huffing and puffing, the bus was unusually quiet. All eyes seemed to be on me while I collapsed in the front seat and tried to catch my breath.

Curiosity got the best of the nice couple seated behind me. "Where are you headed?" the lady asked with an amused smile.

"The convention center," I answered. It was an odd question; weren't we all heading there?

"You're lucky that this bus isn't heading to Albuquerque," he said with a smirk.

"What do you mean?"

"Well, how *did* you know where this bus is headed?"

"It's headed to the convention center, right?"

"Well, yes, but do you always make a habit of flagging buses down in the middle of a street?"

I lay there, sprawled out across two seats, still catching my breath, and realization suddenly dawned on me. This wasn't the bus meant to pick people up from my hotel, but a bus from another hotel a few miles down the road. It was only by coincidence that this bus was going to the convention center!

And I had flagged them down in the middle of the street!

We have a plaque in our house that reminds me, "In his heart a man plans his course, but the LORD determines his steps." This verse from Proverbs 16 crept into my head as I lay there in the front seat of the bus that was going to the convention—not Albuquerque—but God was still in control.

When we walk the Christian walk, we want the Lord to direct our steps. We know that He is going to work in all our circumstances, including our blunders and mishaps. Yes, I've been known to say (quite often), "I wish God would send a note attached to a thunderbolt, telling me what He'd like me to do . . . and I'd do it." But that would be missing God's point—to search His ways, and learn from our trials and situations. We aren't going to live this life error-free. We're meant to learn from our choices, repent, refresh, and renew ourselves in Him.

Learning by trial and error isn't biblical license to mess up on purpose! We need to check our heart-motives. During the process we may not always be getting on the right bus—or always make the right choices. Rather, the process involves praying, learning from our mistakes, then taking the next step. And God will lead us because we all are, in truth, directionally challenged.

Oil Trouble

Faye Landrum

And we know that in all things God works for the good of those who love him.

—Romans 8:28 NIV

O h, my goodness," I said to myself. "I need to send a card!" It was early afternoon when I remembered I hadn't sent a sympathy card to one of the couples in my Sunday school class. His sister had died two days before.

I looked through my cache of cards for one that might express the appropriate sentiments but found nothing appropriate. So I went to the store, bringing along the address and a stamp to help speed the process.

After I purchased the card, addressed the envelope, and affixed the stamp, I went to the post office on my way home. I intended to stop at the drive-by mailbox, but at the last minute, decided that going inside might speed up delivery.

When I came out of the post office, a young man, waved at me. He sat in a blue Ford truck one parking space away from my car. "Do you know your radiator is leaking?" he asked.

"No," I replied. I had no idea I had anything leaking.

I guess the young man felt sorry for me—that's one advantage of being an older female. Anyway, he got out of his truck and came over to inspect my leak.

"That's oil," he said, "not water. If you pop open the hood, I'll take a look inside for you."

I had a little trouble finding the lever that releases the hood—I never pay attention to what's hidden under the engine cover—but I finally got my act together. That was when we discovered the floor of the car's innards was flooded with oil.

"That's not good," the young man quipped.

I probably would've known that without being told.

He reached for the dipstick and checked the oil cylinder. There wasn't a drop of oil on the stick.

"You can't drive the car this way," he said. "You'll burn up the engine. Do you have anyone who can come help you?"

"My son's at home." I fumbled in my purse for my cell phone as my "knight in shining armor" disappeared.

This was one time I was thankful for modern technology—and thankful I was living near my son. I told Gary my problem, and in just a few minutes, he appeared on the scene. He told me which towing company was the best one to call, and we had the car hauled away to a local garage.

The next day, I received the diagnosis that my car's problem was a split O ring. I didn't know until then the car even had an O ring. The garage had done a routine oil change for me a few days before, and they'd apparently overtightened the filter—or something—and that had split the O ring.

A new filter with a healthy O ring solved my problem. I now have my car back in working order, but I continue to be grateful that God puts the right people in the right places at the right times. If I hadn't gone inside the post office to mail my card and left the car in that exact parking space at that exact time, I'd never have known about my oil leak. I could have burned up the engine, ruining my car.

God is gracious. He gives us guidance and protection for everyday problems that might mount up and cripple us. Is it wrong, then, to wish He would send someone to clean up the oil on the garage floor?

Rushin' Roulette

Cindy L. Heflin

Be still, and know that I am God.
—Psalm 46:10 NKJV

I slapped the snooze bar and rolled over for a few more moments of sleep. *It's Saturday, Lord,* I pleaded, as a beam of sunlight pierced the darkened room and poked me in the eye. Heaving a sigh, I threw off the covers and crawled out of bed.

Still slightly comatose, I stumbled past my husband's unpacked luggage and into the shower. While the steamy spray pummeled my scalp, the day's busy schedule swirled inside my head. My need for divine guidance was obvious, so I quickly shot several arrow prayers heavenward. *I'll get to my quiet time a little later, Lord,* I promised.

I pulled on a pair of sweats, dashed downstairs to the kitchen, and pushed a bowl of cereal toward each kid. While they sat at the island crunching on cereal, my husband, Bryant, and I checked our mile-long "to-do" list. After a hectic week of school, sports, and business travel, we knew carving out some family time was important.

"How 'bout a picnic in the park for lunch?" I suggested. My gang was game, but a severe storm in the forecast dampened our outdoor plans. Playing it safe, we opted to catch the newest kid-flick at a nearby cinema. "What if I cook, clean up the house, and finish party preparations," I suggested, "while you shuttle the girls to softball, dance class, and take the dog to the vet. Then we could run errands together, and squeeze the movie in before Grandma's birthday bash."

"Okay, girls. Let's go!" Bryant called as the kids scrambled out the door to our sky-blue Caravan. While he taxied our cherubs all over town, I tackled the chores at home. Fun and frantic! Just an ordinary Saturday—or so it seemed.

The morning evaporated rapidly as I wrapped gifts, layered a lasagna, and mopped a trail of muddy paw prints off the kitchen floor. Time slipped by as I hurried to clean the countertops of clutter—dirty dishes, star-spangled school papers, a slimy science fair project, and a myriad of books. Feeling a twinge of guilt, I thumbed the pages of my daily devotional and placed it on the table with a pile of mail. "Oh, Father!" I said sincerely, "I'll spend time with You as soon as I'm finished." My heart longed for Him, but the clock was ticking.

After crossing each item off my checklist, I made a beeline for the bedroom to change clothes and pop in my contacts. Soon, the honking horn in my driveway jolted my mind—our errands! I scurried from room to room like a squirrel gathering nuts, collecting library books, dry cleaning, and an overdue video. Checking our bedside clock, I glanced at my Bible with a sigh, then hustled out to the van, juggling the load in my arms.

"Just three little errands before the movie, remember?" I panted, and dumped the heap into my lap.

"Awe, Mom!" cried the backseat chorus. My husband cruised down the cul-de-sac as the rushin' roulette continued.

Through the afternoon drizzle, we raced the clock, rushing to finish our rounds before show time. Bryant had just returned after another week of business travel, and we made use of our time between stops, bringing Dad up to speed on family concerns and school activities.

"So, what'd you learn about this week?" he asked each child.

"Stranger-Danger!" said the six-year-old with confidence.

My husband shot a questioning look my way.

"Safety Week at school," I explained with a smile. "First graders read a booklet and learn rules about crossing the street, riding the bus, and avoiding strangers."

The windshield wipers slurped as we cruised the rain-slick streets and continued our "family time." Halfway through an involved conversation, we arrived at the crowded superstore to return the overdue video. Thunder crashed as Bryant parked at the curb by the door and I rushed in with the tape. Lightening crackled and a downpour broke loose. To allow the vehicle behind him access to the entrance, my ever-courteous husband moved ahead. The other driver pulled up and parked his sky-blue Caravan at the curb by the door.

Unaware of this activity, I proceeded through the busy store, straight to the video counter, paid the fee, and headed back. With the grace and speed of a gazelle, I swept by the bargain aisle, squelching my tendency to browse, and maneuvered my way through the maze of shoppers in the checkout line. I could almost taste the popcorn as I exited the store in sixty seconds—or so.

Reaching the van, I flung open the door, dropped into my seat, and continued our discussion, never skipping a beat. *Why isn't he driving on to the cinema?* I wondered. Then I noticed something rolling around at my feet. Puzzled, I picked up a fuzzy, fluorescent green, tennis ball. "Where'd this come from?" I asked. Confusion furrowed my brow as I casually tossed the ball over the backseat—and turned to my husband for his reply. Sheer terror overwhelmed me when I saw a strange man seated behind the wheel of the van!

Realizing Bryant and the girls were missing, my mind wildly raced through all the horrible possibilities. I didn't know whether to pray first—or scream! A dead silence hung in the air. Totally numb, I froze with fear like a deer caught in the headlights. Come to think of it, the guy looked pretty shocked too.

Staring out the windshield, I saw another blue minivan parked straight ahead. Without a word, I bolted out the door and dashed through the rain down the sidewalk. Relief and embarrassment washed over me as I realized my family was safe inside *our* blue minivan!

They were safe—and completely oblivious to my blunder. While catching my breath, my heart still pounding, I described in detail what had just happened. Bryant listened, an astonished expression on his face, then suddenly we exploded with laughter. As tears rolled down our cheeks, we laughed until our sides ached, and wondered if that poor man was amused too, or just plain shocked.

"Mommy!" my first grader cried. With fear in her voice and tears in her eyes, she was visibly shaken. "Don't you remember? It's not *safe* to get in a stranger's car."

After consoling our daughter, we thanked God for His divine protection, and raced to the cinema.

My nerves calmed as I collapsed into a seat in the darkened theater. Since I'd already experienced the action and adventure of a four-star movie, God finally had my undivided attention. *No more rushin' roulette for me, Lord,* I sighed. Then He reminded, "Be still, my child— and know that I am God." At last my heart overflowed with the peace of His presence.

Sitting at the Feet of Jesus

Florence Littauer

Jesus met them and greeted them. And they came up and took hold of His feet and worshiped Him.
—Matthew 28:9 NASB

Each of us had brought enough clothes to outfit the characters on a soap opera. Nance, Jim, Carolyn, and I had arrived at the airport in Rio De Janeiro, eager to embark on our cruise. We'd found our way to baggage claim, but there were no baggage handlers, so we lugged our overstuffed bags onto rented trolleys.

But we looked forward to a comfortable ride to the ship; Nance had made arrangements for a limousine to pick us up at the airport and drive us to the pier. We looked in vain for a uniformed chauffeur to greet us, but no one stepped forward to claim us.

While we pushed our possessions around, looking for a chauffeur with a sign bearing the ship's name, Nance called the ship's phone number. She got an answering machine message in Miami, saying it was too early in the morning to talk with a real person. Driven to the curb in despair, we found an abundance of smiling taxi drivers who spoke only Portuguese. Using sign language, Nance got us two vans, one for us and one for our collective luggage.

We were hot and disheveled as we dragged ourselves into the glamorous lobby entrance, and more closely resembled the cast of *The*

Beverly Hillbillies than *The Bold and the Beautiful*. Nance investigated why no one had met us. She found out that two male cruise passengers had taken our limousine. The driver had been assigned to meet and greet four people—two men and two women—but apparently hadn't noticed the absence of two women.

We'd hardly unpacked when it was time for our first tourist trip—to the monumental statue of Jesus atop Sugar Loaf mountain. There He towers, arms-outstretched, protecting the city of Rio below. Looking forward to a spiritual experience, we hired a tour guide with a minibus. She wove through the city traffic to the base of the mountain, avoiding the plethora of natives selling Jesus trinkets.

We then boarded a red cable car that wound to the mountain top. This was a frightening experience as the car surged and groaned its way along rock ledges. I was sure it was only our prayers that kept it from tumbling over the edge. Twice we met red cars coming down, and we had to pull to a siding and let them hurtle by.

We'd been told to wear light clothes, but by the time we got to the top—8,000 feet up—the weather had turned cold, and we were freezing. The huge statue of Jesus (think Statue of Liberty) was still way above us. Escalators took tourists up to the precipice, but the electricity had been turned off as a thunderstorm approached. We were forced, by the surge of the crowds, to walk up a series of stairs. There was nowhere to sit or get away from the pouring rain and hurricane winds. I took one good look at Jesus and turned back down the slippery, metal stairs, hoping that He would protect my descent. I recited "Lo, I am with you always—even unto the ends of the earth." And I was at the end!

By now, about fifty people huddled against a cliff for protection, waiting for a cable car to come back. Only two benches were available, and our guide got them for the four of us, making us instantly unpopular. Soon word came that a large tree had fallen across the tracks, and our red car couldn't come up. Panic swept over us as we imagined staying on this mountain forever or pictured ourselves being blown off.

We tried humor as we huddled at the foot of Jesus, reciting bits of old church music—Jesus wants me for a sunbeam; safe in the arms of the Savior; brighten the corner where you are. Nance came up with a Texas cowboy song, "I don't care if it rains or freezes as long as I'm in the arms of Jesus." She added, "The higher I tease my hair the closer I am to heaven."

Our humor was dissolving into fear when our guide signaled us to quietly follow her. We sneaked around a rock ledge—and there, thank God, was a taxi! The driver had brought someone up, and he wanted many times the usual fare to take us down. We happily paid to get back to the ship and our long awaited cruise.

Later, as I lounged on a chaise in the sun, I reflected on our trip to Sugar Loaf. A tree on the tracks had placed us in a dilemma. How many times has it happened? We know where we're going, we know what God wants us to do, and we know how we're going to get there. But we let a "tree on the tracks" stop us.

Next time I face an impediment, I'll remember sitting at the feet of Jesus, where God provided a way around that tree. And I'll remember that if God wants me to go somewhere, He will provide a way to get there.

Part 15

Sports

In the Zone

Trish Porter

*It's not that I've already reached the goal or have already
completed the course. But I run to win that which Jesus
Christ has already won for me. Brothers and sisters, I can't
consider myself a winner yet. This is what I do: I don't
look back, I lengthen my stride, and I run straight toward
the goal to win the prize that God's heavenly call offers in
Christ Jesus.*

—Philippians 3:12–14 GW

I'd planned for it. Trained for it. Worked toward it. The day had finally come. My family was there. My boyfriend was there. It was my
moment of glory.

It was October 1988, Seoul, Korea, and I was a member of the U.S.
Olympic Team. The high jump was my event. Electricity charged the
air as each athlete reached for "the zone"—the place where everything
lines up: you're well rested, the weather is in your favor, and you know
you're on top of the world. I was in the zone the day I made the Olympic team, and what an incredible, amazing, wonderful feeling that had
been. What could be better than being in the zone and making the
Olympic team? Being in the zone at the Olympics and winning!

Now I was here. I needed to take good care of myself, so I was in my
room, resting up, having a great dream. From my deep sleep, I was

sure I heard knocking, heavy-handed and insistent. With effort I pulled myself out of dreamland, and then reality slammed me in the face. "Oh, Noooo! What time is it?" I'd overslept. My alarm didn't go off, and my coach was pounding on my door.

With a major adrenaline rush, I jumped out of bed and opened the door. I was freaking out. I'd slept through the Olympics! I screamed at my couch, "Did I miss it? Tell me, I didn't."

My coach was a stabilizing force. Putting his hands on my shoulders, he looked me in the eyes and said, "Trish . . . stop . . . take a deep breath. It will be okay. Get yourself ready."

For me, getting myself ready meant getting up several hours early, drinking my coffee (so I can go to the bathroom), eating oatmeal (so I can go to the bathroom), shower, shave my legs, etc.

I'd done none of those things. My routine was thrown off. All I ate was a Nutri-grain bar on the bus, and I couldn't go to the bathroom.

We arrived at the grounds, and I discovered I'd forgotten my full sweat suit, and it was freezing outside. Great. Now I was cold *and* constipated; I need to be warm and loose when I compete.

Trying to get prepped, I jogged around the track when four-time gold medalist, Daly Thompson, zipped by me, but not so fast that I didn't hear his comment—a rumor about me was circulating around the Olympic track. I was unnerved, self-conscious, and my concentration was shot.

My self-talk, went something like this: "What day is it? Oh, yes. I'm competing at the Olympics. That's it."

Finally it was time to jump, and all of the athletes lined up and were announced to the crowd. I scanned the group of athletes preparing for the high jump. I was one of the two shortest. *Ugh! What am I doing?* This was the high jump—an event where you have to jump over a high bar. It helps to be tall.

This was my first big international competition. I'd been to Canada for a few meets, but this was Seoul, Korea. Women from all over the world stood with me—and I was short.

My turn. I headed for the bar. "I think I'm too far." I moved up. "No! I'm too close. I need to move back." I was so wrapped up in trying to win, in trying for what I wanted, I didn't even hear my coach telling me what to do—the same coach who got me to the Olympics in the first place.

I didn't jump well. Defeated, I left the mat. Pat, a male member of the U.S. Olympic Track and Field Team offered me comfort. Just when it seemed nothing else could go wrong, my boyfriend—of five years—saw Pat give me a hug. Outraged that another man touched me, my boyfriend stormed off, threw the engagement ring he'd planned to give me into the river, and left Korea.

My family took me to lunch, where they told me that my mom's health wasn't good, and she needed to go home immediately. My goals, my dreams, my hopes. All gone—and it was only one o'clock.

It took years to recover. My mom got better, Pat and I got married and now have two beautiful children, and I've been coaching track and field for a local high school.

One day a girlfriend called. "Why don't you train for the National Masters?" she asked. Hmmmm. Did I want to enter competition again? It had been such a hard end. I prayed about my decision, and I felt God telling me to go for it—for His glory. I started to train, but it was much harder now, fifteen years later and at forty years old.

I won a few smaller meets heading up to the big event. Then August 10, 2003, arrived. My family and friends were with me in Eugene, Oregon, and I was wearing a jersey with the number J 4 J—Jump for Jesus. It was a totally different day than that one fifteen years ago. I was in the zone.

I'm now the world record holder in the women's age forty to forty-five high jump and the National Masters champion 2003, high jump age thirty-five to forty-nine. This time, winning wasn't my goal, my hope, or my dream. I was jumping for Jesus.

My efforts have paid off. I've been interviewed by local and national media and had the opportunity to talk about Jesus from this platform. I have the ears of the teens I coach, and they listen to my witness. I remind them that in everything they do, the focus isn't our own goals but God's plan for our lives. My message is a simple one—Jump with joy, jump for Jesus.

Learning to Receive

Raelene Searle

It is more blessed to give than to receive.
—Acts 20:35 NASB

Chip and I really enjoyed serving in our church. We especially enjoyed giving in any way we could. We both struggled, however, with the idea of receiving. I mean, doesn't the Bible say it is better to give than to receive? We tried not to get into a position to need anything from others. But it was time for us to learn a lesson.

It was a beautiful sunny Southern California day. A handful of adult chaperones—including Chip—and our church's youth group headed off for a fun outing to a local water park.

One of the greatest fears of adults who are in charge of a group of teens is losing one of them or having one of them get injured. By late afternoon, though, all youth were accounted for and no injuries had been reported—so far.

As their time was coming to an end, some of the kids wanted to see Chip take a ride down the biggest slide in the park. He'd already ridden it several times, but they wanted to see it for themselves.

The waterslide is a tall black tube, and while standing at the top of it, you can't see the bottom. The rider shoots through a dark tunnel, not knowing when the big splash at the end would come. At the bottom, a lifeguard clears the slide and pool area before the life guard at the top sends the next rider down.

Chip lay down, crossed his right leg over his left, and then was sent flying down the slide by the lifeguard. When he reached the end, instead of a splash, he felt a big "thud" with his left foot. It seems the lower lifeguard had not cleared the tunnel of the previous rider before giving the okay to send the next one down. Chip ended up plowing into the back of a poor teenage girl. During the slide, her shirt had wrapped around her, and she'd been sitting on the edge of the slide, fixing it.

Not willing to show his pain, he simply hobbled away. For the next hour he limped around the park, avoiding any more challenges and any questions about his new walk.

Although he was still limping badly, Chip felt comfortable about piling a bunch of kids into the motor home, dropping them off at church, and heading home on the freeway during rush hour.

When he arrived home, he hobbled through our front door, mumbling that he'd had a good day. The limping was nothing to worry about—we had a barbecue to put on that evening. I couldn't convince him to go to the urgent care center.

The pain got worse, so Chip sat on the back porch with his leg propped up while his friend Mike tended the barbecue. I was in the kitchen preparing the food when I heard a ruckus. I looked out, and Mike had the garden hose, trying to get a very angry skunk out of the yard. Chip flailed around trying to get himself out of the chair and out of the way of the spraying skunk.

The next morning, the pain was still intense, but Chip was sure everything would be okay. By noon, I had him convinced he should go get x-rays.

I stayed in the waiting area while Chip was wheeled into the exam room. The next time I saw my husband, he was being wheeled out in tears, holding the x-rays of not one, but two breaks in his lower left leg. So off we went to Orthopedics to get a cast on his leg.

Chip got wrapped in a bright blue cast all the way up to his hip and was handed crutches. As we left the building, he stumbled and fell forward. Others around rushed to help him up, but he insisted he was able to take care of himself. What a frustrating time he had, learning to walk on those crutches.

Oh, did I mention that Chip had called in to work sick that day so he could go on this outing? Now he had to see his boss with his medical excuse to be off work for the next week. His upper management never commented on the incident. They, in fact, enjoyed smirking at Chip's unfortunate outcome.

The next several weeks were humbling. God taught us that by refusing to allow others to give to us, we were robbing them of the joy of giving—the same joy we had when we gave of ourselves.

First, Chip had to accept assistance and a ride to and from work each day. Second, he could no longer do regular outdoor chores. A single friend, who hated outdoor work, came by regularly to mow the lawn and do other maintenance. Chip couldn't stand to have Ric doing everything, and he'd go outside and stand on his crutches and watch—like his presence helped. Third, the pastor gave us some money; Chip couldn't drive a car so he was unable to take weekend call and earn the overtime we needed for our budget.

It's unfortunate that the lessons we most need to learn usually come from being knocked down so that God can get our attention. As much as those eight weeks in a cast and on crutches were difficult for Chip, we were truly blessed by the love of our church and the help offered by so many. We've learned so much about how the church was truly meant to operate. Receiving is still a little hard—old ways are sometimes difficult to get past. But we experienced a new understanding. We learned of the joy others feel when they give, and we learned that there's joy in receiving too.

Manly Man

Craig Sundheimer

*Just as our bodies have many parts and each part has a
special function, so it is with Christ's body. We are all parts
of his one body, and each of us has different work to do.
And since we are all one body in Christ, we belong to each
other, and each of us needs all the others.*

—Romans 12:4–5 NLT

From my position in left center field, I looked to home plate as our
pitcher readied his next throw. I took a deep breath of cool evening
air and slapped my glove with my right hand. These church-league
softball games were a welcome, relaxing break from the daily routine.
I looked forward to the exercise, competition, and fellowship with my
teammates and opponents.

I watched as the pitch arced high into the air and down toward the
plate. The batter swung, and with a loud "ting!" from the aluminum
bat, the ball shot over the shortstop's head, a line drive heading to my
left. I sprinted to the spot where the ball was headed, knowing I could
make the catch before it hit the ground. I stretched out my left hand,
and reached my right hand over to cover the ball. Since I was running
at full speed, I wanted to make certain I covered the ball so it wouldn't
pop out and cause an error.

At the last split-second, the flight of the ball veered slightly to my

right and struck directly on the tip of my right index finger—snap!—
before landing solidly in my glove. A pain shot like a bolt of electricity
through my arm down to my elbow. My teammates cheered me for a
nice running catch, but as I reached into my glove for the ball, I could
only concentrate on the pain in my forefinger. I tried to bend it, but
the joint just below the nail wouldn't move. I should have taken myself out of the game, but I was the leadoff batter for our next inning.
Despite the pain, I really wanted to bat.

I dropped my glove in the dugout, grabbed my favorite bat, and
stepped toward the plate. The thought entered my mind that this was
a bad idea—I couldn't close my forefinger around the bat because of
the swelling in the first joint. But there were still several innings yet to
play, and it was my turn to bat. In my competitive, male frame of
mind, I just wanted to continue. It was only a small joint. How bad
could this be? So I walked to the plate, took my stance, hoisted the bat
over my shoulder, and eyed the pitcher.

He threw the pitch. As it dropped toward me, I knew immediately
that I could drive it into right field and use my speed for a double,
maybe a triple. I stepped forward and swung the bat. CRACK!

When my bat met the ball, I groaned with pain. Fire seared my
right arm. The ball fell into right field, but I could only stumble toward first base, holding my throbbing right hand with my left. Arriving at first base after what seemed like an eternity, my competitive,
male frame of mind now assured me that I was unable to continue. I
called time out and dragged myself to the bench. One of my teammates looked at my swollen finger and said, "I'm driving you home."
There my wife, a registered nurse, could make an educated diagnosis
and determine what to do next.

As I walked through the door, Cheryl took a look at my finger. It
had turned strange shades of blue around the joint and under the
nail. I replayed how I'd made the catch—even while sustaining the
injury—how badly it hurt, but how I was able to bear the pain, and
still take my turn at bat. But after hitting the single to right field, my
hand was *really* hurting.

Anticipating warmth and sympathy, I was surprised by her piercing eye—what I've come to regard as . . . "The Look." My manly bubble quickly burst. "Now, let me get this straight," she said. "You hurt your finger making the catch but *still* chose to bat?"

It didn't sound quite that stupid when it happened, but I had no choice but to agree with her.

That's when she dropped the bomb. "It's probably broken, but since you're man enough to bat after breaking it, I'm sure you're man enough to wait until tomorrow morning to go to the doctor. It'll be less expensive than a visit to the emergency room."

"W-what?" I gasped through my increasing pain, hoping my injured tone would get her to change her mind. But I knew she was right, although it would go against the code of manliness for me to admit it.

That had to be the worst night of my life. My finger throbbed and ached constantly, and I couldn't find a comfortable sleeping position. Cheryl, in her benevolence, had given me a pain pill that was *supposed* to provide some relief. Despite my tossing and turning, she seemed to sleep quite contentedly, with what appeared to be a wry smile across her lips. I know she's not a vengeful person, but she seemed to take great joy in teaching me a lesson—whatever it was supposed to be. The sunrise couldn't come quickly enough for me, and after the long night we finally went to the doctor.

I ultimately had surgery on the first joint in order to retain range of movement—enough for writing, typing, and playing the guitar. For weeks afterward, I was under doctor's orders not to use my right hand so I wouldn't damage the pins that had been placed into the joint. Every small task, like trying to manipulate a knife or fork, was an adventure. It seemed unfair that an injury to such a small joint could disrupt my entire life.

It made me think about the biblical comparison of the physical body to the Body of Christ. As believers, we're all important. In the family of God, all people—not just the noticeable ones—have an important role to play. Just as my small-joint injury kept me from operating at an optimum level, when one member of the Body is injured, the entire Body is affected. We must work together for healing in order to operate efficiently and effectively.

The finger healed, and although I have reduced range of motion in the joint, I'm still able to work and play as before. The surgical scar below my fingernail, though, is a continual reminder, not only of my competitive male frame of mind, but of the importance of all parts of the body working together.

Now I'm more careful when I play sports and exercise because, while I'm grateful that I'm married to a nurse, I never again want to experience "The Look"!

The Lady with the Hose

Kathy Boyle

Everyone who drinks this water will be thirsty again, but whoever drinks the water I give him will never thirst. Indeed, the water I give him will become in him a spring of water welling up to eternal life.

—John 4:13–14 NIV

The day didn't start out very promising. It was Sunday, April 18, 1999, and a rebelling stomach awakened me around 4:00 A.M. I made a trip to the bathroom about every half an hour until 6:30 A.M. "This is *not* good, Lord! The handbell choir is playing this morning and I *have* to be there to play my part! And this is the day of the 10K CROP Walk for Hunger. I've spent a month rounding up sponsors to help raise money for this worthy cause. I *have* to be able to do this walk!"

Do it, I did. The walk started out fine, and I was okay for the first mile, but . . .

"It's hot out here, Lord! It was supposed to be a lot cooler today. You know how I hate heat. I can't carry enough water to keep myself hydrated. Please help me to take one step at a time."

Then I came to *the hill!* It went straight up with no end in sight. The top just disappeared into heaven.

"I can do this! No problem."

But it didn't take long to realize I couldn't do it. Once the cool ocean breeze disappeared and the water in my system evaporated, I was in trouble. I tried drinking Gatorade and it, too, couldn't fulfill my needs. The stomach cramps were coming back, and I was literally losing it.

"Lord, I think I'm going to pass out—maybe die! Please don't let either happen."

I'm sure my two walking buddies, Kay and Dawn, thought I was going to pass out. Although my mind said, *Quit!* I made it to the top of the hill with the encouragement of Kay and Dawn, prayers from friends and family—and the lady with the hose.

There she was when I needed her. She was watering the grass in the heat of the day. Didn't her mother tell her that water evaporates most quickly between 10:00 A.M. and 6:00 P.M.? She let me use her hose, and I literally drenched myself in water—cool water. What an answer to prayer!

As we said our good-byes, the lady with the hose smiled; actually, I think it was more of a chuckle. She probably thought that I'd never make it to the finish line, but I wondered if she realized how the Lord used her to give life back to my body and spirit.

I know one thing, I slowed down Kay and Dawn, but they never left me. The Lord answered my (our) prayers and, although the event raised money for the hungry, the Lord also supplied *me* with some food for thought:

1. He gave me friends, people who came along side of me when I felt I couldn't take another step. And someone else was with us that day too—Jesus.
2. The Lord uses us when we're willing. He took my focus off myself and my pride and placed it on completing the walk for the hungry. The stomach cramps I had, due to lack of water and food, allowed me to feel their hunger for several hours. Although I knew I could eat within two hours, some do not have that luxury.
3. The Lord provided a gift. The lady with the hose seemed so out of place on a hot afternoon, but the Lord placed her there to quench my thirst. The water in my water bottle couldn't sustain

me, but the lady's hose rejuvenated me. In a similar way, when nothing else can quench my dry spirit, God supplies "a flowing fountain" that "gives eternal life." He asks me to seek Him and have faith and He will supply what I *need*. He is the only One to quench my thirst, literally and spiritually.

The Lord heard and answered my simple prayers. I didn't think I'd make it up that hill, but God, in His infinite wisdom, used the experience. He helped me see that He is in control and that He is with me every step of the way. All I have to do is take one step at a time and He will take me—or maybe even carry me—across that finish line.

Contributors

In addition to the contact information provided below,
all contributors can also be reached at
HappyShallow@kregel.com.

⌘

Lilly Allison lives and writes in Irving, Texas. She is married, has two children, and can be reached at lattelal@yahoo.com.

Nancy C. Anderson (www.NCAwrites.com) is the author of *The "Greener Grass" Syndrome: Growing Affair-Proof Hedges Around Your Marriage* (Kregel Publications, 2005). Nancy lives in Southern California with her husband and their teenage son.

Martin Babb lives in Springfield, Tennessee, and is an associate pastor and published author. He may be reached at mkbabb@bellsouth.net.

Marlene Bagnull (www.writehisanswer.com) is an author, speaker, and director of the Colorado and Greater Philadelphia Christian Writers Conferences. She and her husband, Paul, live in a Philadelphia suburb. They have three grown children and are expecting their first grandbaby.

Marlene Barger lives in Niamey, the capital of Niger Republic in West Africa, where she serves as a tentmaker missionary and directs the activities of Partnership Niger, a nonprofit organization. She can be reached at marlene_barger@yahoo.com.

Jennie Bishop is the author of the best-selling children's book *The Princess and the Kiss*. She lives in the thumb of Michigan with her husband and three daughters. Visit her website at www.jenniebishop.com.

Barb Loftus Boswell is a writer—*Chicken Soup for the Bride's Soul*—and abstinence educator from Aston, Pennsylvania. You may contact Barb at Bx2Boswell@aol.com.

Lanita Bradley Boyd, a freelance writer living in Fort Thomas, Kentucky, is a contented wife, mother of two outstanding adult children, and grandmother to one brilliant granddaughter. Lanita can be reached through www.lanitaboyd.com.

Kathy Boyle (onlyHeisable@yahoo.com) is an up-and-coming writer in the Christian community. Living in Torrance, California, Kathy is a mature single woman who serves on her church council.

Lauren Littauer Briggs (www.Laurenbriggs.com), speaker and author of *The Art of Helping*, gives her audience confidence to bring comfort to hurting hearts. She lives in Redlands, California, with her husband, Randy, and three adult sons.

Elaine Britt is grateful to God for the call to be an author, speaker, wife, and mother of two boys. She resides contentedly in Alabama.

Carolyn Brooks (www.carolynbrooks.com) is a speaker, coauthor of three books, and consultant. She has appeared on national Christian television, has spoken on radio, and is a former model. Carolyn is a single mother and resides in Houston, Texas.

Jan Bryan is a dynamic and powerful Bible teacher, speaking to women even internationally! She can be reached at My2Roads@yahoo.com. She lives with her husband, Peter, in Shrewsbury, Massachusetts. They have five children and four grandchildren.

Sherri Buerkle is a freelance writer, an editor, and a writing instructor. She and her husband live in Albuquerque, New Mexico, with their five surprisingly beautiful daughters.

Tim Burns, author, speaker, and teacher (www.inkwellcommunication .com), is a single parent from Grand Ledge, Michigan. Tim's writing encourages and equips believers toward becoming "vessels of honor, ready for any good purpose" (2 Tim. 2:20–21).

Jennifer Moore Cason writes and speaks to inspire, encourage, and instruct Christians as they fulfill God's calling for their lives. She and her husband, Frank, live in Dacula, Georgia. Learn more about Jennifer's ministry at www.jencason.com.

Kitty Chappell, speaker and author, lives near Phoenix with her husband, Jerry. They have two grown children and one granddaughter. For information about her recently released book *Sins of a Father: Forgiving the Unforgivable,* visit www.kittychappell.com.

Jan Coleman is an author, conference speaker, mom, and gramma to five. When she's not fishing, she's working on her next book in Auburn, California. Get more of the scoop on Jan at www.jancoleman.com.

Laurie Copeland (www.lauriecopeland.com) is a speaker, humorist, actress, and coauthor of the book *The Groovy Chicks Road Trip to Peace.* She lives in Florida with her husband, John, and their daughter, Kailey.

Lisa Copen is author of *Mosaic Moments: Devotions for the Chronically Ill.* She lives in San Diego, California, with her family.

Verna Davis is a speaker, author, minister's wife, mother, grandmother, newspaper columnist, and CLASS grad (of course!). With her husband and their cocker spaniel, Zacchaeus, Verna lives in central Indiana, but you can visit her at www.VernaDavis.com.

Evelyn W. Davison is a television talk show host, businesswoman, publisher, and the author of hundreds of newspaper and magazine articles. She is a grandmother and the wife of Van Ed Davison, a realtor in Austin, Texas.

Judy Dippel, author of the book *Refreshing Hope in God,* is a speaker, wife, mother, and grandmother. She lives in Eugene, Oregon, where she enjoys a variety of outdoor activities. Visit her at www.judydippel.com.

Prior to her death in 2003, **Neva Donald** was a big fan of CLASS. We are honored to include her work here.

Patsy Dooley is an author, a funny and inspirational speaker, and a certified CLASServices Personality Instructor. She lives in Iowa Park, Texas and has three children, twelve grandchildren, and two great-grandchildren. For information, visit pat2funnyd@aol.com.

Dena J. Dyer is the author of *Grace for the Race: Devotionals for Busy Moms* (Barbour, Fall 2004). She makes her home in Granbury, Texas, with her husband and two sons. For more information, visit www.denadyer.com.

Patricia Evans (www.EmptyNestSouls.com) is a ministry leader, nurse-midwife, and writer. She has raised five children with her husband in California.

Paula Friedrichsen is a Christian speaker from Mammoth Lakes, California, where she resides with her husband and two children. For information about her, or about the Abundant Life Seminar, visit her website at www.PFMinistries.com.

Jeff Friend (Words of a Friend Ministries) is an author and speaker. He and his wife, Nancy, live in Largo, Florida. For more information or to contact Jeff, visit www.wordsofafriend.com.

Kim Garrison is a publicist and runs CLASS Promotional Services (www.classervices.com/CS_PromServ.html). She is also a contributor to *You Can Market Your Book* (Write Now Publications, 2003). Kim and her family live in Oceanside, California.

Amanda Graybill is a writer and speaker. She serves as women's minister at a Southern California church. For information, visit www.fromshabbytochicministry.com.

Deb Haggerty, author and speaker, her husband, and Cocoa and Foxy the dogs live in Orlando, Florida. You can contact Deb at www.DebHaggerty.com.

Bonnie Compton Hanson, author of several books including the *Ponytail* series for girls, can be reached at bonnieh1@worldnet.att.net. She and her husband, Don, are thrilled when children and grandchildren can visit their Santa Ana, California, home.

Elaine Hardt, CLASS graduate, loves to share her joy in Jesus. She's had sixteen books and 465 articles published. She and Don, her husband of fifty years, live in Arizona. They have two married sons and two grandchildren.

Cindy L. Heflin (heflin.1976@prodigy.net) writes with a passion for spiritual encouragement. Her inspirational articles have appeared in numerous publications. She and her husband, Bryant, coauthors of *Proclaim His Glory* (Kregel, 2005), live in Ohio with their two daughters.

Kirk Hine, twenty-year Navy veteran and training specialist, and his wife, Judi, live in Colorado with their last single daughter.

Brenda Hughes is an author and speaker. She lives in New Mexico with her husband and two sons.

Linda LaMar Jewell is a CLASS graduate, author, and speaker who encourages and equips others to express themselves. Linda and her husband, Jim, live in Albuquerque, New Mexico. Her son, Tymon, is married to Anna. Visit Linda at www.PowerOfYourPen.com.

Kim Johnson, grandmother of four, writer, speaker, and creator of Double Honor—a ministry to teach congregations how to minister to their ministers—resides in Anaheim, California, with her husband. Contact her at kim@a-circle-of-friends.org.

Anna Jones (anna@classervices.com), a native to Albuquerque, New Mexico, is happily married to Chad. They have two daughters, Suzanne and Savanna. Anna is a CLASS graduate, author, and speaker, and serves as seminar coordinator with CLASSServices.

Caryl Jones is an author and registered nurse. She lives in Oregon with her loving husband and yellow lab. Caryl may be reached at wcaryl2003@yahoo.com.

Donna Jones is a conference speaker, Bible teacher, pastor's wife, and mom. She is the author of *Taming Your Family Zoo* and can be reached at Donna-Jones@cox.net.

Chris Karcher is a speaker and author of *Relationships of Grace*, a companion workbook, and *Amazing Things I Know About You*. She lives with her husband and daughter in Utah. For more information visit www.relationshipsofgrace.com.

Erin K. Kilby has been writing freelance for two years while teaching English in Kingwood, Texas. You may reach her at erinkilby@hotmail.com.

Debi King resides in Vista, California, with her husband and their four teenagers. A CLASS graduate and aspiring author and speaker, she loves to share how God's mercy has given her a new hope. Learn more about Debi's life and ministry at www.debiking.com.

Cynthia Komlo is a hospital chaplain and published writer seeking to publish her book, *Purple Prayers*. She lives in Grand Junction, Colorado, with her husband and children, and may be reached at CKomlo@aol.com.

Faye Landrum is the author of four books and more than 250 articles and short stories. She lives in Patskala, Ohio, with her miniature white schnauzer, Jewel. She has two sons and four grandchildren. See www.fayeland.org for more information.

John Leatherman is a software engineer and a cartoonist from Sanford, Florida. His website is www.springycam.com.

Peggy Levesque writes for and edits several news publications for the Arizona Department of Education. A member of two local Christian critique groups, she is presently marketing her first novel. She can be contacted at plevesque10@msn.com.

Florence Littauer is known for being entertaining, encouraging, and educational. Her speaking and writing inspires people to lead legendary lives. She has written more than thirty books and lives in Southern California. For more information, visit www.florencelittauer.com.

Marita Littauer, as a speaker and author, (www.maritalittauer.com) helps people have more success in who they are and more joy in getting where they're going. Married since 1983, she and Chuck Noon live in Albuquerque, New Mexico.

Patricia Lorenz is a speaker, author of five books, top contributor to *Chicken Soup for the Soul* books, columnist, mother of four, and grandmother of seven. She lives in Oak Creek, Wisconsin. To find more information, visit www.patricialorenz.com.

Gena Maselli lives in Texas with her husband, children's author Christopher P. N. Maselli. She is the author of two books and coauthor of

Divine Wisdom for Working Women (Barbour, winter 2004). Visit GenaMaselli.com for more information.

Mary Maynard is a writer and speaker whose favorite sport is discussion. She lives with her husband, David, and two children in Monument, Colorado. You can reach Mary at writesouth@aol.com.

Kathy Collard Miller (KathyCollardMiller.com) lives in Indio, California, with her husband. She is mom to two grown children. Kathy is a popular conference speaker and the author of forty-seven books including *Princess to Princess*.

Janet Lynn Mitchell is a wife, mother, CLASS speaker, and coauthor of *A Special Kind of Love*. You can reach Janet in Southern California at Janetlm@prodigy.net.

Mary Lapé Nixon is an author, speaker, and CLASS graduate. She also researches immune cell disorders in a clinical laboratory. Married since 1992, she lives with her husband and their doberman pinscher in Southern California.

Chuck Noon (www.chucknoon.com), L.P.C.C., is a counselor specializing in marriage. His writings have been featured in books and magazines including *HomeLife* and *Marriage Partnership*. Married to Marita Littauer, they have written *Love Extravagantly* and speak together.

Karen J. Olson is a writer and columnist for various newspapers and magazines. She lives in Wisconsin and has quit watching infomercials.

Golden Keyes Parsons is a CLASS speaker, author, and pastor. She has three grown daughters and lives in Red River, New Mexico, with her husband. For further information, Golden can be reached at GPar0719@aol.com.

Ginger Plowman, speaker and author of *Don't Make Me Count to*

Three, lives with her husband, Jim, in Opelika, Alabama, where she homeschools their two children. For more information, visit www.gingerplowman.com.

Trish Porter was a 1988 U.S. Olympic Team member, is the world record holder (ages 40–44) for the high jump, and is married to two time Olympian Pat Porter. She has two children and lives in Albuquerque, New Mexico.

Amanda Rankin lives in Live Oak, Florida, with her husband, Tony. Their website for caregivers and those who have had strokes is www.ahelpfulhand.com. To reach Amanda for her life-enriching seminars and books, contact www.buddycoaching.com.

Debbie Robbins, a Louisville, Kentucky, native, is a singer and pianist. As a speaker and writer, her ministry has taken on a deeper dimension. She is happily married to Scott. For more information, visit www.debbierobbins.net.

Kathryn Robbins is a speaker, certified CLASServices Personality Trainer, and president of *Stones of Glory* ™ jewelry. She lives in St. Louis, Missouri with her husband of twenty-seven years and their five sons.

Gayle Roper is the award-winning author of thirty-eight books, a speaker and teacher, and a CLASSeminar staff member. She lives in Coatesville, Pennsylvania, with her husband. They have two grown children. You can visit Gayle at www.gayleroper.com.

Tonya Ruiz wears many hats. She is a popular conference speaker, professional writer, pastor's wife, mother of four, and grandmother who calls Southern California home. To contact her, visit www.TonyaRuiz.com.

Renee Coates Scheidt is an author and speaker who knows how to connect with her audience. Renee, her husband, and their two daughters reside in China Grove, North Carolina. Visit www.reneescheidt.com for more information.

Doris Schuchard is a wife and mother of two teenagers. She enjoys writing for the family from her Atlanta home.

Raelene Searle (www.raelenesearle.com) is a CLASS speaker and author, with a unique creativity for encouraging abundant joy in the lives of women. She lives in Albuquerque, New Mexico, with her husband, Chip, and their two grown children.

Georgia Shaffer, author of *A Gift of Mourning Glories* and producer of the syndicated radio feature *The Mourning Glory Minute,* is a professional speaker and life coach for communicators and ministry leaders. Visit her garden at www.GeorgiaShaffer.com.

Gail Cawley Showalter is an author and speaker. She inspires audiences of adults who touch the lives of children. Gail and her husband, Sam, have a total of six children and four grandchildren. Contact her at www.seeinguthrough.com.

Lynne Cooper Sitton (LynneCooperSitton@cs.com) is an author and illustrator, and president of the Broward County Florida Chapter of American Christian Writers.

Bonnie Skinner (www.bonieskinner.com) is a writer, speaker, and founder of "Happiness on a Shoestring Ministries." She and her husband of fifty-two years live in San Antonio, and enjoy three grown children and eight grandchildren.

Daphne V. Smith, speaker and author, enjoys life with her husband, David, and their two children in Arkansas. She considers juggling family and career a privilege. Contact Daphne at www.daphnesmith.com for your speaking needs.

Gail Snow is a writer and speaker. She and her husband of thirty-one years live in Rogue River, Oregon.

Betty Southard (www.bettysouthard.com) enjoys mentoring others in the choices and challenges of life. She lives in Newport Beach, California, with her husband.

Lynette Sowell writes to entertain and inspire readers. She lives in Texas with her husband (who runs the real "Daddy Day Care") and two kids. You can learn about Lynette and her writing at www.geocities.com/lynsow.

Elaine Stone is a freelance writer, speaker, pastor's wife, and mother of three who makes her home in Fredericksburg, Virginia. She can be reached at estone@spotswood.org.

Craig Sundheimer is worship pastor for Cottonwood Church (www.cottonwoodchurch.net), speaker services manager for CLASServices, and "Dad" to Jay and Amanda. He and his wife, Cheryl, call the beautiful southwestern landscape of Albuquerque, New Mexico, home.

Gaylynne Sword is a novelist and speaker. She lives and writes in Orlando, Florida, where she lives with her husband and three children.

Gayle Team-Smith is an inspirational speaker and nationally published author. Her inspirational devotions are included in both the *Chicken Soup* and *God Allows U Turns* books. Gayle and her family live in Edmond, Oklahoma. Contact her at gayle.smith@lmscpa.com.

Deborah Fuller Thomas is a five-year breast cancer survivor and pastor's wife. She lives in Northern California with her husband and teenaged son and daughter. She writes both children's and women's fiction.

Nanette Thorsen-Snipes (www.nanettesnipes.com) has published Christian articles and devotions in over fifty publications. She and her husband live in north Georgia and have four children, three grandchildren, and a cat named Possum. Contact her at jsnipes212@aol.com.

Judy Wallace is a speaker and author and is the founder of *Principles on Purpose*. She lives in Arkansas with her husband, Tommy. For more information, visit www.principlesonpurpose.com.

Sharen Watson is a freelance journalist, the founder of Words for the Journey Christian Writer's Guild (www.wordsforthejourney.org), and a mother of three. She lives in Texas with her husband, Ray, and is currently working on her first book.

Karen H. Whiting (www.karenhwhiting.com) has written *Family Devotional Builder, Let's Chat About the Bible, God's Girls* series, and other books that creatively connect families and women to God. Karen lives in Miami, Florida with her family.

Lori Wildenberg, speaker, educator, and coauthor of *Empowered Parents,* lives in Colorado with her husband and four children. She speaks to various groups on parenting from a Christian perspective. See www.loriwildenberg.com for more information.

Dr. Anne Worth recently retired after twenty-five years as a family therapist. She is joyfully serving in her ministry of writing, leading women's retreats, and teaching at Fellowship Bible Church in Dallas, Texas.

Dr. Jason S. Wrench (www.roadspeakers.com/jwrench) is assistant professor at Ohio University Eastern in the School of Communication Studies and a professional speaker and author.

Jeanne Zornes's books include *When I Prayed for Patience . . . God Let Me Have It!* (Kregel). She lives in Wenatchee, Washington with her husband and two children. Learn more about Jeanne at www.allaboutquotes.com/awsa/search/asp.

Permissions

When I Prayed for Patience . . .
God Let Me Have It

Jeanne Zornes (Foreword by Jerry Jenkins)

Instant gratification. It doesn't just describe our society it has also impacted the way we view our own spiritual develoment at times. Jeanne breaks in with reality, sharing a humor-laced blend of anecdotes from everyday life that offers practical and biblical suggestions for developing perseverance, endurance, patience, longsuffering, forbearance, and trust.

When I Got on the Highway to Heaven . . . I Didn't Expect Rocky Roads

Jeanne Zornes (Foreword by Lucinda Secrest McDowell)

Life, liberty, and—especially—the pursuit of happiness is what we often seek. We are surprised and discouraged when we face discomfort on our journey through life. Jeanne offers a humorous and poignant look at the tough times of life through real-life stories of people who have faced insurmountable obstacles and have overcome them. These examples provide encouragement for anyone who needs a fresh perspective and redirects us from the hopelessness we sometimes feel we're living in.

Living Whole Without a Better Half

Wendy Widder

From sad Country tunes, to box-office hits, to the recesses of our own minds we are permeated by them—thoughts of loneliness, fears, and rejection. Using the lessons of Bible characters, the author shows singles how to find abundance in life instead of letting it slip away while waiting for marriage. This book delves into the deep issues and provides solid principles for living.

To Love, Honor, and Vacuum

Sheila Wray Gregoire (Foreword by Carla Barnhill, *Christian Parenting Today*)

Overworked and under-appreciated is sometimes the way we feel, especially when our families view us as the maid. A syndicated writer and popular speaker helps women grow and thrive in the midst of their hectic lives, even if their circumstances never change.

> "Sheila grabs every area of a woman's life and helps to make sense of it. Not only does she address problems, she offers simple, biblical solutions in a succinct, easy to read way."
>
> —LEANNE ELY,
> Talk show host and author